Religion in America

Primary Sources in

U.S. History Series

Volume I

James T. Baker
Western Kentucky University

THOMSON
™
WADSWORTH

Australia • Canada • Mexico • Singapore • Spain
United Kingdom • United States

THOMSON

✦
™

WADSWORTH

*For the two men who taught me the most
about religion—in America and around the world:
Glenn Hinson and Charles Wellborn*

Publisher: *Clark Baxter*
Senior Acquisitions Editor: *Ashley Dodge*
Editorial Assistant: *Lucinda Bingham*
Technology Project Manager: *David Lionetti*
Marketing Manager: *Lori Grebe-Cook*
Marketing Assistant: *Teresa Jessen*
Project Manager, Editorial Production:
　Katy German
Print Buyer: *Doreen Suruki*

Permissions Editor: *Sarah Harkrader*
Production Service: *Buuji, Inc.*
Photo Researcher: *Sue Howard*
Copy Editor: *Kristina Rose McComas*
Cover Designer: *Lee Anne Dollison*
Cover Image: *Getty Images*
Compositor: *Cadmus*
Printer: *Webcom*

Printed in Canada
1 2 3 4 5 6 7 09 08 07 06 05

For more information about our
products, contact us at:
**Thomson Learning Academic
Resource Center
1-800-423-0563**

For permission to use material from this
text or product, submit a request online at
http://www.thomsonrights.com.

Any additional questions about permissions
can be submitted by email to
thomsonrights@thomson.com.

Library of Congress Control Number: 2005923046

ISBN 0-495-00511-8

**Thomson Higher Education
10 Davis Drive
Belmont, CA 94002-3098
USA**

Asia (including India)
Thomson Learning
5 Shenton Way
#01-01 UIC Building
Singapore 068808

Australia/New Zealand
Thomson Learning Australia
102 Dodds Street
Southbank, Victoria 3006
Australia

Canada
Thomson Nelson
1120 Birchmount Road
Toronto, Ontario M1K 5G4
Canada

UK/Europe/Middle East/Africa
Thomson Learning
High Holborn House
50–51 Bedford Row
London WC1R 4LR
United Kingdom

Latin America
Thomson Learning
Seneca, 53
Colonia Polanco
11560 Mexico
D.F. Mexico

Spain (including Portugal)
Thomson Paraninfo
Calle Magallanes, 25
28015 Madrid, Spain

Contents

The Importance of Religious Education in the British Colonies   45

Insecurity and Witchcraft   52

The First "Great Awakening"   62

The First American "Enlightenment"   76

CHAPTER 3 BIRTH OF A NATION: THE STRUGGLE FOR AMERICAN INDEPENDENCE 87

Native American Religious Reaction to White Encroachment   175

Religion and the Abolitionist Movement   184

Preface

"When I find in people narrow religion,
I find narrow reading."
RALPH WALDO EMERSON

The American psyche is deeply divided. Americans are the offspring both of Calvin and Voltaire, whose early American representatives were Cotton Mather and Benjamin Franklin. Americans have through their history wrestled with the contradictory tugs of their Puritan and Enlightenment heritages, and the struggle has made their experiments in government, social development, and religion a fascinating, multidimensional spectacle.

Americans have never agreed on whether the nation they founded in the seventeenth and eighteenth centuries should be the Holy Experiment, the "city set on a hill as a light to the nations," envisioned by the Puritans—or the Secular Society, with freedom of religious choice and separation of church and state, established by the authors of the United States Constitution.

Americans have never decided whether their nation should, through governmental intervention and planning, strive to achieve equality for all, in a true social and economic democracy—or should, through governmental restraint, encourage free enterprise and the freedom for rugged individualists to achieve their full potential, even at the expense of those weaker than they are.

Americans have never determined whether America's place in the world should be the Power its industrial and military might has in the last century made possible, dealing with ambiguous circumstances with amoral actions, serving as police officer to the world—or whether it should be an Inspiration for democracy and morality around the world while maintaining a benign posture of military restraint.

All of these conflicts appear in religious documents written by Americans across the last three centuries. While there is no "American religion" as such, while we have no established Church as some European countries have had and some still do have, Americans have always been and continue to be religious people; and their religious side, deeply divided as it has been and continues to be, is just as evident to observers as their political and social sides. Religion in America has inspired many historical events, criticized many others, and interpreted them all.

ACKNOWLEDGEMENTS

I would like to thank the following reviewers of *Religion in America* for their helpful suggestions while preparing this text:
David Bains, Samford University
Wayne Flynt, Auburn University (retired) and Samford University
Karin E. Gedge, West Chester University
Barry Hankins, Baylor University
David J. McCowin, Boston College
Karin Gedge, West Chester University
Peter W. Williams, Miami University

✳

CHAPTER 1

Religious Life in the Americas Before and Beyond the British Colonies

Religion, of course, did not arrive in what is today the United States with the English-speaking settlers at Jamestown (1607) and at Plymouth (1620). To study the religious thought and practices of Native Americans before the arrival of Europeans and that of the Spanish and French who shared command of the North American continent with the English is both fascinating and essential to gaining an understanding of the peculiar themes, nuances, and flavors of religion in America.

Native American, Spanish, and French religious thought and practice were not only influential in bygone days. They continue to exert an influence over such thought and practice today, not only among their descendants but among many descendants of the English-speaking colonists as well.

NATIVE AMERICAN RELIGIOUS THOUGHT AND PRACTICE

Native Americans came to this continent over ten thousand years ago. Their religious teachings and practices, although widely varied among the many tribal groups, were established long before Europeans arrived to alter the continent so dramatically.

Two problems arise in the study of Native American religion, its thought and practice. One, nothing was committed to paper before the arrival of the Europeans, and much that was recorded thereafter was filtered through the assumptions and prejudices of the newcomers. Two, by the time Native Americans began speaking for themselves, they had been so deeply influenced by European thought and practice that it is difficult to know precisely the nature of their religious thought and practice before the sixteenth century. Nevertheless, reading passages recorded during the past two centuries can open windows through which we can catch glimpses of the religious world of America before the arrival of Europeans and their Christian faith.

In the passages that follow, despite the fact that they were captured long after the myths were first taught and the rituals first practiced, we can see something of what Native Americans believed and how they worshiped. The **Myth of the Tsimshian,** which was probably recited in ceremonies, recounts a Native American view of the world's creation. The **Kwakiutl Ritual for the Dying** demonstrates the way Native Americans dealt with illness and death, which they considered to be a part of the great circle of life. The **Zuni and Apache Predictions of the World's End** reflect the pessimism Native Americans felt in fighting their losing battle for cultural survival with the white man.

1.1

Myth of the Tsimshian
on the Creation

It was in the beginning, before anything that lives in our world was created. There was only the chief in heaven. There was no light in heaven. There were only emptiness and darkness.

The chief had two sons and one daughter. His people were numerous. Indeed, they were the tribe of the chief.

Source: *Thirty-First Annual Report of the Bureau of American Ethnology,* 1909–1910.
(Washington; DC Government Printing Office, 1916) pp. 113–116.

These were the names of his three children. The name of the eldest one was Walking About Early; the name of the second, The One Who Walks All Over The Sky. The name of the girl was Support Of Sun. They were very strong. The younger boy was wiser and abler than the elder one. Therefore one day he was sad, and he pondered why darkness was continuing all the time. Therefore one day he spoke to his sister, "Let us go and get pitch wood!" They went and they cut very good pitch wood. They made a ring of a slender cedar twig, and measured it according to the size of a face. Then they tied pitch wood all round it, so that it looked like a mask. After they had finished, they told their sister, who was accompanying them while they were getting pitch wood, not to tell the people about what they were doing. Then The One Who Walks All Over The Sky went to where the Sun rises and showed himself to the people. The pitch wood that was tied around his face was burning.

Suddenly the people saw the great light rising in the east. They were glad when they saw the light. Then he ran in full sight across the sky. He came from the east and went westward. He was carrying the pitch mask. That is the reason why he was running quickly, because else the pitch wood would have been burned up. Therefore he was running quickly across the sky. Then the chief's tribe assembled. They sat down together to hold a council, and said, "We are glad because your child has given us light, but he is running too quickly. He ought to go a little more slowly, so that we may enjoy the light for a longer time." Therefore the chief told his son what the people had said. His son replied, asking him what he should do, since the pitch wood would burn before he could reach the west. Therefore he went that way every day.

The people assembled again and held a council, and requested him to go slowly along the sky. That is what they asked of him; and therefore his sister said, "I will hold him when he is running along the sky."

Then the people blessed the woman, and the father also blessed his daughter. Next time when The One Who Walks All Over The Sky started on his journey, Support Of Sun started too. She went southward. Her brother rose in the east, and then the girl turned back and ran to meet her brother.

The woman said, "Wait for me until I catch up with you!" She ran as fast as she could, and held her brother in the middle of the sky. For this reason the Sun stops for a little while in the middle of the sky.

The woman stood firm, holding her brother. Therefore we see the Sun stopping for a little while in the middle of the sky. . . .

When The One Who Walks All Over The Sky was asleep, sparks flew out of his mouth. Those are the stars; and at night the moon receives its light from the shining face of the Sun, who is asleep when he is tired and when his light shoots out of the smoke hole.

Sometimes when the Sun is glad he adorns himself. He takes his sister's red ocher to paint his face. Then the people know what kind of weather it is going to be on the following day. When the people see the red sky in the evening, they know that it will be good weather the following day; and when they see the red sky in the morning, they know that the weather is going to be bad the whole day. That is what the people say.

1.2

Kwakiutl Ritual for the Dying

When a beloved child is dying, the parents keep on praying to the spirit not to try to take away their child. "I will pay you with these clothes of this my child, Sitting-on-Fire." Thus they say, while they put on the fire the clothes of the one who is lying there sick.

Then the parents of the one who is lying there sick pay Sitting-on-Fire, that he may pray to the souls of the grandparents of the one who lies sick, that they may not wish to call their grandson. And the parents of the one who lies there sick take four kinds of food, dry salmon first. They break it into four pieces. When it is ready, they take cinquefoil-roots and fold them up in four pieces. And when that is ready, they take dried berry-cakes and break them into four pieces. And when that is ready, they take viburnum-berries, four spoonfuls. When all this is ready, the father of the one who is lying sick in bed takes the dry salmon and throws the pieces into the fire, one by one. And the mother of the one who lies sick in bed says, "O Sitting-on-Fire! now eat, and protect my child, Sitting-on-Fire!"

Then the father of the one who lies sick in bed takes also cinquefoil roots; he takes one (root) and dips it into the oil. And the mother of the one who lies sick in bed says again, "O Sitting-on-Fire! go on, and pray to the spirits, that they may have mercy on my child!" Thus she says.

Then the father takes also one of the dried berry-cakes dips it into oil, and throws it into the fire. Then he himself says "O Sitting-on-Fire! now do have mercy on me, and keep alive my child here, Sitting-on-Fire! Have mercy and press back my child here, spirit, and I will take care of this, supernatural one, that I may still have for a while my son here! Long-Life-Maker!"

And when he has put all the berry-cakes on the fire of the house, then he takes one of the spoonfuls of viburnum-berries, and three times he aims at the fire of the house. The fourth time he pours them on the fire; and he says, "Take this, Sitting-on-Fire! and pray to the spirits of those behind us that they have mercy on me and my wife here! Pray to the Long-Life-Maker that he may come and take away the sickness of my child here! Take pity on me, and ask the supernatural one to come! Wa!" Thus says the father to Sitting-on-Fire. Then that is finished. . . .

In the morning, when day comes, the hearts of the parents of the one who lies sick abed feel bad, for they know that their child will die. Then the one who is lying sick abed is growing weak very fast. His parents now take

Source: *Thirty-Fifth Annual Report of the Bureau of American Ethnology,* 1913–1914, (Washington: Government Printing Office, 1921) pp. 705–709.

all the best kinds of food and the best clothing for the one who is sick abed, who is dying.

As soon as (the breath) of the one lying sick abed breaks, the parents take the best clothing and put it on the one who had been sick abed. After the parents have done so, the mother kicks her dead child four times. And when she first kicks him, she says, "Don't turn your head back to me." Then she turns around, and again she kicks him. And as she kicks him, she says, "Don't come back again." Then she turns around again. She kicks him; and she says as she kicks him, "Just go straight ahead." And then she kicks him again; and says, "Only protect me and your father from sickness." Thus she says, and she leaves him.

1.3

Predictions of the World's End

ZUNI

Many Years Ago when our grandparents foresaw what our future would be like, they spoke their prophecies among themselves and passed them on to the children before them.

"Cities will progress and then decay to the ways of the lowest beings. Drinkers of dark liquids will come upon the land, speaking nonsense and filth. Then the end shall be nearer.

"Population will increase until the land can hold no more. The tribes of men will mix. The dark liquids they drink will cause the people to fight among themselves. Families will break up: father against children and the children against one another.

"Maybe when the people have outdone themselves, then maybe, the stars will fall upon the land, or drops of hot water will rain upon the earth. Or the land will turn under. Or our father, the sun, will not rise to start the day. Then our possessions will turn into beasts and devour us whole.

"If not, there will be an odor from gases, which will fill the air we breathe, and the end for us shall come.

"But the people themselves will bring upon themselves what they receive. From what has resulted, time alone will tell what the future holds for us."

Source: Peter Nabokov (ed.), *Native American Testimony* (New York Viking, 1991) pp. 439–440.

APACHE

The Old People used to tell us that when the end of the earth is coming all the water will begin to dry up. For a long time there will be no rain.

There will be only a few places, about three places, where there will be springs. At those three places the water will be dammed up and all the people will come in to those places and start fighting over the water.

That's what old Nani used to tell us. Those old Indians found out somehow, I don't know how. And the way it looks, I believe it is the truth.

Many old Chiricahua used to tell the same story. They say that in this way most of the people will kill each other off. Maybe there will be a few good people left.

When the new world comes after that the white people will be Indians and the Indians will be white people.

THE SPANISH EMPIRE:
"GOLD, GLORY, AND GOD"

The first Europeans to have a religious impact on the Americas were the Spanish. In **"The Treaty of Tordesillas,"** issued in 1494 from the village of Tordesillas, near the Spanish border with Portugal, the Holy Father of Rome gave his blessings to the Spanish monarchs Fernando and Isabel to make a part of their newly united kingdom the lands 370 degrees west of the Cape Verde Islands. While he did not know it at the time, only two years after Columbus' first voyage, he had effectively given the Americas to the Spanish. They could exploit their new domain to gain riches, so long as they converted and protected the natives of that nebulous region.

It is clear in the **Commission King Fernando of Aragon gave to Ponce de León** that the Spanish intended to conquer the world given to them by any means necessary. Fernando's representatives converted the natives (most often by force) but exploited without protecting them. **Bartholomew De Las Casas** recorded their abuses and appealed to the king and the pope for action. In his **"Sublimus Deus,"** the pope responded with fine words that did not alter practices. Not all Native Americans surrendered peacefully to Spanish rule, and missionaries were at times massacred, as the record of the **Martyrdom of the Dominican Friar Luis Cancér** in Florida demonstrates. Spaniards such as **Juan De Escalona** sought to explain the reasons for such violence against the conquerors.

Among the most effective missionary-administrators of the Spanish Empire was Junípero Serra, who worked in California, serving the Church and the Spanish crown. His **Letter Upon Leaving Spain,** written as he departed for the New World, reflects the great missionary impulse that drove such men. His **Letter to the Viceroy** makes clear his dual role as servant of Christ and of the King. He was and remains a controversial figure, as demonstrated by the fact that late twentieth century plans to make him a saint were thwarted by Native American protests.

The Spanish governors and their Christian missionaries did, however, succeed in creating a new Hispanic Catholic culture in the New World, not just in what is today Latin America but also in large parts of what is today the United States. The effects of that cultural establishment are still an important element of religion in America.

1.4

The Treaty of Tordesillas (1494)

Whereas a certain controversy exists between the said lords, their constituents, as to what lands, of all those discovered in the ocean sea up to the present day, the date of this treaty, pertain to each one of the said parts respectively; therefore, for the sake of peace and concord, and for the preservation of the relationship and love of the said King of Portugal for the said King and Queen of Castile, Aragon, etc., it being the pleasure of their Highnesses, they . . . covenanted and agreed that a boundary or straight line be determined and drawn north and south, from pole to pole, on the said ocean sea, from the Arctic to the Antarctic pole. This boundary or line shall be drawn straight, as aforesaid, at a distance of three hundred and seventy leagues west of the Cape Verde Islands, being calculated by degrees . . . And all lands, both islands and mainlands, found and discovered already, or to be found and discovered hereafter, by the said King of Portugal and by his vessels on this side of the said line and bound determined as above, toward the east, in either north or south latitude, on the eastern side of the said bound

Source: J. Gordon Melton, *American Religions* (Santa Barbara, CA: ABC-CLIO, 2000) p. 43.

provided the said bound is not crossed, shall belong to, and remain in the possession of, and pertain forever to, the said King of Portugal and his successors. And all other lands, both islands and mainlands, found or to be found hereafter . . . by the said King and Queen of Castile, Aragon, etc., and by their vessels, on the western side of the said bound, determined as above, after having passed the said bound toward the west, in either its north or south latitude, shall belong to . . . the said King and Queen of Castile, Leon, etc., and to their successors.

Item, the said representatives promise and affirm, that from this date no ships shall be dispatched—namely as follows: the said King and Queen of Castile, Leon, Aragon, etc., for this part of the bound, . . . which pertains to the said King of Portugal . . . nor the said King of Portugal to the other part of the said bound which pertains to the said King and Queen of Castile, Aragon, etc.—for the purpose of discovering and seeking any mainlands or islands, or for the purpose of trade, barter, or conquest of any kind. But should it come to pass that the said ships of the said King and Queen of Castile . . . on sailing thus on this side of the said bound, should discover any mainlands or islands in the region pertaining, as abovesaid, to the said King of Portugal, such mainlands or islands shall pertain to and belong forever to the said King of Portugal and his heirs, and their Highnesses shall order them to be surrendered to him immediately. And if the said ships of the said King of Portugal discover any islands and mainlands in the regions of the said King and Queen of Castile . . . all such lands shall belong to and remain forever in the possession of the said King and Queen of Castile . . . and their heirs, and the said King of Portugal shall cause such lands to be surrendered immediately.

And by the present agreement they . . . entreat our most Holy Father that his Holiness be pleased to confirm and approve this said agreement according to what is set forth therein, and that he order his bulls in regard to it to be issued to the parties or to whichever of the parties may solicit them with the tenor of this agreement incorporated therein, and that he lay his censures upon those who shall violate or oppose it at any time whatsoever.

1.5

To Ponce de León, Governor of Florida (1514)

KING FERNANDO OF ARAGON

The agreement that was made by Our command with you, Juan Ponce de Leon, for the expedition to colonize the island of Beniny and the island of Florida which you discovered by Our command, in addition to the articles and agreement that were made with you when you took action for discovery, is as follows:

First, whereas, in the said articles and agreement made with you by Our command, concerning the discovering and colonizing of the said islands, I gave license and authority, for the time and limitation of three years to commence from the day of delivery to you of the said articles, to conduct at your cost and charge the vessels that you might wish, provided that you stood obligated to begin the expedition of discovery within the first year; and because until now you have occupied yourself in matters of Our service and you have not had time to start the voyage of discovery, it is My will and pleasure that the said three years may commence to run and be reckoned from the day you may embark on your voyage to the said islands.

Item, that as soon as you embark [sic] at the said islands you may summon the chiefs and Indians thereof, by the best device or devices there can be given them, to understand what should be said to them, conformably to a summons that has been drawn up by several learned men . . . by all the ways and means you may be able to devise, that they should come into the knowledge of Our Catholic Faith and should obey and serve as they are bound to do; and you will take down in signed form before two or three notaries, if such there be, and before as many witnesses and these the most creditable, as may be found there, in order that it may serve for Our justification, and you will send the said document; and the summons must be made once, twice, thrice.

And if after the aforesaid they do not wish to obey what is contained in the said summons, you can make war and seize them and carry them away for slaves; but if they do obey, give them the best treatment you can and endeavor, as is stated, by all the means at your disposal, to convert them to Our Holy Catholic Faith; and if by chance, after having once obeyed the said summons, they again rebel, I command that you again make the said summons before making war or doing harm or damage.

Source: D. B. Quinn, ed., *New American World* (New York: Arno Press 1979) pp. 238–239.

1.6

Complaint on Spanish Treatment
of Native Americans

BARTOLOMÉ DE LAS CASAS

There is nothing more detestable or more cruel, than the tyranny which the Spaniards use toward the Indians for the getting of pearl. Surely the infernal torments cannot much exceed the anguish that they endure, by reason of that way of cruelty; for they put them under water some four or five ells [15 to 18 feet] deep, where they are forced without any liberty of respiration, to gather up the shells wherein the pearls are; sometimes they come up again with nets full of shells to take breath, but if they stay any while to rest themselves, immediately comes a hangman row'd in a little boat, who as soon as he has well beaten them, drags them again to their labor. Their food is nothing but filth, and the very same that contains the pearl, with a small portion of that bread which that country affords; in the first whereof there is little nourishment; and as for the latter, it is made with great difficulty; besides that they have not enough of that neither for sustenance; they lie upon the ground in fetters, lest they should run away; and many times they are drown'd in this labor, and are never seen again till they swim upon the top of the waves: oftentimes they also are devoured by certain sea monsters, that are frequent in those seas. Consider whether this hard usage of the poor creatures be consistent with the precepts which God commands concerning charity to our neighbor, by those that cast them so undeservedly into the dangers of a cruel death, causing them to perish without any remorse or pity, or allowing them the benefit of the sacraments, or the knowledge of religion; it being impossible for them to live any time under the water; and this death is so much the more painful, by reason that by the constricting of the breast, while the lungs strive to do their office, the vital parts are so afflicted that they die vomiting the blood out of their mouths. Their hair also, which is by nature black, is hereby changed and made of the same color with that of the sea wolves; their bodies are also so besprinkled with the froth of the sea, that they appear rather like monsters than men.

Source: F. A. Macnut, *Bartholomew de las Casas* (New York: Putnam, 1909), p. 429.

POPE PAUL III'S RESPONSE: "SUBLIMUS DEUS" (1537)

We . . . consider, however, that the Indians are truly men and that they are not only capable of understanding the catholic faith but, according to our information, they desire exceedingly to receive it. Desiring to provide ample remedy for these evils, we define and declare by these our letters, or by any translation thereof signed by any notary public and sealed with the seal of any ecclesiastical dignitary, to which the same credit shall be given as to the originals, that, notwithstanding whatever may have been or may be said to the contrary, the said Indians and all other people who may later be discovered by Christians, are by no means to be deprived of their liberty or the possession of their property, even though they be outside the faith of Jesus Christ; and that they may and should, freely and legitimately, enjoy their liberty and the possession of their property; nor should they be in any way enslaved; should the contrary happen, it shall be null and of no effect.

1.7

Martyrdom of the Dominican Friar Luis Cáncer in Florida (1549)

When I saw the Indians I sent ashore the interpreter, who was an Indian girl we had brought from Havana and came from those parts, and the good man Fuentes went with her. The Pilot would not let me go, but I was sure that with the interpreter and giving them something they would do no harm to the monk, so I lifted up my habit without telling the Pilot and plunged into the sea waist-deep, and the Lord knows the speed at which I went to stop them dealing with the monk before they heard the reason for our voyage. When I reached the shore I fell to my knees and begged for God's grace and help, then I went up to the flat bit where I found them all together; before I reached them I did again what I had done on the beach, and then got up and began to take out from my sleeve some things from Flanders, which may not seem very important or valuable to Christians, but which they regarded as valuable and great gifts.

Source: D. B. Quinn, ed., *New American World*, (New York: Arno, 1979), II, 192, 194.

Then they came to me, and I gave them part of what I was carrying, then I went to the monk, who came to me, and I embraced him with great pleasure, and we both knelt down, with Fuentes and the Indian girl, took out the book and recited the litanies, commending ourselves to the Lord and His Saints. The Indians knelt, some of them squatting, which pleased me very much, and once they had got up I left the litanies in the middle and sat down with them on a log and soon found out where the port and the bay we were looking for were, about a day and a half's journey by land from where we were; we told them of our aims and wishes.

When the Indian girl saw it was all so peaceful she was very pleased and said to me "Father, didn't I tell you that if I spoke to them they would not kill you? These people are from my land and this one speaks my language." Our Lord knows how pleased we were to see them as peaceful as they were being then; I was getting covered in their red dye from all the embracing that was going on, although I managed to get the worst of it on my habit to leave the skin untouched. To see if I was free to do so, if they would let me go to the launch, I was careful to tell them that I had more to give them and I was going back to get it, although in fact I had it already in my sleeve, but I had not wanted to give them all of it since I had intended to do this: I went, and came back, and found so many who wanted to embrace me that I could not get away from them. This friendship and affection was obviously based on what they thought they could get from us than on ourselves, but since this world is the route to the other, and as we all know from experience and say that love is good deeds and that gifts can break rocks, I was pleased that they should receive us so well for these material matters: the spiritual and true would come bit by bit, like the fear of being bad is considered a good thing because afterwards there enters the true and good. . . .

When we arrived at the ship, thinking we were carrying great news, we found others waiting both much better and much worse: they told us that there had come there one of the Spaniards that Soto had taken, who had fled from his master in a canoe. I was very pleased with such good news, and it would have been a great help to our purpose if he had not added other sadder and more terrible information, saying that the Indians who had taken the monk and his companion had killed them as soon as I left them, and that they were holding the seaman alive. When he was asked how he had found this out, he said "I have often heard it from other Indians who saw them being killed, and I also saw the skin from the head of the monk, which an Indian showed me who was taking it about as an exhibit, and he said that they were doing and saying many things when they killed them." All this is a most terrible thing and very distressing for us all, but even so it could be endured, and is the kind of event involved in these affairs of the faith, and I always used to think, whenever I considered the importance of this matter, that, as it was with the Apostles, it would be with our own blood that we would plant and establish the law and the faith of the one who even to give it and preach it to us suffered and died; and since this is the way it is, and is only to be expected in the preaching of so great a law, there is no reason to despair of future success because of something like this happening.

1.8

Juan de Escalona Explains
Indian Violence (1610)

JUAN DE ESCALONA

Would that I could have spoken to your lordship in person and have given you more directly the information that now I must of necessity put down in writing, lest I be an unfaithful servant of the Lord. I cannot help the situation as much in this way as by a personal conference and I would have preferred that someone else should make this report. As prelate and protector, however, sent to this land to prevent evil and to seek what is good for God's children, I must inform your lordship of what is and has been transpiring here, for although reports and communications have been sent from here about matters in this land, they do not tell the actual truth about what has been going on since the arrival of Governor Don Juan de Oñate in this province. I shall tell about these matters, not because I wish to meddle in the affairs of others, but because, as prelate, I am under obligation, by informing his majesty and your lordship, to seek a remedy for the difficulties and obstacles that prevent the preaching of the gospel and the conversion of these souls.

The first and foremost difficulty, from which have sprung all the evils and the ruin of this land, is the fact that this conquest was entrusted to a man of such limited resources as Don Juan de Oñate. The result was that soon after he entered the land, his people began to perpetrate many offenses against the natives, and to plunder their pueblos of the corn they had gathered for their own sustenance; here corn is God, for they have nothing else with which to support themselves. Because of this situation and because the Spaniards asked the natives for blankets as tribute, even before teaching them the meaning of God, the Indians began to get restless, abandon their pueblos, and take to the mountains.

The governor did not want to sow a community plot to feed his people, although we friars urged him to do so, and the Indians agreed to it so that they would not be deprived of their food. This effort was all of no avail, and now the Indians have to provide everything. As a result, all the corn they had saved for years past has been consumed, and not a kernel is left over for them. The whole land has thus been reduced to such need that the Indians drop dead from starvation wherever they live; and they eat dirt and charcoal ground up with some

Source: G. P. Hammond, *Don Juande Oñate* (Alba: University of New Mexico Press, 1953) III 692–695. Reprinted by permission.

seeds and a little corn in order to sustain life. Any Spaniard who gets his fill of tortillas here feels as if he has obtained a grant of nobility. Your lordship must not believe that the Indians part willingly with their corn, or the blankets with which they cover themselves; on the contrary, this extortion is done by threats and force of arms, the soldiers burning some of the houses and killing the Indians. This was the cause of the Acoma war, as I have clearly established after questioning friars, captains, and soldiers. And the war which was recently waged against the Jumanas started the same way. In these conflicts, more than eight hundred men, women, and children were killed, and three pueblos burned. Their supplies of food were also burned, and this at a time when there was such great need. . . .

In addition to the aforesaid, all of the provisions which the governor and his men took along on this new expedition they took from the Indians. I was to have gone on this journey, but on observing the great outrages against the Indians and the wars waged against them without rhyme or reason, I did not dare to accompany the governor; instead I sent two friars to go with him. This expedition would have been impossible if the Indians had not furnished him with the provisions and supplies needed, and if I, in the name of his majesty, had not provided him with sixty mules, six carts, and two negroes that your lordship had given us to come to this land. My reason for giving this assistance, even though your lordship had ordered just the opposite, was that the said exploration could not have been undertaken without it, nor could the gospel have been preached to these people; and this was important, especially when we were already at the borders of their lands and the church and his majesty had sent us for this purpose. Furthermore, if this expedition had not been made, all the soldiers would have run away, for all are here against their will, owing to the great privations they endure. To protect his majesty's interests, the governor assumed responsibility for the damages caused by his people and gave me three honorable men with property in New Spain as guarantors. The soldiers and captains provided the rest of the arms and horses, as he had nothing of his own. For lack of these he left here some servants whom he could not take along.

I have told all this to make it clear that the governor does not have the resources to carry out the discovery of these lands. I do not hesitate to say that even if he were to stay here for twenty thousand years, he could never discover what there is to be discovered in this land, unless his majesty should aid him or take over the whole project. Moreover, the governor has oppressed his people so that they are all discontented and anxious to get away, both on account of the sterility of the land and of his harsh conduct toward them. I do not hesitate to say that his majesty could have discovered this land with fifty well-armed Christian men, giving them the necessary things for this purpose, and that what these fifty men might discover could be placed under the royal crown and the conquest effected in a Christian manner without outraging or killing these poor Indians, who think that we are all evil and that the king who sent us here is ineffective and a tyrant. By so doing we would satisfy the wishes of our mother church, which, not without long consideration and forethought and illuminated by the Holy Spirit, entrusted these conquests and the conversions of souls to the kings of Castile, our lords, acknowledging in them the means, Christianity, and holiness for an undertaking as heroic as is that of winning souls for God.

Because of these matters (and others that I am not telling), we cannot preach the gospel now, for it is despised by these people on account of our great offenses and the harm we have done them. At the same time it is not desirable to abandon this land, either for the service of God or the conscience of his majesty since many souls have already been baptized. Besides, this place where we are now established is a good stepping stone and site from which to explore this whole land.

1.9

Letter upon Leaving Spain (1750)

JUNÍPERO SERRA

To Father Fray Francisco Serra:

This is my letter of farewell. We are all packed. In four days the *Villasota* will have weighed anchor and we shall have left Cadiz.

My dear, dear friend, words cannot express what I am feeling at this hour of separation. I know that my parents are in mortal grief; at this moment I commend them to you once more, and tell you again that it is you upon whom I rely for their comforting. Ah, if it were only possible for me to make them share my own immeasurable happiness, they themselves would urge me on! Could they dream, indeed, of a nobler vocation for their son than that of apostolic missionary?

Advanced in age as they are, and with their days numbered, the life that remains to them on this earth is only a moment in relation to eternity. Brief, alas, would have been the consolation which my presence would have given them. Would it be reasonable, and in conformity with the will of God, to cling henceforth to that? It is better to renounce seeing each other again in this world, so that we may deserve to be united forever in heaven.

Tell them, make them realize, that I suffer deeply in no longer being near them, as I once was, to solace their old age. But they know that what is essential must come before all else; and what is essential is for us to carry out the divine will. God alone, indeed, is responsible for my going away; it is His love alone which has snatched me beyond reach of their tenderness. May this same love so inspire them that they may generously accept our separation! Their

Source: Omer Englebert, *The Last of the Congustidors—Junípero Serra,* trans. Katherine Woods (New York: Harcourt, 1954). Reprinted by permission.

confessor will say this to them again; may they listen well to his counsel: they will derive from it that holy patience, that resignation to the divine will, which will restore their souls' serenity, and they will feel that the Lord has never called down such a blessing upon their home. By grace of repeating to themselves, as I repeat to them, that it is Our Lord and no one else who is the author of their ordeal, they will come to find, at last, that His yoke is easy, and their tribulation will be transformed into a calm happiness.

Since nothing in this world is worthy of our finding affliction in its loss, is it not better to concentrate our endeavors on fulfilling God's will and preparing ourselves for a good death? With a righteous death, everything is saved; without a death in righteousness, all is lost.

May they come to esteem themselves happy, these dear parents of mine, in having a son who, unworthy and a sinner as he is, prays at the altar for them every morning, with all his heart, imploring that God will give them the necessities of life, patience in trials, resignation to His holy will, the grace to live in peace and friendship with those about them, and, when at last God's summons comes, the grace of a sanctified death! In thinking of me—my beloved parents, and also my little sister Juanita and my brother-in-law Miguel—may they devote themselves wholly to beseeching God that I may become a good priest and a good friar. . . .

You remember, my dear Father, what you said to me some fifteen years ago, when, having received extreme unction, you believed yourself close to appearing before God?. . . I recall your words as if they had fallen this very moment from your lips; and with them I recall the promise I made to you, as you asked me, then: "Always to be a good son of St. Francis." Very well, then! It is to carry out your will, which is also the will of God, that I am now on the way to Mexico.

My dear Mother, as for you, I know that this is what you too have always asked of God for me, in your prayers. He has answered them already, in setting me upon the path on which I have entered. Be happy then, beloved Mother, and when you suffer say again, with your son, "Blessed be God! May His holy will be done!". . .

May she [Serra's sister Juanita], and her husband with her, show patience, respect, and compassion toward them; may they two live together as a good husband and wife who love each other; may they bring up their three children well; may the entire family continue in the practice of piety, going regularly to church, keeping close to the sacraments, assiduously making the Stations of the Cross.

And now we are parting, promising, as we do so, to pray for one another a very great deal. God will be the close protector of us all; He will give us His grace in this life and His glory in the life to come. Farewell then, my cherished Father! farewell, my fond Mother! farewell, little sister Juanita! farewell, Miguel, my dear brother-in-law! You will be able, each and all of you, to count upon the deep feeling in the heart of the one who is going away. Farewell! Farewell!

Farewell to you, Father Serra, my very dear colleague [and cousin, Fray]! Henceforth my letters will be of necessity less frequent; but you love my parents and they love you. That is why I commend them to you again, to you first of all; I commend them also to the loving-kindness of the Father Guardian, the Father Vicar, and the Father Master of Novices. If the last-named two could be present at the reading of this letter, I am sure that this would give pleasure to my parents and would add to their solace. . . .

Your affectionate friend in Our Lord,
FRAY JUNÍPERO SERRA, VERY UNWORTHY PRIEST.

1.10

Letter to the Viceroy (1773)

JUNÍPERO SERRA

Your Excellency should notify the said Officer and the soldiers that the training, governance, punishment and education of baptized Indians, or of those who are being prepared for Baptism, belong exclusively to the Missionary Fathers, the only exception being for capital offenses. Therefore no chastisement or ill-treatment should be inflicted on any of them whether by the Officer or by any soldier, without the Missionary Father's passing upon it. This has been the time-honored practice of this kingdom ever since the conquest; and it is quite in conformity with the law of nature concerning the education of the children, and an essential condition for the rightful training of the poor neophytes. Having these as his basic reasons, as well as others that might be adduced, the Most Illustrious Inspector General gave instructions to this effect before leaving California. Yet, on the contrary practice has prevailed, which has resulted in the worst of evils. I had intended to explain myself at greater length on this most important topic but I leave it for later, should circumstances make it necessary.

Concerning the number of soldiers required in the missions as escort, I give my opinion as follows:

For Mission San Carlos de Monterey, established on the banks of the Carmel River, in consideration of its proximity to the presidio, eight leather-jacket soldiers are sufficient.

Note: Footnotes have been deleted from this reading—ED.

Source: *Writings of Junípero Serra,* ed. Antonina Tibesar (Washington, DC: Academy of American Franciscan History, 1955), I, 307. Reprinted by permission.

For San Antonio de Padua de los Robles: ten leather-jacket soldiers.

For San Luis Obispo de los Tichos: ten leather-jacket soldiers also.

For San Gabriel de los Temblores: likewise ten leather-jacket soldiers.

And for San Diego of the Port: thirteen or fourteen leather-jacket soldiers also. The reason for this increase in number is that, from this mission, very frequently a courier has to start, either for California, or for Monterey. If the number were less, what occurred when the boat last came there might happen again. Captain Don Juan Pérez found so few soldiers in the mission, that he deemed it advisable to order a number of sailors to disembark for the proper protection of the mission. This I mentioned in my letter to Your Excellency, if my memory serves me well.

As for the Missions of San Buenaventura and Santa Clara, at first sight it would seem to me that, there should be twenty for the first mentioned, on account of its closeness to the Santa Barbara Channel, and for Santa Clara, fifteen.

With regard to the Mission of our Seraphic Father San Francisco, in his famous Port, I say nothing, because I am unaware of the manner and place in which Your Excellency has decided that it should be established.

The conclusion of all this seems to me to be as follows: that, for the presidio, and the missions already established or yet to be founded, it will be necessary and most suitable that the number of a hundred leather-jacket soldiers be realized, and that they be attached as a separate unit to the Presidio of Monterey, and should not be linked up, in any way, with those of Old California.

THE FRENCH EMPIRE:
"FISH, FURS, AND THE FAITH"

Because the French army and navy left North America after their defeat in the Seven Years War (called the French and Indian War here) in 1763, it is easy to forget that for over two centuries the French claimed much of the continent. French trappers, colonial administrators, and Catholic missionaries travelled, mapped, and attempted to subdue an enormous territory that extended down the St. Lawrence River to the Great Lakes and down the Mississippi River to the Gulf of Mexico.

French control of North America was tenuous because, except for the large population of Francophone Catholics along the northern shores of the St. Lawrence, in Quebec, France failed to send adequate numbers of colonists to people and control their empire. Unlike Spanish men, who came to the New World to stay and married Native American women, unlike English men who either brought or sent back for English wives, most French men preferred to make their fortunes and return home, as observers of the French mind have noted "to be buried in the yard of the church where as infants they were baptized."

Yet French Catholic missionaries did come to New France to stay. They kept the faith alive among the fishermen of the Atlantic coast, the fur trappers of the interior, and the farmers of Quebec; and they made an effort, which proved much less successful than that of their Spanish counterparts, to convert Native Americans. Since the French religious influence on the United States is far less noticeable today than that of the Spanish, two letters from French missionaries will illustrate their dreams and concerns. **Pierre Baird's Letter to His Jesuit Superior** reflects not just French but the general European impression of Native Americans. **Jean de Brebeuf's Instructions to Prospective Missionaries** mirrors not just the practical side of the missionary enterprise but its biases as well.

1.11

Letter to His Jesuit Superior (1611)

PIERRE BAIRD

And now you have had, my Reverend Father, an account of our voyage, of what happened in it, and before it, and since our arrival at this settlement. It now remains to tell you that the conversion of this country, to the Gospel, and of these people to civilization, is not a small undertaking nor free from great difficulties; for, in the first place, if we consider the country, it is only a forest, without other conveniences of life than those which will be brought from France, and what in time may be obtained from the soil after it has been cultivated. The nation is savage, wandering and full of bad habits; the people few and isolated. They are, I say, savage, haunting the woods, ignorant, lawless and rude: they are wanderers, with nothing to attach them to a place, neither homes nor relationship, neither possessions nor love of country; as a

Source: D. B. Quinn, ed., *New American World* (New York: Arno, 1979), II, 392–394.

people they have bad habits, are extremely lazy, gluttonous, profane, treacher-
ous, cruel in their revenge, and given up to all kinds of lewdness, men and
women alike, the men having several wives and abandoning them to others,
and the women only serving them as slaves, whom they strike and beat unmer-
cifully, and who dare not complain; and after being half killed, if it so please
the murderer, they must laugh and caress him.

With all these vices, they are exceedingly vainglorious: they think they are
better, more valiant and more ingenious than the French; and, what is difficult
to believe, richer than we are. They consider themselves, I say, braver than we
are, boasting that they have killed Basques and Malouins, and that they do a
great deal of harm to the ships, and that no one has ever resented it, insinuating
that it was from a lack of courage. They consider themselves better than the
French; "For," they say, "you are always fighting and quarreling among yourselves; we live peaceably. You are envious and are all the time slandering each
other; you are thieves and deceivers: you are covetous, and are neither generous
nor kind; as for us, if we have a morsel of bread we share it with our neighbor."

They are saying these and like things continually, seeing the above-
mentioned imperfections in some of us, and flattering themselves that some of
their own people do not have them so conspicuously, not realizing that they all
have much greater vices, and that the better part of our people do not have
even these defects, they conclude generally that they are superior to all christians. It is self-love that blinds them, and the evil one who leads them on, no
more nor less than in our France, we see those who have deviated from the
faith holding themselves higher and boasting of being better than the catholics,
because in some of them they see many faults; considering neither the virtues
of the other catholics, nor their own still greater imperfections; wishing to
have, like Cyclops, only a single eye, and to fix that one upon the vices of a few
catholics, never upon the virtues of the others, nor upon themselves, unless it
be for the purpose of self-deception.

Also they [the savages] consider themselves more ingenious, inasmuch as
they see us admire some of their productions as the work of people so rude
and ignorant; lacking intelligence, they bestow very little admiration upon
what we show them, although much more worthy of being admired. Hence
they regard themselves as much richer than we are, although they are poor and
wretched in the extreme. . . .

All these things, added to the difficulty of acquiring the language, the time
that must be consumed, the expenses that must be incurred, the great distress,
toil and poverty that must be endured, fully proclaim the greatness of this
enterprise and the difficulties which beset it. Yet many things encourage me to
continue in it. . . .

In conclusion, we hope in time to make them susceptible of receiving the
doctrines of the faith and of the christian and catholic religion, and later, to
penetrate farther into the regions beyond, which they say are more populous
and better cultivated. We base this hope upon Divine goodness and mercy,
upon the zeal and fervent charity of all good people who earnestly desire the
kingdom of God, particularly upon the holy prayers of Your Reverence and of

our Reverend Fathers and very dear Brothers, to whom we most affectionately commend ourselves.

From Port Royal, New France, this tenth day of June, one thousand six hundred and eleven.

PIERRE BAIRD

1.12

Instructions to Prospective Missionaries (1637)

JEAN DE BREBEUF

You must have sincere affection for the Savages, —looking upon them as ransomed by the blood of the son of God, and as our brethren, with whom we are to pass the rest of our lives.

To conciliate the Savages, you must be careful never to make them wait for you in embarking.

You must provide yourself with a tinder box or with a burning mirror, or with both, to furnish them fire in the daytime to light their pipes, and in the evening when they have to encamp; these little services win their hearts.

You should try to eat their sagamité or salmagundi in the way they prepare it, although it may be dirty, half-cooked, and very tasteless. As to the other numerous things which may be unpleasant, they must be endured for the love of God, without saying anything or appearing to notice them.

It is well at first to take everything they offer, although you may not be able to eat it all; for, when one becomes somewhat accustomed to it, there is not too much.

You must try and eat at daybreak unless you can take your meal with you in the canoe; for the day is very long, if you have to pass it without eating. The Barbarians eat only at Sunrise and Sunset, when they are on their journeys.

Source: R. G. Thwaites, ed., *Jesuit Relations and Allied Documents* (Cleveland: Burrows Brothers, 1896–1901), XII, 117, 119, 121.

You must be prompt in embarking and disembarking; and tuck up your gowns so that they will not get wet, and so that you will not carry either water or sand into the canoe. To be properly dressed, you must have your feet and legs bare; while crossing the rapids, you can wear your shoes, and, in the long portages, even your leggings.

You must so conduct yourself as not to be at all troublesome to even one of these Barbarians.

It is not well to ask many questions, nor should you yield to your desire to learn the language and to make observations on the way; this may be carried too far. You must relieve those in your canoe of this annoyance, especially as you cannot profit much by it during the work. Silence is a good equipment at such a time. . . .

Be careful not to annoy any one in the canoe with your hat; it would be better to take your nightcap. There is no impropriety among the Savages.

Do not undertake anything unless you desire to continue it; for example, do not begin to paddle unless you are inclined to continue paddling. Take from the start the place in the canoe that you wish to keep; do not lend them your garments, unless you are willing to surrender them during the whole journey. It is easier to refuse at first than to ask them back, to change, or to desist afterwards.

CHAPTER 2

✳

Religion in the British American Colonies

"Land, Liberty, and the Lord"

Unlike the Spanish colonists, whose marriages to Native American women created a mestizo population, unlike the French, who came to America only for riches and, except for Quebec, failed to establish a permanent culture, English colonists either brought wives with them or arranged for wives or marriagable women to make the voyage soon thereafter. The English were interested in transplanting their culture, including their religious beliefs and practices, intact from the Old to the New World.

Unlike the Catholic Spanish and French settlers, the religious quilt of the English-speaking colonies, while predominantly Protestant, was multicolored; and the variety proved both controversial and creative. Anglican dominated the southern colonies, while Puritans ruled the northern ones, with a few Catholics, Quakers, Lutherans, and Jews joining those two in the middle colonies; but the challenges and opportunities of the North American landscape tended to transform the religious denominations as they had been known in Europe; and colonists showed a tendency, which grew stronger with time, to abandon the established churches and join independent sects such as the Baptists and the Methodists.

Perhaps the most important of the early religious groups, a people whose influence extended far beyond their New England home turf and farther into the future than their registered numbers would have predicted, were the

Puritans. Some historians of religion believe that Americans are, in their moral and social conventions, even today quite Puritan.

THE PURITAN WORLD

The very first English settlers in New England were not Puritans but a small group of dissident nonconformists that we have come to call Pilgrims. They arrived in 1620, just thirteen years after the first successful English colony was established in Virginia. Although they were soon outnumbered and over-whelmed by the more aggressive Puritans, the Pilgrim spirit of religious adventure lived on. While still aboard the Mayflower, they put down their reasons for making their dangerous voyage and what they hoped to accomplish on the new continent. **"The Mayflower Compact"** was a civil agreement, but it was done "in the name of God."

Within ten years, shiploads of Puritans were pouring into the Massachusetts Bay colony. Puritans were Anglicans who were directed by the theology of the reformer John Calvin to demand that English Christianity be purified of its Catholic debris. Their theology was strongly Biblical, as is evident in a sermon by John Cotton, **"The Divine Right to Occupy the Land,"** which demonstrates the Puritan conviction that they were a New Israel arriving in a latter-day promised land. The Bay Colony's Governor John Winthrop captured in his **"A Model of Christian Charity"** the spirit of the Puritanism that so dramatically affected the course of American religious life.

After almost a full century in New England, during which time Puritans for all practical purposes left the Anglican Church to become Congregational-ists, the Puritan spirit and the culture it fashioned were still vibrant. One of its most illustrious products, the theologian Cotton Mather, who played a prominent role in the witchcraft controversy of 1692, wrote in 1710 **"A Christian at His Calling,"** making clear that the Puritan ethic of hard work and devotion to God still ruled his part of the world.

2.1

The Mayflower Compact (1620)[1]

In the Name of God, Amen.

We whose names are underwritten, the loyal subjects of our dread Sovereign Lord King James, by the Grace of God of Great Britain, France, and Ireland King, Defender of the Faith, etc.

Having undertaken, for the Glory of God and advancement of the Christian Faith and Honour of our King and Country, a Voyage to plant the First Colony in the Northern Parts of Virginia, do by these presents solemnly and mutually in the presence of God and one of another, Covenant and Combine ourselves together into a Civil Body Politic, for our better ordering and preservation and furtherance of the ends aforesaid; and by virtue hereof to enact, constitute and frame such just and equal Laws, Ordinances, Acts, Constitutions and Offices, from time to time, as shall be thought most meet and convenient for the general good of the Colony, unto which we promise all due submission and obedience. In witness whereof we have hereunder subscribed our names at Cape Cod, the 11th of November, in the year of the reign of our Sovereign Lord King James, of England, France and Ireland the eighteenth, and of Scotland the fifty-fourth. Anno Domini 1620.

2.2

The Divine Right to Occupy the Land[2]

JOHN COTTON

Moreover I will appoint a place for my people Israel, and I will plant them, that they may dwell in a place of their own, and move no more. . . [II Sam 7:10]

---

1. Source: www./law.ou.edu/hist/mayflow.html

2. Source: Common.

The placing of a people in this or that country is from the appointment of the Lord. . .

Quest. Wherein doth this work of God stand in appointing a place for a people?

Answ. First, when God espies or discovers a land for a people, as in Ezek. 20:6: "He brought them into a land that He had espied for them." And, that is, when either He gives them to discover it themselves, or hears of it discovered by others, and fitting them.

Second, after He hath espied it, when He carrieth them along to it, so that they plainly see a providence of God leading them from one country to another, as in Ex. 19:4: "You have seen how I have borne you as on eagles' wings, and brought you unto Myself." So that though they met with many difficulties, yet He carried them high above them all, like an eagle, flying over seas and rocks, and all hindrances.

Third, when He makes room for a people to dwell there, as in Ps. 80:9: "Thou preparedst room for them. . . ."

Now, God makes room for a people three ways: First, when He casts out the enemies of a people before them by lawful war with the inhabitants, which God calls them unto, as in Ps. 44:2: "Thou didst drive out the heathen before them." But this course of warring against others and driving them out without provocation depends upon special commission from God, or else it is not imitable.

Second, when He gives a foreign people favor in the eyes of any native people to come and sit down with them, either by way of purchase, as Abraham did obtain the field of Machpelah; or else when they give it in courtesy, as Pharaoh did the land of Goshen unto the sons of Jacob.

Third, when He makes a country, though not altogether void of inhabitants, yet void in that place where they reside. Where there is a vacant place, there is liberty for the sons of Adam or Noah to come and inhabit, though they neither buy it nor ask their leaves. . . . So that it is free from that common grant for any to take possession of vacant countries. Indeed, no nation is to drive out another without special commission from Heaven, such as the Israelites had, unless the natives do unjustly wrong them, and will not recompense the wrongs done in a peaceable fort [manner]. And then they may right themselves by lawful war and subdue the country unto themselves. . . .

This may teach us all, where we now dwell or where after we may dwell: Be sure you look at every place appointed to you from the hand of God. We may not rush into any place and never say to God, "By Your leave." But we must discern how God appoints us this place. There is poor comfort in sitting down in any place that you cannot say, "This place is appointed me of God." Canst thou say that God made room for thee, and there hath settled thee above all hindrances? Didst thou find that God made room for thee either by lawful descent, or purchase, or gift, or other warrantable right? Why, then, this is the place God hath appointed thee; here He hath made room for thee, He hath placed thee in Rehoboth, in a peaceable place. This we must discern or else we are but intruders upon God. And when we do withal discern that God giveth us these outward blessings from His love in Christ, and maketh comfortable provision as well for our soul as for our bodies by the means of grace, then do we enjoy our present possession as well by gracious promise as by the common, and just, and bountiful providence of the Lord. Or, if a man do remove, he must see that God hath espied out such a country for him.

2.3

A Model of Christian Charity (1630)

JOHN WINTHROP

1. For the persons, we are a Company professing ourselves fellow members of Christ. In which respect only, though we were absent from each other many miles, and had our employments as far distant, yet we ought to account ourselves knit together by this bond of love, and live in exercise of it. . . .

2. For the work we have in hand, it is by a mutual consent through a special overruling providence, and a more than ordinary approbation of the Churches of Christ, to seek out a place of Cohabitation and Consortship under a due form of Government both civil and ecclesiastical. In such cases as this, the care of the public must oversway all private respects, by which not only conscience, but mere Civil policy doth bind us. For it is a rule that particular estates cannot subsist in the ruin of the public.

3. The end is to improve our lives to do more service to the Lord, the comfort and increase of the body of Christ, whereof we are members, that ourselves and posterity may be the better preserved from the Common corruptions of this evil world, to serve the Lord and work out our Salvation under the power and purity of his holy Ordinances.

4. For the means whereby this must be effected, they are twofold: a Conformity with the work and end we aim at—these we see are extraordinary; therefore, we must not content ourselves with usual ordinary means. Whatsoever we did or ought to have done when we lived in England,

Source: *Winthrop Papers*, Vol II. (Boston: Massachusetts Historical Society, 1931).

the same must we do, and more also, where we go. That which the most (in their Church) maintain as a truth in profession only, we must bring into familiar and constant practice. As in this duty of love, we must love brotherly without dissimulation. We must love one another with a pure heart fervently; we must bear one another's burdens; we must not look only on our own things, but also on the things of our brethren. Neither must we think that the Lord will bear with such failings at our hands as he doth from those among whom we have lived. . . .

. . . Thus stands the cause between God and us. We are entered into Covenant with him for this work, we have taken out a Commission, the Lord hath given us leave to draw our own Articles. We have professed to enterprise these Actions upon these . . . ends, we have hereupon besought him of favor and blessing. Now if the Lord shall please to hear us, and bring us in peace to the place we desire, then hath he ratified this Covenant and sealed our Commission, [and] will exact a strict performance of the articles contained in it; but if we shall neglect the observation of these Articles which are the ends we have propounded, and dissembling with our God, shall fall to embrace this present world and prosecute our carnal intentions, seeking great things for ourselves and our posterity, the Lord will surely break out in wrath against us, be revenged of such a perjured people, and make us know the price of the breach of such a Covenant.

Now the only way to avoid this shipwreck and to provide for our posterity is to follow the Counsel of Micah, to do Justly, to love mercy, to walk humbly with our God. For this end, we must be knit together in this work as one man; we must entertain each other in brotherly Affection; we must be willing to abridge ourselves of our superfluities, for the supply of others' necessities; we must uphold a familiar Commerce together in all meekness, gentleness, patience and liberality; we must delight in each other, make others' Conditions our own, rejoice together, mourn together, labor and suffer together, always having before our eyes our Commission and Community in the work, our Community as members of the same body. So shall we keep the unity of the spirit in the bond of peace. The Lord will be our God and delight to dwell among us, as his own people and will command a blessing upon us in all our ways, so that we shall see much more of his wisdom, power, goodness, and truth than formerly we have been acquainted with. We shall find that the God of Israel is among us, when ten of us shall be able to resist a thousand of our enemies, when he shall make us a praise and glory, that men shall say of succeeding plantations: the Lord make it like that of New England. For we must Consider that we shall be as a City upon a Hill, the eyes of all people are upon us. So that if we shall deal falsely with our God in this work we have undertaken and so cause him to withdraw his present help from us, we shall be made a story and a by-word through the world; we shall open the mouths of enemies to speak evil of the ways of God and all professors for God's sake; we shall shame the faces of many of God's worthy servants, and cause their prayers to be turned into Curses upon us till we be consumed out of the good land whither we are going. And to shut up this discourse with that exhortation of Moses, that faithful servant of the Lord, in his last farewell to Israel, . . . Beloved, there is now set before us life and good, death and evil in that we are Commanded this day to love the Lord our God, and to love one another, to walk in his ways and to keep his Commandments and his Ordinance and his laws and the Articles of our Covenant with him, that we live and be multiplied, and that the Lord our God may bless the land whither we go to possess it. But if our hearts shall turn away so that we will not obey, but shall be seduced and worship . . . other gods, our pleasures, and profits, and serve them, it is propounded unto us this day, we shall surely perish out of the good Land whither we pass over this vast Sea to posess it.

Therefore, let us choose life, that we, and our Seed, may live; obeying his voice, and leaving to him, for he is our life, and our prosperity.

2.4

A Christian at His Calling (1701)

COTTON MATHER

Every Christian ordinarily should have a calling. That is to say, there should be some special business, and some settled business, wherein a Christian should for the most part spend the most of his time; and this, that so he may glorify God . . .

There is a variety of callings in the world; even as there are various objects, about which the callings of men are conversant, and various designs unto which the callings of men are intended. Some callings, are more immediately, to serve the souls of our neighbors; and some their safety and some their defense; and some their bodies; and some their estates; and some their delights. But it is not lawful for a Christian ordinarily to live without some calling or another, until infirmities have unhappily disabled him. Indeed a man cannot live without the help of other men. But how can a man reasonably look for the help of other men, if he be not in some calling helpful to other men? . . .

Source: http://personal.pitnet.net/primarysources/mather

© Bettmann/Corbis

A Portrait of Cotton Mather,
Puritan divine

A Christian should have it contrived, that his calling be agreeable, as well as allowable. It is a wonderful inconvenience for a man to have a calling that won't agree with him. See to it, O parents, that when you choose callings for your children, you wisely consult their capacities, and their inclinations; lest you ruin them . . .

It is the singular favor of God, unto a man, that he can attend his occupation with contentment and satisfaction. That one man has a spirit formed and fitted for one occupation, and another man for another, this is from the operation that God, who forms the spirit of man within him . . . Count not your business to be your burden or your blemish. Let not a proud heart make you ashamed of that business wherein you may be a blessing. For my part, I can't see an honest man hard at work in the way of his occupation, be it never so [insignificant] (and tho perhaps driving of a wheel barrow) [without finding] my heart sensibly touched with respect for such man. It is possible, you may think, that you may see others in some greater and richer business; and you may think that you might be, yourselves greater and richer, if you were in some other business. Yea, but has not the God of heaven cast you into that business, which now takes you up?

THE RAPID DIVERSIFICATION
OF RELIGION IN THE ENGLISH COLONIES

America may have started out strongly Puritan and its Puritan heritage may still cling to it, but early in the colonial experience Puritanism was challenged by alternative religious thought and practices. In 1635, a dissident Puritan minister named Roger Williams caused the Puritan establishment so many problems that he was exiled from Massachusetts to a region set aside for religious misfits, a colony later called Rhode Island. In 1644, he protested in his ***Bloudy Tenet of Persecution*** against authoritative controls in matters of conscience.

In 1637, Anne Hutchinson followed Williams into exile. Although she was a women, Hutchinson insisted on preaching the Gospel, under the direct inspiration of the Holy Spirit, with men present; and her **Creed,** as recorded by Reverend Theodore Welde, brought her before Governor John Winthrop. After her **Trial at the Court of Newton,** she was banished for behavior unbecoming to her sex. She went first to Rhode Island, proved too radical even to live in Roger Williams' free colony, and was eventually killed in an Indian raid on Long Island.

Not all challenges to Puritan and Anglican establishments came from domestic dissidents. In 1632, Charles I granted to the Calvert family a colony on the northern shores of the Chesapeake as a refuge for Roman Catholics, a colony named Maryland. In 1634, Andrew White described the first **Catholic Arrival in Virginia.** Seven years later the Virginia colony passed a **Law Banning Catholics from Public Office** or proselyting there. In 1700, **New York Anglicans** spoke out against them. Colonial diversification was never smooth sailing, and Catholics were the first victims of religious bigotry.

In 1681, Charles II granted to William Penn a colony inland from the mid-Atlantic region for another dissident religious group, the Society of Friends, called Quakers by their detractors. In his 1686 **"Defense of Freedom of Religion,"** he made it a Pennsylvania tradition to welcome people of all religious persuasions.

2.5

Bloudy Tenet
of Persecution (1644)

ROGER WILLIAMS

THE ARGUMENT

. . . that the blood of so many hundred thousand souls of Protestants and Papists, spilt in the Wars of present and former Ages, for their respective Consciences, is not required nor accepted by Jesus Christ the Prince of Peace. . . .

. . . All Civil States with their Officers of justice in their respective constitutions and administrations are proved essentially Civil, and therefore not Judges, Governors or Defenders of the Spiritual or Christian State and Worship.

. . . It is the will and command of God, that (since the coming of his Son the Lord Jesus) a permission of the most paganish, Jewish, Turkish, or Antichristian consciences and worships, be granted to all men in all Nations and Countries: and they are only to be fought against with that Sword which is only (in Soul matters) able to conquer, to wit, the Sword of God's Spirit, the Word of God.

. . . The state of the Land of Israel, the Kings and people thereof in Peace and War, is proved figurative and ceremonial, and no pattern nor precedent for any Kingdom or civil state in the world to follow.

. . . God requireth not an uniformity of Religion to be enacted and enforced in any civil state; which enforced uniformity (sooner or later) is the greatest occasion of civil War, ravishing of conscience, persecution of Christ Jesus in his servants, and of the hypocrisy, and destruction of millions of souls.

. . . In holding an enforced uniformity of Religion in a civil state, we must necessarily disclaim our desires and hopes of the Jews' conversion to Christ.

. . . An enforced uniformity of Religion throughout a Nation or civil state, confounds the Civil and Religious, denies the principles of Christianity and civility, and that Jesus Christ is come in the Flesh.

. . . The permission of other consciences and worships than a state professeth, only can (according to God) procure a firm and lasting peace, (good assurance

Source: Roger Williams, *Bloudy Tenet of Persecution*, (London, 1644).

being taken according to the wisdom of the civil state for uniformity of civil obedience from all sorts).

. . . I acknowledge that to molest any person, Jew or Gentile, for either professing doctrine, or practising worship merely religious or spiritual, is to persecute him, and such a person (what ever his doctrine of practice be true or false) suffereth persecution for conscience.

The church or company of worshippers (whether true or false) is like unto a Body or College of Physicians in a City; like unto a Corporation, Society, or Company of East-Indie or Turkie-Merchants, or any other Society or Company in London: which Companies may hold their Courts, keep their Records, hold disputations; and in matters concerning their Society, may dissent, divide, break into Schisms and Factions, sue and implead each other at the Law, yea, wholly break up and dissolve into pieces and nothing, and yet the peace of the City not be in the least measure impaired or disturbed; because the essence or being of the City, and so the well-being and peace thereof is essentially distinct from those particular Societies; the City Courts, City Laws, City punishments distinct from theirs. The City was before them, and stands absolute and entire, when such a Corporation or Society is taken down.

. . . as God needeth not the help of a material sword of steel to assist the sword of the Spirit in the affairs of conscience, so those men, those Magistrates, Yea, the Commonwealth which makes such Magistrates, must needs have power and authority from Christ Jesus to fit Judge and to determine in all the great controversies concerning doctrine, discipline, government, etc. . . .

Either there is no lawful Commonwealth nor civil State of men in the world, which is not qualified with this spiritual discerning. . . .

Or, . . . the Commonwealth and Magistrates, thereof must judge and punish as they are persuaded in their own belief and conscience, (be their conscience Paganish, Turkish, or Antichristian) what is this but to confound Heaven and Earth together, and not only to take away the being of Christianity out of the World, but to take away all civility, and the world out of this world, and to lay all upon heaps of confusion? . . .

Christ Jesus would not be pleased to make use of the Civil Magistrate to assist him in his Spiritual Kingdom; nor would he yet be daunted or discouraged in his Servants by all their threats and terrors: for Love is strong as death, and the coals thereof give a most vehement flame, and are not quenched by all the waters and floods of mightiest opposition.

Christ's Church is like a chaste and loving wife, in whose heart is fixed her Husband's love, who hath found the tenderness of his love towards her, and hath been made fruitful by him, and therefore seeks she not the smiles, nor fears the frowns of all the Emperors in the World to bring her Christ unto her, or keep him from her.

As it is most true that Magistracy in general is of God for the preservation of Mankind in civil order and peace, (the World otherwise would be like the Sea, wherein Men, like Fishes would hunt and devour each other, and the greater devour the less:) so also it is true, that Magistracy in special for the several kinds of it is of Man. Now what kind of Magistrate soever the people shall agree to set up, whether he receive Christianity before he be set in office, or whether he receive Christianity after, he receives no more power of Magistracy, than a Magistrate that hath received no Christianity. For neither of them both can receive more, than the Commonwealth, the Body of People and civil State, as men, communicate unto them, and betrust with them.

All lawful Magistrates in the World, both before the coming of Christ Jesus, and since . . . are but Derivatives and Agents immediately derived and employed as eyes and hands, serving for the good of the whole: Hence they have and can have no more Power, than fundamentally lies in the Bodies or Fountains themselves, which Power, Might, or Authority, is not Religious, Christian, etc. but natural, humane and civil.

And hence it is true, that a Christian Captain, Christian Merchant, Physician, Lawyer, Pilot, Father, Master, and (so consequently) Magistrate, etc. is no more a Captain, Merchant, Physician, Lawyer, Pilot, Father, Master, Magistrate, etc. than a Captain, Merchant, etc. of any other Conscience or Religion.

. . . In his season God will glorify himself in all his truths: but to gratify thy desire, thus: A pagan or Antichristian Pilot may be as skillful to carry the Ship to its desired Port, as any Christian Mariner or Pilot in the World, and may perform that work with as much safety and speed: yet have they not command over the souls and consciences of their passengers or mariners under them, although they may justly see to the labor of the one, and the civil behavior of all in the ship: A Christian Pilot he performs the same work (as likewise doth the Metaphorical Pilot in the ship of the Commonweal) from a principle of knowledge and experience: but more than this, he acts from a root of the fear of God and love to mankind, in his whole course. Secondly, his aim is more to glorify God than to gain his pay, or make his voyage. Thirdly, he walks heavenly with Men, and God, in a constant observation of God's hand in storms, calms, etc. so that the thread of Navigation being equally spun by a believing or unbelieving Pilot, yet is it drawn over with the gold of Godliness and Christianity by a Christian Pilot, while he is holy in all manner of Christianity. . . . But lastly, the Christian Pilot's power over the Souls and consciences of his Sailors and Passengers is not greater than of the Antichristian, otherwise than he can subdue the souls of any by the two-edged sword of the Spirit, the Word of God, and by his holy demeanor in his place, etc.

2.6

Creed (1644)

ANNE HUTCHINSON

- That the Law and the preaching of it, is of no use at all to drive a man to Christ.
- That a man is united to Christ and justified, without faith; yea, from eternity.
- That faith is not a receiving of Christ, but a man's discerning that he hath received him already.
- That a man is united to Christ only by the work of the Spirit upon him, without any act of his.
- That a man is never effectually Christ's, till he hath assurance.
- This assurance is only from the witness of the Spirit.
- This witness of the Spirit is merely immediate, without any respect to the word, or any concurrence with it.
- When a man hath once this witness he never doubts more.
- To question my assurance, though I fall into murder or adultery, proves that I never had true assurance.
- Sanctification can be no evidence of a man's good estate.
- No comfort can be had from any conditional promise.
- Poverty in spirit (to which Christ pronounced blessedness, Matt v. 3) is only this, to see I have no grace at all.
- To see I have no grace in me, will give me comfort; but to take comfort from sight of grace, is legal.
- An hypocrite may have Adam's graces that he had in innocence.
- The graces of Saints and hypocrites differ not.
- All graces are in Christ, as in the subject, and none in us, that Christ believes, Christ loves, etc.
- Christ is the new Creature.
- God loves a man never the better for any holiness in him, and never the less, be he never so unholy.
- Sin in a child of God must never trouble him.

Source: The Reverend Theodore Welde, written 1644, found at
www.annehutchinson.com/creed.htm

- Trouble in conscience for sins of Commission, or for neglect of duties, shows a man to be under a covenant of works.
- All covenants to God expressed in works are legal works.
- A Christian is not bound to the Law as a rule of his conversation.
- A Christian is not bound to pray except the Spirit moves him.
- A minister that hath not this new light is not able to edify others: that have it.
- The whole letter of the Scripture is a covenant of works.
- No Christian must be pressed to duties of holiness.
- No Christian must be exhorted to faith, love, and prayer, etc., except we know he hath the Spirit.
- A man may have all graces, and yet want Christ.
- All a believer's activity is only to act sin.

2.7

Hutchinson's Trial at the Court at Newton (1637)

Gov. John Winthrop: Mrs. Hutchinson, you are called here as one of those that have troubled the peace of the commonwealth and the churches here; you are known to be a woman that hath had a great share in the promoting and divulging of those opinions that are the cause of this trouble, and to be nearly joined not only in affinity and affection with some of those the court had taken notice of and passed censure upon, but you have spoken divers things, as we have been informed, very prejudicial to the honour of the churches and ministers thereof, and you have maintained a meeting and an assembly in your house that hath been condemned by the general assembly as a thing not tolerable nor comely in the sight of God nor fitting for your sex, and notwithstanding that was cried down you have continued the same. Therefore we have thought good to send for you to understand

Source: http://personal.pitnet.net/primarysources/hutchinson.html

how things are, that if you be in an erroneous way we may reduce you that so you may become a profitable member here among us. Otherwise if you be obstinate in your course that then the court may take such course that you may trouble us no further. Therefore I would intreat you to express whether you do assent and hold in practice to those opinions and factions that have been handled in court already, that is to say, whether you do not justify Mr. Wheelwright's sermon and the petition.

Mrs. Anne Hutchinson: I am called here to answer before you but I hear no things laid to my charge.

Gov. John Winthrop: I have told you some already and more I can tell you.

Mrs. Anne Hutchinson: Name one, Sir.

Gov. John Winthrop: Have I not named some already?

Mrs. Anne Hutchinson: What have I said or done?

Gov. John Winthrop: Why for your doings, this you did harbor and countenance those that are parties in this faction that you have heard of.

Mrs. Anne Hutchinson: That's matter of conscience, Sir.

Gov. John Winthrop: Your conscience you must keep, or it must be kept for you.

[After hours of haggling]

Mrs. Anne Hutchinson: If you please to give me leave I shall give you the ground of what I know to be true. Being much troubled to see the falseness of the constitution of the Church of England, I had like to have turned Separatist. Whereupon I kept a day of solemn humiliation and pondering of the thing; this scripture was brought unto me—he that denies Jesus Christ to be come in the flesh is antichrist. This I considered of and in considering found that the papists did not deny him to be come in the flesh, nor we did not deny him—who then was antichrist? Was the Turk antichrist only? The Lord knows that I could not open scripture; he must by his prophetical office open it unto me. So after that being unsatisfied in the thing, the Lord was pleased to bring this scripture out of the Hebrews, he that denies the testament denies the testator, and in this did open unto me and give me to see that those which did not teach the new covenant had the spirit of antichrist, and upon this he did discover the ministry unto me; and ever since, I bless the Lord, he hath let me see which was the clear ministry and which the wrong.

Since that time I confess I have been more choice and he hath left me to distinguish between the voice of my beloved and the voice of Moses, the voice of John the Baptist and the voice of antichrist, for all those voices are spoken of in scripture. Now if you do condemn me for speaking what in my conscience I know to be truth I must commit myself unto the Lord.

Mr. Nowel (assistant to the Court): How do you know that was the spirit?

Mrs. Anne Hutchinson: How did Abraham know that it was God that bid him offer his son, being a breach of the sixth commandment?

Dep. Gov. Thomas Dudley: By an immediate voice.

Mrs. Anne Hutchinson: So to me by an immediate revelation.

Dep. Gov. Thomas Dudley: How! an immediate revelation.

Mrs. Anne Hutchinson: By the voice of his own spirit to my soul. I will give you another scripture, Jeremiah 46:27–28—out of which the Lord showed me what he would do for me and the rest of his servants. But after he was pleased to reveal himself to me I did presently, like Abraham, run to Hagar. And after that he did let me see the atheism of my own heart, for which I begged of the Lord that it might not remain in my heart, and being thus, he did show me this (a twelve-month after) which I told you of before. . . .

Therefore, I desire you to look to it, for you see this scripture fulfilled this day and therefore I desire you as you tender the Lord and the church and commonwealth to consider and look what you do.

You have power over my body but the Lord Jesus hath power over my body and soul; and assure yourselves thus much, you do as much as in you lies to put the Lord Jesus Christ from you, and if you go on in this course you begin, you will bring a curse upon you and your posterity, and the mouth of the Lord hath spoken it.

Dep. Gov. Thomas Dudley: What is the scripture she brings?

Mr. Stoughton (assistant to the Court): Behold I turn away from you.

Mrs. Anne Hutchinson: But now having seen him which is invisible I fear not what man can do unto me.

Gov. John Winthrop: Daniel was delivered by miracle; do you think to be deliver'd so too?

Mrs. Anne Hutchinson: I do here speak it before the court. I look that the Lord should deliver me by his providence. . . . (because God had said to her) though I should meet with affliction, yet I am the same God that delivered Daniel out of the lion's den, I will also deliver thee.

Mr. Harlakenden (assistant to the Court): I may read scripture and the most glorious hypocrite may read them and yet go down to hell.

Mrs. Anne Hutchinson: It may be so. . . .

Gov. John Winthrop: I am persuaded that the revelation she brings forth is delusion.

(All the court but some two or three ministers cry out, we all believe it—we all believe it. Mrs. Hutchinson was found guilty.)

Gov. John Winthrop: The court hath already declared themselves satisfied concerning the things you hear, and concerning the troublesomeness of her spirit and the danger of her course amongst us, which is not to be suffered. Therefore if it be the mind of the court that Mrs. Hutchinson for these things that appear before us is unfit for our society, and if it be the mind of the court that she shall be banished out of our liberties and imprisoned till she be sent away, let them hold up their hands.

(All but three did so.)

Gov. John Winthrop: Mrs. Hutchinson, the sentence of the court you hear is that you are banished from out of our jurisdiction as being a woman not fit for our society, and are to be imprisoned till the court shall send you away.

Mrs. Anne Hutchinson: I desire to know wherefore I am banished?

Gov. John Winthrop: Say no more. The court knows wherefore and is satisfied.

2.8

On a Catholic Arrival in Virginia (1634)

ANDREW WHITE

At length, sailing from this place, we reached the *cape,* which they call *Point Comfort,* in Virginia, on the 27th of February, full of apprehension, lest the English inhabitants, who were much displeased at our settling, should be plotting something against us. Nevertheless the letters we carried from the King, and from the high treasurer of England, served to allay their anger, and to procure those things, which would afterwards be useful to us. For the Governor of Virginia hoped, that by this kindness toward us, he would more easily recover from the Royal treasury a large sum of money which was due him. They only told us that a rumor prevailed, that six ships were coming to reduce everything under the power of the Spaniards, and that for this reason, all the natives were in arms; this we afterwards found to be true. Yet I fear the rumor had its origin with the English.

After being kindly treated for eight or nine days, we set sail on the third of March, and entering the Chesapeak Bay, we turned our course to the north to reach the *Potomeack* River. The Chesopeacke Bay, ten leagues (30 Italian miles) wide, flows gently between its shores: it is four, five and six fathoms deep, and abounds in fish when the season is favorable; you will scarcely find a more

Source: *Relatio Inteneris: Narrative of a Voyage to Maryland* (Baltimore: Maryland Hist. Soc, 1844), pp. 30–34.

beautiful body of water. Yet it yields the palm to the Potomeack River, which we named after St. Gregory.

Having now arrived at the wished-for country, we allotted names according to circumstances. And indeed the Promontory, which is toward the south, we consecrated with the name of St. Gregory (now Smith Point,) naming the northern one (now Point Lookout) St. Michael's, in honor of all the angels. Never have I beheld a larger or more beautiful river. The Thames seems a mere rivulet in comparison with it; it is not disfigured with any swamps, but has firm land on each side. Fine groves of trees appear, not choked with briers or bushes and undergrowth, but growing at intervals as if planted by the hand of man, so that you can drive a four-horse carriage, wherever you choose, through the midst of the trees. Just at the mouth of the river, we observed the natives in arms. That night, fires blazed through the whole country, and since they had never, seen such a large ship, messengers were sent in all directions, who reported that a *Canoe,* like an island had come with as many men as there were trees in the woods. We went on, however, to Herons' Islands, so called from the immense numbers of these birds. The first island we came to, [we called] St. Clement's Island, and as it has a sloping shore, there is no way of getting to it except by wading. Here the women, who had left the ship, to do the washing, upset the boat and came near being drowned, losing also a large part of my linen clothes, no small loss in these parts.

This island abounds in cedar and sassafras trees, and flowers and herbs, for making all kinds of salads, and it also produces a wild nut tree, which bears a very hard walnut with a thick shell and a small but very delicious kernel. Since, however, the island contains only four hundred acres, we saw that it would not afford room enough for the new settlement. Yet we looked for a suitable place to build only a Fort (perhaps on the island itself) to keep off strangers, and to protect the trade of the river and our boundaries; for this was the narrowest crossing-place on the river.

On the day of *the Annunciation of the Most Holy Virgin* Mary in the year 1634, we celebrated the mass for the first time, on this island. This had never been done before in this part of the world. After we had completed the sacrifice, we took upon our shoulders a great cross, which we had hewn out of a tree, and advancing in order to the appointed place, with the assistance of the Governor and his associates and the other Catholics, we erected a trophy to Christ the Saviour, humbly reciting, on our bended knees, the Litanies of the Sacred Cross, with great emotion.

2.9

Virginia Law Banning Catholics from Public Office (1641)

I t is enacted by the authority aforesaid, that according to a Statute made in the third year of the reign of our sovereign Lord King James, of blessed memory, no popist [sic] recusant shall at any time hereafter exercise the place or places of secretary, counsellor, register, commissioner, surveyor or sheriff, or any other public place, but be utterly disabled for the same;

And further, be it enacted by the authority aforesaid, that none shall be admitted into any of the aforesaid offices or places before he or they have taken the oaths of supremacy and allegiance. And if any person or persons whatsoever shall by any sinister or secret means contrive to himself any of the aforesaid places, or any other public office whatsoever, and refuse to take the aforesaid oaths, he or they so convicted before any assembly shall be dismissed of his said office, and for his offense herein, forfeit a thousand pounds weight of tobacco, to be disposed of by the next grand assembly after conviction.

And it is enacted by the authority aforesaid that the statutes in force against popish recusants be duly executed in the government; and that it shall not be lawful, under the penalty aforesaid, for any popish priest that shall hereafter arrive here to remain above five days, after warning given for his departure by the governor or commander of that place where he or they shall be, if wind and weather hinder not his departure; this act to be in force after ten days from the publication here at James City.

Source: Francis X. Curran, S.J. (ed.), *Catholics in Colonial Law* (Chicago: Loyola University Press, 1963) p. 22.

2.10

New York Anglicans Speak
Out on Catholics (1700)

Whereas divers Jesuits preists and popish missionaries have of late, come and for Some time have had their residence in the remote parts of this Province and other his ma'tys adjacent Colonies, who by their wicked and Subtle Insinuations Industriously Labour to Debauch Seduce and w'thdraw the Indians from their due obedience unto his most Sacred ma'ty and to Excite and Stir them up to Sedition Rebellion and open Hostility against his ma'tys Goverm't for prevention whereof Bee it Enacted by his Excel the Gov'r Council and Representatives Convened in Generall Assembly and it is hereby Enacted by the Authority of the Same, That all and every Jesuit and Seminary Preist missionary or other Spirituall or Ecclesiasticall person made or ordained by any Authority power or Jurisdicon derived Challenged or p'tended from the Pope or See of Rome now resideing w'th in this province or any part thereof shall depart from and out of the Same at or before the first day of November next in this present year Seaventeen hundred.

And be it further Enacted by the authority aforesaid, That all and every Jesuit Seminary Preist Missionary or other Spirituall or Ecdesiasticall person made or Ordained by any Authority power or Jurisdiction derived Challenged or p'tended from the pope or See of Rome or that shall profess himself or otherwise appear to be Such by preaching & teaching of others to Say any popish prayers by Celebrating masses granting of absolutions or using any other of the Romish Ceremonies & Rites of worship by what name title or degree So ever such a person shall be called or known who shall Continue abide remaine or come into this province or any part thereof after ye first day of November aforesaid shall be deemed and Accounted an incendiary and disturber of the publick peace and Safety and an Enemy to the true Christian Religion and shal be adjudged to Suffer perpetuall Imprisonm't and if any person being So Sentenced and actually Imprisoned shall break prison and make his Escape and be afterwards retaken he shall Suffer such paines of Death penalties and forfeitures as in Cases of ffelony.

And it is further Enacted by the authority aforesaid, That every person that shall wittingly and willingly receive, harbour, Conceale aid Succour and releive any Jesuit preist missionary or other Ecclesiastical person of the Romish Clergy knowing him to be Such and be thereof lawfully Convicted before any of his

Source: Hugh Hastings (ed.), *Ecclesiastical Records, State of New York* (Albany, 1901), II, 1368–1370.

ma'tys Courts of Records w'thin this Province w'ch Courts are hereby Impowered and Authorized to hear try and Determine the Same he shall forfeit the Sum of two hundred pounds Currant mony of this Province one half to his Maty for and towards the Support of the Governm't and the other half to the Informer who shall sue for ye Same in any Court of Record w'thin this province wherein no Essoyn protection or wager of Law shall be allowed and Such person shall be further punished by being Set in ye pillory on three Severall dayes and also be bound to the good behaviour at the discretion of the Court.

And be it further Enacted by the Authority aforesaid That it shall and may be Lawfull to and for every Justice of the peace to cause any person or persons Suspected of being a Jesuit, Seminary Preist or of the Romish Clergy to be apprehended & Convented before himself & Some other of his ma'tys Justices and if Such person do not give Satisfactory acco't of himself he shall be committed to prison in order to a Tryall also it shall and may be Lawfull to and for any person or persons to app'rehend w'thout a warrant any Jesuit Seminary preist or other of the Romish Clergy as aforesaid and to Convent him before ye Gov'r or any two of the Council to be Examined and Imprisoned in order to a Tryall unless he give a Satisfactory acco't of himself and as it will be Esteemed and accepted as a good Service don for ye King by the person who shall Seiz & apprehend any Jesuit Preist missionary or Romish Ecclesiactick as aforesaid So the Gov'r of this province for ye time being w'th ye advice & Consent of the Council may Suitably reward him as they think fitt.

Provided this act shall not Extend, or be Construed to Extend unto any of the Romish Clergy, who shall happen to be Shipwrackt, or thro' other adversity shall be cast on shoure or driven into this province, So as he Continue or abide no Longer w'thin ye Same than untill he may have opportunity of passage for his Departure So also as Such person Immediately upon his arrivall shall forthw'th attend ye Gov'r if near to ye place of his Residence or otherwise on one or more of ye Council or next Justices of the peace, & acquaint y'm w'th his Circumstances & observe ye Direccons w'ch they shall give him during his stay in ye province.

2.11

Defense of Freedom
of Religion (1686)

WILLIAM PENN

Moderation, the subject of this discourse, is, in plainer English, liberty of conscience to church-dissenters: a cause I have, with all humility, undertaken to plead, against the prejudices of the times.

That there is such a thing as conscience, and the liberty of it, in reference to faith and worship towards God, must not be denied, even by those that are most scandalized at the ill use some seem to have made of such pretences. But to settle the terms: by conscience, I understand, the apprehension and persuasion a man has of his duty to God: by liberty of conscience, I mean, a free and open profession and exercise of that duty; especially in worship: but I always premise this conscience to keep within the bounds of morality, and that it be neither frantic or mischievous, but a good subject, a good child, a good servant, in all the affairs of life; as exact to yield to Caesar the things that are Caesar's, as jealous of withholding from God the thing that is God's.—In brief, he that acknowledges the civil government under which he lives, and that maintains no principle hurtful to his neighbour in his civil property.

For he that in any thing violates his duty to these relations, cannot be said to observe it to God, who ought to have his tribute out of it. Such do not reject their prince, parent, master, or neighbour, but God, who enjoins that duty to them. Those pathetic words of Christ will naturally enough reach the case, "In that ye did it not to them, ye did it not to me:" for duty to such relations hath a divine stamp; and divine right runs through more things of the world, and acts of our lives, than we are aware of; and sacrilege may be committed against more than the church. Nor will a dedication to God, of the robbery from man, expiate the guilt of disobedience: for though zeal could turn gossip to theft, his altars would renounce the sacrifice.

The conscience then that I state, and the liberty I pray, carrying so great a salvo and deference to public and private relations, no ill design can, with any justice, be fixed upon the author, or reflection upon the subject, which by this time, I think, I may venture to call a toleration.

But to this so much craved, as well as needed, toleration, I meet with two objections of weight, the solving of which will make way for it in this

Source: *The Silent Works of William Penn*, 4th ed. (London: Wm. Philips, 1825), II, 507–508.

kingdom. And the first is, a disbelief of the possibility of the thing. 'Toleration of dissenting worships from that established, is not practicable,' say some, 'without danger to the state, with which it is interwoven.' This is political. The other objection is, 'That admitting dissenters to be in the wrong, (which is always premised by the national church) such latitude were the way to keep up the disunion, and instead of compelling them into a better way, leave them in the possession and pursuit of their old errors.' This is religious. I think I have given the objections fairly; it will be my next business to answer them as fully.

THE IMPORTANCE OF RELIGIOUS EDUCATION IN THE BRITISH COLONIES

A common theme of early colonial American thought was the importance of higher education. Although Calvinists were biblically orthodox, they considered it essential that their clergy be well educated. In 1636, only sixteen years after the arrival of the Pilgrims, the Puritans in New England founded a college across the river from Boston, at a site they named Cambridge after the university city in England, and named it for one of its benefactors John Harvard. **Thomas Shephard's Letter to His Son at Harvard** in the seventeenth century indicates the purpose of the school: to train young men for the ministry. **The Yale College "Rules,"** written the year of its founding, 1701, give the same impression, as do the **"Statutes,"** written in 1723, of Virginia's College of William and Mary, founded in 1693.

Religious fervor and the ideal of an educated clergy gave birth to the first centers of American higher education. From these early provincial, ecclesiastical beginnings, America's first universities expanded both in enrollment and offerings. While curricula remained for many years closely tied to classical and clerical training, their doors were gradually opened to students preparing for careers not only in the ministry but in education and law. The move toward secular education was slow, but it was steady and unrelenting.

2.12

Letter to Son
at Harvard College

THOMAS SHEPARD

Dear Son, I think meet (partly from the advice of your renowned Grandfather to myself att my admission into the College, and partly from some other observation I have had respecting studies in that society) to leave the Remembrances and advice following with you, in this great Change of your life, rather in writing, than viva voce only; that so they may be the better considered and improved by you, and may abide upon your heart when I shall be (and that may be sooner than you are aware) taken from thee, and speak no more: requiring you frequently to read over, and seriously to ponder, and digest, as also conscientiously to putt in practice the same through the Lord[']s assistance.

I. Remember the end of your life, which is acoming back again to God, and fellowship with God; for as your great misery is your separation, and estrangement from him, so your happiness, or last end, is your Return again to him; and because there is no coming to God but by Christ[']s Righteousness, and no Christ to be had but by faith, and no Faith without humiliation or sense of your misery, hence therefore let all your Prayers, and tears be, that God would first humble you, that so you may fly by faith to Christ, and come by Christ to God.

II. Remember the End of this turn of your life, viz the Holy Ministry; that you may declare the Name of God to the Conversion and salvation of souls; for this End, your Father has sett you apart with many Tears, and hath give you up unto God, that he may accept of you; and that he would delight in you.

III. Remember therefore that God looks for and calls for much holiness from you: I had rather see you buried in your Grave, than grow light, loose, wanton, or prophane. God's secretts in the holy scriptures, which are left to instruct Ministers, are never made known to common and prophane Spirits: and therefore be sure you begin and end every Day wherein you study with Earnest prayer to God, lamenting after the favour of God; reading some part of the Scriptures daily; and setting

Source: Website on American Education: www.skidmore.edu/stkuroda/HI107/sheplet.htm

apart some time every Day (tho' but one Quarter of an hour) for meditation of the things of God.

IV. Remember therefore, that tho' you have spent your time in the vanity of Childhood; sports and mirth, little minding better things, yet that now, when come to this ripeness of Admission to the College, that now God and man expects you should putt away Childish things: now in the time come, wherein you are to be serious, and to learn sobriety, and wisdom in all your ways which concern God and man.

V. Remember that these are times and Days of much Light and Knowledge and that therefore you had as good be no Scholar as not excell in Knowledge and Learning. Abhorr therefore one hour of idleness as you would be ashamed of one hour of Drunkenness: Look that you loose not your precious time by falling in with Idle Compansions, or by growing weary of your Studies, or by Love of any filthy lust; or by discouragement of heart that you shall never attain to any exellency of Knowledge, or by thinking too well of your self, that you have gott as much as is needfull for you, when you have gott as much as your Equals in the same year; no verily, the Spirit of God will not communicate much to you in a way of Idleness, but will curse your Soul, while this sin is nourished, which hath spoiled so many hopeful youths in their first blossoming in the College: And therefore tho' I would not have you neglect seasons of recreation a little before and after meals (and altho' I would not have you Study late in the night usually, yet look that you rise early and loose not your morning thoughts, when your mind is most fresh, and fitt for Study) butbe no wicked example all the Day to any of your Fellows in spending your time Idly: And do not content yourself to do as much as your Tutor setts you about, but know that you will never excell in Learning unless you do Somewhat else in private Hours, wherein his Care cannot reach you: and do not think that Idling away your time is no great Sin, if so be you think you can hide it from the Eyes of others: but Consider that God, who always sees you, and observes how you Spend your time, will be provoked for every hour of that precious time you now misspend, which you are like never to find the like to this in the College, all your Life after.

★ ★ ★

VII. Remember that not only heavenly and spiritual and Supernatural knowledge descends from God, but also all naturall, and humane learning, and abilities; and therefore pray much, not only for the one but also for the other from the Father of Lights, and mercies; and remember that prayer att Christs feet for all the learning you want, shall fetch you in more in an hour, than possibly you may gett by all the books, and helps you have otherwise in many years.

VIII. Remember to be Grace (not Childish) and amiable and loving toward all the Scholars, that you may win their hearts and Honour.

IX. Remember now to be watchful against the two great Sins of many Scholars; the first is youthful Lusts, speculative wantoness, and secret filthiness, which God sees in the Dark, and for which God hardens and blinds young men[']s hearts, his holy Spirit departing from such, unclean Styes. The second is malignancy and secret distaste of Holiness and the Power of Godliness, and the Professors of it, both these sins you will quickly fall into, unto your own perdition, if you be not carefull of your Company, for there are and will be such in every Scholasticall Society for the most part, as will tech you how to be filthy and how to jest, and Scorn at Godliness, and the professors thereof, whose Company I charge you to fly from as from the Devil, and abhor: and that you may be kept from these, read often that Scripture Prov[erbs] 2.10.11.12, 16.

X. Remember to intreat God with Tears before you come to hear any Sermon, that thereby God would powerfully speak to your heart, and make his truth precious to you: neglect not to write after the preacher always, and write not in loose sheets but in handsome Paper-books; and be carefull to preserve and peruse the Same. And upon the Sabbath days make exceeding Conscience of Sanctification, mix not your other Studies, much less Idleness, or vain and casual discourses with the Duties of that holy Day; but remember that Command Lev[iticus] 19.30. Ye shall keep my Sabbaths and reverence my Sanctuary, I am the Lord.

XI. Remember that whensoever you read, hear or conceive of any Divine truth, you Study to affect your heart with it and the Goodness of it. Take heed of receiving Truth into your head without the Love of it in your heart, lest God give you up to strong Delusions to believe lyes, and that in the Conclusion all your learning shall make you more fitt to decieve [sic] your Self and others. Take heed lest by seeing things with a form of Knowledge, the Lord do not bind you by that Knowledge the more, that in seing [sic] you shall not see: If therefore God revealth any truth to you att any time, be sure you be humbly and deeply thankfull: and when he hides any truth from you, be sure you lie down, and loath yourself, and be humble: the first degree of wisdom is to know and feel your own folly.

2 Tim[othy] 2. 7. Consider what I say and the Lord give thee understanding in all things.

Prov[erbs] 23. 15. My Son, if thine heart be wise, my heart shall rejoice, even mine.

Pater tuus
T. SHEPARD

2.13

Yale College "Rules" (1701)

1. All Scholars Shall Live Religious, Godly and Blameless Lives according to the Rules of Gods Word, diligently Reading the holy Scriptures the Fountain of Light and Truth; and constantly attend upon all the Duties of Religion both in Publick and Secret.

2. That the President, or in his absence One of the Tutors Shall constantly Pray in the College-Hall every morning and Evening: and Shall read a Chapter or Suitable Portion of the Holy Scriptures, unless there be Some other Theological Discourse or Religious Exercise: and Every Member of the College whether Graduates or Undergraduates, whether Residing in the College or in the Town of New-Haven Shall Seasonably Attend upon Penalty that every Undergraduate who Shall be absent (without Sufficient Excuse) Shall be Fined one Penny and for comeing Tardy after the Introductory Collect is made Shall be fin'd one half penny.

3. The President is hereby Desired as he hath Time & Opportunity to make and Exhibit in the Hall Such a publick Exposition, Sermon or Discourse as he shall think proper for the Instruction of ye Scholars, and when He Shall See cause So to do and Give public Notice thereof, Every Undergraduate Shall be Obliged to Attend upon the Same Penalty as aforesaid.

4. Every Student of the College Shall diligently attend upon the Duties of Religious Worship, both Private and Publick of the Sabbath Day, and Shall attend upon the Said Public Worship of God in the Meeting-House with the President and Tutors on the Lord's Day and on Days of public Fasting and Thanksgiving appointed by Authority, and all Public Lectures appointed by the Minister of the first Society of New Haven, upon Penalty of Four Pence for absence (without Sufficient reason) on either Part of the Sabbath or any Day of Public Fasting or Thanksgiving and three Pence for Absence on a Lecture, one Penny for comeing Tardy. And if any Student Shall be Detain'd by Sickness or a necessary Occasion He Shall Signifie the Same to the President or any of the Tutors on the morning; or otherwise his Excuse Shall be judged as Groundless unless it otherwise manifestly appear to be Sufficient.

5. No Student of this College Shall attend upon any Religious Meetings either Public or Private on the Sabbath or any other Day but Such as are appointed by Public Authority or Approved by the President upon

Source: F. B. Dexter, *Biographical Sketches of the Graduates of Yale College* (New York: Henry Halto Co. 1896), I, 3–5.

Penalty of a Fine, Public Admonition, Confession or Otherwise according to the Nature or Demerit of the Offence.

6. That if any Student Shall Prophane the Sabbath by unnecessary Business, Diversion, Walking abroad, or makeing any Indecent Noise or Disorder on the Said Day, or on the Evening before or after, or Shall be Guilty of any Rude, Profane or indecent Behaviour in the Time of Publick Worship, or at Prayer at any Time in the College Hall, He Shall be punished, Admonished or otherwise according to the Nature and Demerit of his Crime.

7. Every Student of this College Shall in Words and Behaviour Shew all Due Honour, Respect and Reverence towards all their Superiours, Such as their natural Parents, Magistrates and Ministers, and Especially to the President, Fellows and Tutors of this College; and Shall in no case use any Reproachful, reviling, Disrespectful or contumacious Language: but on the contrary Shall Shew Them all proper Tokens of Reverence, Obedience and Respect: Such as Uncovering their Heads, Rising up, Bowing and Keeping Silence in their Presence. And particularly all Undergraduates Shall be uncovered in the College Yard when the President or either of the Fellows or Tutors are there: and when They are in their Sight and View in any other Place: and all the Bacchelors of Arts Shall be uncovered in the College Yard when the President is there; and all the Scholars shall Bow when he Goes in or out of the College Hall, or into the Meeting-House, provided that the Public Worship is not Begun. And Scholars Shall Shew due Respect and Distance to those who are in Senior and Superiour Classes.

2.14

College of William and Mary "Statutes" (1723)

There are three things which the Founders of this College proposed to themselves, to which all its Statutes should be directed. The First is, That the Youth of Virginia should be well educated to Learning and good Morals. The Second is, That the Churches of America, especially Virginia,

Source: E. W. Knight (ed.), *A Documentary History of Ed in the South before 1860* (Chapel Hill: UNC Press, 1949), I, 509ff.

should be supplied with good Ministers after the Doctrine and Government of the Church of England; and that the College should be a constant Seminary for this Purpose. The Third is, That the Indians of America should be instructed in the Christian Religion, and that some of the Indian Youth that are well-behaved and well-inclined, being first well prepared in the Divinity School, may be sent out to preach the Gospel to their Countrymen in their own Tongue, after they have duly been put in Orders of Deacons and Priests. . . .

[Concerning Grammar School students,] Special Care likewise must be taken of their Morals, that none of the Scholars presume to tell a Lie, or curse or swear, or talk or do any Thing obscene, or quarrel and fight, or play at Cards or Dice, or set in to Drinking, or do any Thing else that is contrary to good Manners. And that all such Faults may be so much the more easily detected, the Master shall chuse some of the most trusty Scholars for public Observators, to give him an Account of all such Transgressions, and according to the Degrees of Heinousness of the Crime, let the Discipline be used without Respect of Persons.

As to the Method of teaching, and of the Government of the School, let the Usher be obedient to the Master in every Thing, as to his Superior.

On Saturdays and the Eves of Holidays, let a sacred Lesson be prescribed out of Castalio's Dialogues, or Buchanan's Paraphrase of the Psalms, or any other good Book which the President and Master shall approve of, according to the Capacity of the Boys, of which an Account is to be taken on Monday, and the next Day after the Holidays.

The Master shall likewise take Care that all the Scholars learn the Church of England Catechism in the vulgar Tongue; and that they who are further advanced learn it likewise in Latin.

Before they are promoted to the Philosophy School, they who aim at the Privileges and Revenue of a Foundation Scholar, must first undergo an Examination before the President and Masters, and Ministers skilful in the learned Languages; whether they have made due Progress in their Latin and Greek. And let the same Examination be undergone concerning their Progress in the Study of Philosophy, before they are promoted to the Divinity School. And let no Blockhead or lazy Fellow in his Studies be elected. . . .

For avoiding the Danger of Heresy, Schism, and Disloyalty, let the President and Masters, before they enter upon these Offices, give their Assent to the Articles of the Christian Faith, in the same Manner, and in the same Words, as the Ministers in England, by Act of Parliament are obliged to sign the Articles of the Church of England. And in the same Manner too they shall take the Oaths of Allegiance to the King or Queen of England. And further, they shall take an Oath that they will faithfully discharge their Office, according to the College Statutes, before the President and Masters, upon the Holy Evangelists. All this under the Penalty of being deprived of their Office and Salary.

INSECURITY AND WITCHCRAFT

The fervor and devotion that inspired, motivated, and gave direction to early New England religious life did not free the English colonists from spiritual insecurity. The best example both of religious zeal and the way fear of the unknown led it astray was the curious episode called the witchcraft craze.

King James I strongly believed in witches, and his royal paranoia spawned a pandemic. In 1688, the Massachusetts Puritan divine, Cotton Mather, delivered a famous **"Discourse on Witchcraft,"** which he confirmed theologically the existence and malevolence of witches, thus giving religious sanction to the search for human purveyors of evil designs. By 1692, the small community of Salem plantations had executed nineteen people accused of nefarious relations with Satan, and fifty-five more were awaiting execution before Governor William Phips halted the carnage.

The **Examinations of Sarah Good** in March 1692, and **Mary Easty** in April of that same year illustrate the assumptions, methods, and conclusions of the ruling religious elite. But by May even Cotton Mather was having second thoughts about the use of **Spectral Evidence** and feared that innocent people might be suffering. In October, his father Increase Mather, also a Puritan minister, published his **"Cases of Conscience Concerning Evil Spirits."** While continuing to argue that witches did exist and when proven to be such should be exterminated, while refusing to cast any doubt on the validity of the executions already carried out, he tried to determine what constituted sufficient proof of guilt. In his conclusions—that proof should rest only on the testimony of two independent witnesses—he inadvertently contributed to the establishment of a distinctively American principle of jurisprudence.

2.15

Discourse on Witchcraft (1688)

COTTEN MATHER

It should next be proved THAT Witchcraft *is*.

The *Being* of such a thing is denied by many that place a *great part* of their *small wit* in deriding the Stories that are told of it. Their chief Argument is, that they never *saw* any Witches, therefore there are *none*. Just as if you or I should say, we never met with any *Robbers* on the Road, therefore there was never any *Padding* there.

Indeed the *Devils* are loath to have true Notions of *Witches* entertained with us. I have beheld them to put out the Eyes of an Enchanted Child, when a Book that proves, *There is Witchcraft,* was laid before her. But there are especially two Demonstrations that Evince the Being of that Infernal mysterious thing.

First, We have the Testimony of *Scripture* for it. We find *Witchcrafts* often mentioned, sometimes by way of *Assertion,* sometimes by way of *Allusion,* in the Oracles of God. Besides that, We have there the *History of divers Witches* in these infallible and inspired Writings. Particularly, the Instance of the *Witch* at *Endor,* in I *Sam.* 28. 7. is so plain and full that *Witchcraft* itself is not a more amazing thing than any *Dispute* about the Being of it, after this. The Advocates of *Witches* must use more *Tricks* to make Nonsense of the *Bible,* than ever the *Witch* of *Endor* used in her Magical Incantations, if they would Evade the Force of that Famous History. They that will believe no *Witches,* do imagine that *Jugglers* only are meant by them whom the Sacred Writ calleth so. But what do they think of that Law in *Exod.* 22. 18. *Thou shalt not suffer a Witch to live?* Methinks 'tis a little too hard to punish every silly *Juggler* with so great severity.

Secondly, We have the *Testimony* of *Experience* for it. What will those *Incredulous,* who must be the only *Ingenious* Men say to this? Many *Witches* have like those in *Acts* 19. 18. *Confessed and showed their Deeds.* We see those things done, that it is impossible any *Disease,* or any *Deceit* should procure. We see some hideous *Wretches* in hideous *Horrors* confessing, *That they did the Mischiefs.* This Confession is often made by them that are owners of as much Reason as the people that laugh at all *Conceit* of *Witchcraft:* The Exactest Scrutiny of Skillful Physicians cannot find any distraction in their minds. This *Confession* is often made by them that are apart one from another, and yet they *agree* in all the Circumstances of it. This *Confession* is

Source: David Levin, *What Happened in Salem?* (New York: Harcourt-Brace, 1960).

often made by them that at the same time will produce the *Engines* and *Ensigns* of their *Hellish Trade,* and give the standers-by an *Ocular Conviction* of what they do, and how. There can be no Judgment left of any *Human Affairs,* if such *Confessions* must be Ridiculed: all the *Murders,* yea, and all the *Bargains* in the World must be mere *Imaginations* if such *Confessions* are of no Account.

★ ★ ★

WITCHCRAFT is a most Monstrous and Horrid *Evil.* Indeed there is a vast Heap of Bloody Roaring Impieties contained in the *Bowels* of it. *Witchcraft,* is a Renouncing of *God,* and Advancing of a filthy *Devil* into the Throne of the Most High; 'tis the most nefandous *High-Treason* against the MAJESTY on High. *Witchcraft,* is a Renouncing of *Christ,* and preferring the Communion of a loathesome lying *Devil* before all the Salvation of the Lord Redeemer; 'tis a Trampling under foot that *Blood* which is more precious than *Hills* of *Silver,* or whole *Mountains* of *Gold.* There is in *Witchcraft,* a most explicit *Renouncing* of all that is *Holy,* and *Just* and *Good.* The *Law* given by *God,* the *Prayer* taught by *Christ,* the *Creed* left by the *Apostles,* is become *Abominable* where *Witchcraft* is Embraced: The very Reciting of those blessed things is commonly burdensome where *Witchcraft* is. All the *sure Mercies* of the *New Covenant,* and all the *just Duties* of it, are utterly abdicated by that *cursed Covenant* which *Witchcraft* is Constituted with. *Witchcraft* is a Siding with *Hell* against *Heaven* and *Earth;* and therefore a *Witch* is not to be endured in either of them. 'Tis a *Capital* Crime; and it is to be prosecuted as a piece of *Devilism* that would not not only deprive *God* and *Christ* of all His Honor, but also plunder Man of all his Comfort. *Witchcraft,* it's an impotent, but an impudent *Essay* to make an *Hell* of the Universe, and to allow Nothing but a *Tophet* in the World. *Witchcraft*—What shall I say of it! It is the furthest Effort of our *Original Sin;* and all that can make any Practice or Persons odious, is here in the *Exalt[at]ion* of it.

2.16

Examinations of Sarah Good
(March 1, 1692) and Mary Easty
(April 22, 1692)

EXAMINATION OF SARAH GOOD

[The examination of Sarah Good before the worshipfull Assts John Harthorn [and] Jonathan Curren.]

    (H) Sarah Good what evil spirit have you familiarity with

    (S G) none

    (H) have you made no contract with the devil,

    (g) good answered no

    (H) why doe you hurt these children

    (g) I doe not hurt them. I scorn it.

    (H) who doe you imploy then to doe it

    (g) no creature but I am falsely accused

    (H) why did you go away muttering from mr Parris his house

    (g) I did not mutter but I thanked him for what he gave my child

    (H) have you made no contract with the devil

    (g) no

    (H) desired the children all of them to look upon her, and see, if this were the person that had hurt them and so they all did looke upon her and said this was one of the persons that did torment them—presently they—were all tormented.

    (H) Sarah good doe you not see now what you have done why doe you not tell us the truth, why doe you thus torment these poor children

    (g) I doe not torment them,

    (H) who do you imploy then

    (g) I imploy nobody I scorn it

    (H) how came they thus tormented,

    (g) what doe I know you bring others here and now you charge me with it

    (H) why who was it.

    (g) I doe not know but it was some you brought into the meeting house with you

Source: Salem trials home page:
http://www.law.umkc.edu/faculty/projects/ftrials/salem/ASA_Goox.htm

(H) wee brought you into the meeting house

(g) But you brought in two more

(H) Who was it then that tormented the children

(g) it was osburn

(H) what is it that you say when you goe muttering away from persons houses

(g) if I must tell I will tell

(H) doe tell us then

(g) if I must tell I will tell, it is the commandments I may say my commandments I hope

(H) what commandment is it

(g) if I must tell you I will tell, it is a psalm

(H) what psalm

(g) after a long time shee muttered over some part of a psalm

(H) who doe you serve

(g) I serve god

(H) what god doe you serve

(g) the god that made heaven and earth

[Though shee was not willing to mention the word God her answers were in a very wicked, spitfull manner reflecting and retorting aganst the authority with base and abusive words and many lies shee was taken in.it was here said that her housband had said that he was afraid that shee either was a witch or would be one very quickly the worsh mr Harthon asked him his reason why he said so of her whether he had ever seen any thing by her he answered no not in this nature but it was her bad carriage to him and indeed said he I may say with tears that shee is an enimy to all good.]

EXAMINATION OF MARY EASTY

At a Court held at Salem village 22 Apr. 1692
By the Hon. John Hathorne & Jonathan Corwin.
[At the bringing in of the the accused severall fell into fits.]

(H) Doth this woman hurt you? [EXAMINERS' NOTE: Many mouths were stopt, & several other fits seized them Abig: Williams said it was Goody Eastie, & she had hurt her, the like said Mary Walcot, & Ann Putman, John indian said her saw her with Goody Hobbs.] What do you say, are you guilty?

(E) I can say before Christ Jesus, I am free.

Source: Salem trials home page.
www./aw.umkc.edu/faculty/projects/ftrizls/salem/ASA_EASX.HTM

(H) You see these accuse you. There is a God—Hath she brought the book to you? Their mouths were stopt. What have you done to these children?

(E) I know nothing.

(H) How can you say you know nothing, when you see these tormented, & accuse you that you know nothing? Would you have me accuse my self?

(E) Yes if you be guilty.

(H) How far have you complyed w'th Satan whereby he takes this advantage ag't you?

(E) Sir, I never complyed but prayed against him all my dayes, I have no complyance with Satan in this. What would you have me do?

(H) Confess if you be guilty.

(E) I will say it, if it was my last time, I am clear of this sin.

(H) Of what sin?

(E) Of witchcraft.

(H) Are you certain this is the woman?

[Never a one could speak for fits. By and by Ann Putman said that was the woman, it was like her, & she told me her name; It is marvailous to me that you should sometimes think they are bewitcht, & sometimes not, when severall confess that I never knew? Her hands were clincht together, & then the hands of Mercy Lewis was clincht Look now you hands are open, her hands are open. Is this the woman? They made signes but could not speak, but Ann Putman afterwards Betty Hubbard cryed out Oh, Goody Easty, Goody Easty you are the woman, you are the woman Put up her head, for while her head is bowed the necks of these are broken.]

(H) What do you say to this?

(E) Why God will know.

(H) Nay God knows now.

(E) I know he dos.

(H) What did you think of the actions of others before your sisters came out, did you think it was Witchcraft?

(E) I cannot tell.

(H) Why do you not think it is Witchcraft?

(E) It is an evil spirit, but wither it be witchcraft I do not know,

[Sevrall said she brought them the Book and then they fell into fits.]

2.17

On Spectral Evidence
(May 31, 1692)

COTTON MATHER

And yet I must humbly beg you that in the management of the affair in your most worthy hands, you do not lay more stress upon pure specter testimony than it will bear. When you are satisfied or have good, plain, legal evidence that the demons which molest our poor neighbors do indeed represent such and such people to the sufferers, tho' this be a presumption, yet I suppose you will not reckon it a conviction that the people so represented are witches to be immediately exterminated. It is very certain that the devils have sometimes represented the shapes of persons not only innocent, but also very virtuous, tho' I believe that the just God then ordinarily provides a way for the speedy vindication of the persons thus abused. Moreover, I do suspect that persons who have too much indulged themselves in malignant, envious, malicious ebullitions of their souls, may unhappily expose themselves to the judgment of being represented by devils, of whom they never had any vision, and with whom they have much less written any covenant. I would say this: if upon the bare supposal of a poor creature's being represented by a specter, too great a progress be made by the authority in ruining a poor neighbor so represented, it may be that a door may be thereby opened for the devils to obtain from the courts in the invisible world a license to proceed unto most hideous desolations upon the repute and repose of such as have yet been kept from the great transgression. If mankind have thus far once consented unto the credit of diabolical representations, the door is opened! Perhaps there are wise and good men that may be ready to style him that shall advance this caution, a witch advocate; but in the winding up, this caution will certainly be wished for. . . .

Albeit the business of this witchcraft be very much transacted upon the stage of imagination, yet we know that, as in treason there is an imagining which is a capital crime, and here also the business thus managed in imagination yet may not be called imaginary. The effects are dreadfully real. Our dear neighbors are most really tormented, really murdered, and really acquainted

Source: Kenneth Silverman (ed.), *Selected Letters of Cotton Mather* (Baton Rouge: LSU Press, 1971) pp. 36–40.

with hidden things, which are afterwards proved plainly to have been realities. I say, then, as that man is justly executed for an assassinate, who in the sight of men shall with a sword in his hand stab his neighbor into the heart, so suppose a long train laid unto a barrel of gunpowder under the floor where a neighbor is, and suppose a man with a match perhaps in his mouth, out of sight, set fire unto the further end of the train, tho' never so far off. This man also is to be treated as equally a malefactor. Our neighbors at Salem Village are blown up, after a sort, with an infernal gunpowder; the train is laid in the laws of the kingdom of darkness limited by God himself. Now the question is, who gives fire to this train? and by what acts is the match applied? . . .

I begin to fear that the devils do more easily proselyte poor mortals into witchcraft than is commonly conceived. When a sinful child of man distempers himself with some exorbitant motions in his mind (and it is to be feared the murmuring phrensies of late prevailing in the country have this way exposed many to sore temptations) a devil then soon presents himself unto him, and he demands, Are you willing that I should go do this or that for you? If the man once comply, the devil hath him now in a most horrid snare, and by a permission from the just vengeance of God he visits the man with buffetings as well as allurements, till the forlorn man at first only for the sake of quietness, but at length out of improved wickedness, will commission the devil to do mischief as often as he requires it. And for this cause 'tis worth considering, whether there be a necessity always by extirpations by halter or fagot every wretched creature that shall be hooked into some degrees of witchcraft. What if some of the lesser criminals be only scourged with lesser punishments, and also put upon some solemn, open, public, and explicit renunciation of the devil? I am apt to think that the devils would then cease afflicting the neighborhood whom these wretches have stood them upon, and perhaps they themselves would now suffer some impressions from the devils, which if they do, they must be willing to bear till the God that hears prayer deliver them.

2.18

Cases of Conscience Concerning Evil Spirits (October 3, 1692)

INCREASE MATHER

That there are Devils and Witches, the Scripture asserts, and experience confirms, That they are common enemies of Mankind, and set upon mischief, is not to be doubted: That the Devil can (by Divine Permission) and often doth vex men in Body and Estate, without the Instrumentality of Witches, is undeniable: That he often hath, and delights to have the concurrence of Witches, and their consent in harming men, is consonant to his native Malice to Man, and too lamentably exemplified: That Witches, when detected and convinced, ought to be exterminated and cut off . . .

[He then asked: What is sufficient proof?]

1. *That a free and voluntary Confession of the Crime made by the Person suspected and accused after Examination, is a sufficient Ground of Conviction.*

    Indeed, if Persons are Distracted, or under the Power of *Phrenetic Melancholy,* that alters the Case; but the Jurors that examine them, and their Neighbors that know them, may easily determine that Case; or if Confession be extorted, the Evidence is not so clear and convictive; but if any Persons out of Remorse of Conscience, or from a Touch of God in their Spirits, confess and show their Deeds, as the Converted Magicians in *Ephesus* did, *Acts* 19. 18, 19. nothing can be more clear. . . .

    . . . But as for the Testimony of Confessing Witches against others, the case is not so clear as against themselves, they are not such credible Witnesses, as in a Case of Life and Death is to be desired: It is beyond dispute, that the Devil makes his Witches to dream strange things of themselves and others which are not so. . . . What Credit can be given to those that say they can turn Men into Horses? If so, they can as well turn Horses into Men; but all the Witches on Earth in Conjunction with all the Devils in Hell, can never make or unmake a rational Soul. . . . In a word, there is no more Reality in what many Witches confess of strange things seen or done by them, whilst Satan had them in his full Power, than there is in *Lucian's* ridiculous Fable of his being Bewitched into an

Source: David Levin, *What happened in Salem?* (New York: Harcourt-Brace, 1960).

Ass, and what strange Feats he then played; so that what such persons relate concerning Persons and Things at Witch-meetings, ought not to be received with too much Credulity.

2. *If two credible Persons shall affirm upon Oath that they have seen the party accused speaking such words, or doing things which none but such as have Familiarity with the Devil ever did or can do, that's a sufficient Ground for Conviction.*
    . . . The Devil never assists men to do supernatural things undesired. When therefore such like things shall be testified against the accused Party not by *Specters* which are Devils in the Shape of Persons either living or dead, but by real men or women who may be credited; it is proof enough that such an one has that Conversation and Correspondence with the Devil, as that he or she, whoever they be, ought to be exterminated from amongst men. This notwithstanding I will add; It were better that ten suspected Witches should escape, than that one innocent Person should be Condemned; that is an old saying, and true, *Prestat reum nocentem absolvi, quam ex prohibitis Indiciis & illegitima probatione condemnari.* It is better that a Guilty Person should be Absolved, than that he should without sufficient ground of Conviction be condemned. I had rather judge a Witch to be an honest woman, than judge an honest woman as a Witch. The Word of God directs men not to proceed to the execution of the most capital offenders, until such time as upon searching diligently, the matter is *found to be a Truth, and the thing certain,* Deut. 13. 14, 15.

★ ★ ★

Boston, New-England, Octob. 3. 1692.

POSTSCRIPT

The Design of the preceding *Dissertation,* is not to plead for Witchcrafts, or to appear as an Advocate for Witches. . . .

Nor is there designed any Reflection on those worthy Persons who have been concerned in the late Proceedings at *Salem:* They are wise and good Men, and have acted with all Fidelity according to their Light, and have out of tenderness declined the doing of some things, which in our own Judgments they were satisfied about: Having therefore so arduous a Case before them, Pity and Prayers rather than Censures are their due; on which account I am glad that there is published to the World (by my Son) a *Breviate of the Trials* of some who were lately executed, whereby I hope the thinking part of Mankind will be satisfied, that there was more than that which is called *Specter Evidence* for the Conviction of the Persons condemned. I was not myself present at any of the Trials, excepting one, *viz.* that of *George Burroughs;* had I been one of his Judges, I could not have acquitted him: For several Persons did upon Oath testify, that they saw him do such things as no Man that has not a Devil to be his Familiar could perform: And the Judges affirm, that they have not convicted anyone

merely on the account of what *Specters* have said, or of what has been represented to the Eyes or Imaginations of the sick bewitched Persons. . . . It becomes
those of my Profession to be very tender in Cases of Blood, and to imitate our
Lord and Master, *Who came not to destroy the Lives of Men, but to save them.*

★ ★ ★

Some I hear have taken up a Notion, that the Book newly published by my
Son, is contradictory to this of mine: 'Tis strange that such Imaginations should
enter into the Minds of Men: I perused and approved of that Book before it was
printed; and nothing but my Relation to him hindered me from recommend-
ing it to the World: But myself and Son agreed unto the humble Advice which
twelve Ministers concurringly presented before his Excellency and Council,
respecting the present Difficulties, which let the World judge, whether there be
anything in it dissentany from what is attested by either of us. . . .

THE FIRST "GREAT AWAKENING"

A century after the first settlers arrived in the English-speaking colonies, the
religious picture had changed. Many later immigrants came more for material
gain than for religious freedom, and they had little interest in spiritual matters.
There was widespread religious and ecclesiastical apathy among the population, which now extended inland some distance from the sea and beyond the
influence of organized churches. In the first half of the eighteenth century,
from a religious perspective "just in time," came a revival of religion.

The "Great Awakening" was accompanied by the kind of emotional fervor
that John Wesley was at the same time reporting in his services in England. It
had some of the characteristics (crying out in agony, swooning) that only two
decades earlier had been identified as marks of demon possession. It brought
"unchurched" Americans into the fold and divided Americans who were
already "churched" into two religious camps: New Lights, who favored the
excitement of the revival; and Old Lights, who viewed the emotionalism of
the revival with skepticism and at times hostility.

One New Light leader was English Wesleyan transplant, George
Whitefield, whose **Journal Entries** capture the spirit of the movement.
Another was Jonathan Edwards, a Puritan who was for a time president of
Princeton College. His account of the **Revival in Northampton** and his

sermon **"Sinners in the Hands of an Angry God"** provide vivid glimpses of how powerful the awakening was.

A vital part of the awakening was the growing conviction that being born into a Christian home did not make a person a Christian, that an emotional conversion experience was necessary for salvation. New Light churches encouraged people to experience such conversion, and men like Gilbert Tennant warned against the *Dangers of an Unconverted Ministry,* ministers serving without the benefit of a redemptive experience. For obvious reasons, New Light churches grew much faster than Old Lights, and the New Light style became the dominant form of American Protestant Christianity.

2.19

Journal Entries (1740)

GEORGE WHITEFIELD

1

Sunday, October 12 [1740]. Spoke to as many as I could, who came for spiritual advice. Preached, with great power, at Dr. Sewall's meeting-house, which was so exceedingly thronged, that I was obliged to get in at one of the windows. Dined with the Governor, who came to me, after dinner, when I had retired, and earnestly desired my prayers. The Lord be with and in him, for time and eternity! Heard Dr. Sewall preach, in the afternoon. Was sick at meeting, and, also, after it was over. Went with the Governor, in his coach, to the common, where I preached my farewell sermon to near twenty thousand people, —a sight I have not seen since I left Blackheath, —and a sight, perhaps never seen before in America. It being nearly dusk before I had done, the sight was more solemn. Numbers, great numbers, melted into tears, when I talked of leaving them. I was very particular in my application, both to rulers,

Source: *George Whitefield's Journals* (London: Banner of Truth Trust, 1960) pp. 472–473, 476, 477, 489–491.

ministers, and people, and exhorted my hearers steadily to imitate the piety of their forefathers; so that I might hear, that with one heart and mind, they were striving together for the faith of the Gospel. After sermon, the Governor went with me to my lodgings. I stood in the passage, and spoke to a great company, both within and without doors; but they were so deeply affected, and cried so loud, that I was obliged to leave off praying. The Governor took his leave in the most affectionate manner, and said he would come and take me in his coach to Charleston ferry the next morning. . . .

Boston is a large, populous place, and very wealthy. It has the form of religion kept up, but has lost much of its power. I have not heard of any remarkable stir for many years. Ministers and people are obliged to confess, that the love of many is waxed cold. Both seem to be too much conformed to the world. There is much of the pride of life to be seen in their assemblies. Jewels, patches, and gay apparel are commonly worn by the female sex. The little infants who were brought to baptism, were wrapped up in such fine things, and so much pains taken to dress them, that one would think they were brought thither to be initiated into, rather than to renounce, the pomps and vanities of this wicked world. There are nine meeting-houses of the Congregational persuasion, one Baptist, one French, and one belonging to the Scots-Irish. There are two monthly, and one weekly lectures; and those, too, but poorly attended. I mentioned it in my sermons, and I trust God will stir up the people to tread more frequently the courts of His house. One thing Boston is very remarkable for, viz., the external observance of the Sabbath. Men in civil offices have a regard for religion. The Governor encourages them; and the ministers and magistrates seem to be more united than in any other place where I have been. Both were exceedingly civil during my stay. I never saw so little scoffing, and never had so little opposition. Still, I fear, many rest in a head-knowledge, are close Pharisees, and have only a name to live.

2

Sunday, October 19. Felt great satisfaction in being at the house of Mr. [Jonathan] Edwards. A sweeter couple I have not yet seen. Their children were not dressed in silks and satins, but plain, as become the children of those who, in all things, ought to be examples of Christian simplicity. Mrs. Edwards is adorned with a meek and quiet spirit; she talked solidly of the things of God, and seemed to be such a helpmeet for her husband, that she caused me to renew those prayers, which, for some months, I have put up to God, that He would be pleased to send me a daughter of Abraham to be my wife. Lord, I desire to have no choice of my own. Thou knowest my circumstances; Thou knowest I only desire to marry in and for Thee. Thou didst choose a Rebecca for Isaac, choose one to be a helpmeet for me, in carrying on that great work which is committed to my charge. Preached this morning, and good Mr. Edwards wept during the whole time of exercise. The people were equally affected; and, in the afternoon, the power increased yet more. Our Lord seemed to keep the good wine till the last. I have not seen four such gracious meetings together since my arrival. Oh, that my soul may be refreshed with the joyful news, that Northampton people have recovered their first love; that the Lord has revived His work in their souls, and caused them to do their first works!

3

Sunday, Nov. 9. Several came to see me, with whom I prayed. Preached at eleven in the morning, to several thousands, in a house built for that purpose since my departure from Philadelphia. It is a hundred feet long, and seventy feet broad. A large gallery is to be erected all round it. Both in the morning and the evening, God's glory filled the house. It was never preached in before. The roof is not yet up, but the people raised a convenient pulpit, and boarded the bottom. Great was the joy of most of the hearers when they saw me; but some still mocked. Between the services I received a packet of letters from England, dated in March last. May the Lord heal, and bring good out of the divisions which at present seem to be among the brethren there. Many friends being in the room, I kneeled down, prayed, and exhorted them all. I was greatly rejoiced to look round them, because there were some who had been marvellous offenders against God. . . . Whatever men's reasoning may suggest, if the children of God fairly examine their own experiences, —if they do God justice, they must acknowledge that they did not choose God, but that God chose them. And if He chose them at all, it must be from eternity, and that too without anything foreseen in them. Unless they acknowledge this, man's salvation must be in part owing to the free-will of man; and if so, unless men descend from other parents than I did, Christ Jesus might have died, and never have seen the travail of His soul in the salvation of one of His creatures. But I would be tender on this point, and leave persons to be taught it of God. I am of the martyr [John] Bradford's mind. Let a man go to the grammar school of faith and repentance, before he goes to the university of election and predestination. A bare head-knowledge of sound words availeth nothing. I am quite tired of Christless talkers. From such may I ever turn away. Amen.

2.20

On the Revival
in Northampton (1734)

JONATHAN EDWARDS

The town of Northampton is about 82 years standing, and has now about 200 families; which mostly dwell more compactly together than any town of such a size in these parts of the country. This probably has been an occasion, that both our corruptions and reformations have been, from time to time, the more swiftly propagated from one to another through the town. Take the town in general, and so far as I can judge they are as rational and intelligent a people as most I have been acquainted with. . . .

Just after my grandfather's death, it seemed to be a time of extraordinary dullness in religion. Licentiousness for some years greatly prevailed among the youth of the town; they were many of them very much addicted to night-walking, and frequenting the tavern, and lewd practices, wherein some, by their example, exceedingly corrupted others. It was their manner very frequently to get together, in conventions of both sexes, for mirth and jollity, which they called frolics; and they would often spend the greater part of the night in them, without regard to any order in the families they belonged to; and indeed family government did too much fail in the town. It was become very customary with many of our young people to be indecent in their carriage at meeting, . . . There had also prevailed in the town a spirit of contention between two parties, into which they had for many years been divided; . . .

And then it was, in the latter part of December (1734) that the spirit of God began extraordinarily to set in, and wonderfully to work amongst us; and there were very suddenly, one after another, five or six persons, who were all savingly converted, and some of them wrought upon in a very remarkable manner. . . .

Presently upon this, a great and earnest concern about the great things of religion and the eternal world became universal in all parts of the town, and among persons of all degrees and all ages. The noise amongst the dry bones waxed louder and louder; all other talk but about spiritual and eternal things was soon thrown by; all the conversation, in all companies and upon all occasions, was upon these things only, unless so much as was necessary for people carrying on their ordinary secular business. Other discourse than of the things

Note: Footnotes have been deleted from this reading—ED.

Source: Sereno Dwight (ed.), *The Works of President Edwards* (New York: B. Franklin, 1847).

of religion would scarcely be tolerated in any company. The minds of people were wonderfully taken off from the world, it was treated amongst us as a thing of very little consequence. . . .

Religion was with all sorts the great concern, and the world was a thing only by the bye. The only thing in their view was to get the kingdom of heaven, and every one appeared pressing into it. . . . It then was a dreadful thing amongst us to lie out of Christ, in danger every day of dropping into hell; and what persons' minds were intent upon was to escape for their lives and to fly from the wrath to come. All would eagerly lay hold of opportunities for their souls; and were wont very often to meet together in private houses for religious purposes: and such meetings when appointed were greatly thronged.

There was scarcely a single person in the town, old or young, left unconcerned about the great things of the eternal world. Those who were wont to be the vainest and loosest; and those who had been most disposed to think and speak slightly of vital and experimental religion, were now generally subject to great awakenings. And the work of conversion was carried on in a most astonishing manner, and increased more and more; souls did as it were come by flocks to Jesus Christ. From day to day, for many months together, might be seen evident instances of sinners brought out of darkness into marvellous light, and delivered out of a horrible pit and from the miry clay and set upon a rock with a new song of praise to God in their mouths.

This work of God, as it was carried on, and the number of true saints multiplied, soon made a glorious alteration in the town; so that in the spring and summer following, anno 1735, the town seemed to be full of the presence of God: it never was so full of love, nor of joy, and yet so full of distress, as it was then. It was a time of joy in families on account of salvation being brought into them; parents rejoicing over their children as new born, and husbands over their wives, and wives over their husbands. . . . Our public assemblies were then beautiful; the congregation was alive in God's service, every one earnestly intent on the public worship, every hearer eager to drink in the words of the minister as they came from his mouth; the assembly in general were, from time to time, in tears while the word was preached; some weeping with sorrow and distress, others with joy and love, others with pity and concern for the souls of their neighbors. . . .

On whatever occasions persons met together, Christ was to be heard and seen in the midst of them. Our young people when they met, were wont to spend the time in talking of the excellency and dying love of Jesus Christ, the glory of the way of salvation, the wonderful, free, and sovereign grace of God, his glorious works in the conversions of a soul, the truth and certainty of the great things of God's word. . . . Those among us who had been formerly converted were greatly enlivened and renewed with fresh and extraordinary incomes of the spirit of God; . . . Many who before had laboured under difficulties about their own state had now their doubts removed by more satisfying experience and more clear discoveries of God's love.

When this work first appeared and was so extraordinarily carried on amongst us in the winter, others round about us seemed not to know what to make of it. Many scoffed at and ridiculed it; and some compared what we called conversion to certain distempers. But it was very observable of many, who occasionally came amongst us from abroad with disregardful hearts, that what they saw here cured them of such a temper of mind. Strangers were generally surprised to find things so much beyond what they had heard, and were wont to tell others that the state of the town could not be conceived of by those who had not seen it. . . . Many who came to town on one occasion or other had their consciences smitten and awakened; and went home with wounded hearts, and with those impressions that never wore off till they had hopefully a saving issue; and those who had before had serious thoughts, had their awakenings and convictions greatly increased. There were many instances of persons who came from abroad on visits or on business, who had not been long here before, to all appearance, they were savingly wrought upon and partook of that shower of divine blessing which God rained down here, and went home rejoicing; til at length the same work began evidently to appear and prevail in several other towns in the country, . . .

★ ★ ★

This seems to have been a very extraordinary dispensation of providence. God has in many respects gone out of and much beyond his usual and ordinary way. The work in this town, and some others about us, has been extraordinary on account of the universality of it, affecting all sorts, sober and vicious, high and low, rich and poor, wise and unwise. It reached the most considerable families and persons, to all appearance, as much as others. In former stirrings of this nature, the bulk of the young people have been greatly affected; but old men and little children have been so now. . . .

This dispensation has also appeared very extraordinary in the numbers of those on whom we have reason to hope it has had a saving effect. We have about six hundred and twenty communicants, which include almost all our adult persons. The church was very large before: but persons never thronged into it, as they did in the late extraordinary time.—Our sacraments are eight weeks [apart], and I received into our communion about a hundred before one sacrament, fourscore of them at one time, whose appearance when they presented themselves together to make an open explicit profession of Christianity, was very affecting to the congregation. I took in near sixty before the next sacrament day: and I had very sufficient evidence of the conversion of their souls through divine grace, though it is not the custom here, as it is in many other churches in this country, to make a credible relation of their inward experience the ground of admission to the Lord's supper.

I am far from pretending to be able to determine how many have lately been the subjects of such mercy; but if I may be allowed to declare anything that appears to me probable in a thing of this nature, I hope that more than 300 souls were savingly brought home to Christ, in this town, in the space of half a year, and about the same number of males as females.

God has also seemed to have gone out of his usual way, in the quickness of his work and the swift progress his Spirit has made in operations on the hearts of many. It is wonderful that persons should be so suddenly and yet so greatly changed. Many have been taken from a loose and careless way of living and seized with strong convictions of their guilt and misery, and in a very little time old things have passed away, and all things have become new with them. . . .

These awakenings when they have first seized on persons have had two effects: one way, that they have brought them immediately to quit their sinful practices; and the looser sort have been brought to forsake and dread their former vices and extravagances. When once the spirit of God began to be so wonderfully poured out in a general way through the two, people had soon done with their old quarrels, backbitings, and intermeddling with other men's matters. The tavern was soon left empty, and persons kept very much at home; . . . The other effect was, that it put them on earnest application to the means of salvation, reading, prayer, meditation, the ordinances of God's house, and private conference; their cry was, What shall we do to be saved?

As to those in whom awakenings seem to have a saving issue, commonly the first thing that appears is a conviction of the justice of God in their condemnation, appearing in a sense of their own exceeding sinfulness, and the vileness of all their performances. . . .

It has been very wonderful to see how personal affections were sometimes moved—when God did as it were suddenly open their eyes and let into their minds a sense of the greatness of his grace, the fullness of Christ, and his readiness to save—after having been broken with apprehension of divine wrath, and sunk into an abyss under a sense of guilt which they were ready to think was beyond the mercy of God. Their joyful surprise has caused their hearts as it were to leap, so that they have been ready to break forth into laughter, tears often at the same time issuing forth like a flood, and intermingling a loud weeping. Sometimes they have not been able to forbear crying out with a loud voice, expressing their great admiration.

2.21

Sinners in the Hands of an Angry God (1741)

JONATHAN EDWARDS

Enfield, Connecticut
July 8, 1741

Their foot shall slide in due time
DEUTERONOMY 32:35

In this verse is threatened the vengeance of God on the wicked unbelieving Israelites, who were God's visible people, and who lived under the means of grace; but who, notwithstanding all God's wonderful works towards them, remained (as vers 28.) void of counsel, having no understanding in them. Under all the cultivations of heaven, they brought forth bitter and poisonous fruit; as in the two verses next preceding the text.—The expression I have chosen for my text, **their foot shall slide in due time,** seems to imply the following things, relating to the punishment and destruction to which these wicked Israelites were exposed.

1. That they were always exposed to **destruction;** as one that stands or walks in slippery places is always exposed to fall. This is implied in the manner of their destruction coming upon them, being represented by their foot sliding. The same is expressed, Psalm 72:18. "*Surely thou didst set them in slippery places; thou castedst them down into destruction.*"

2. It implies, that they were always exposed to **sudden unexpected** destruction. As he that walks in slippery places is every moment liable to fall, he cannot foresee one moment whether he shall stand or fall the next; and when he does fall, he falls at once without warning: Which is also expressed in Psalm 73:18,19. "*Surely thou didst set them in slippery places; thou castedst them down into destruction: How are they brought into desolation as in a moment!*"

3. Another thing implied is, that they are liable to fall **of themselves,** without being thrown down by the hand of another; as he that stands or

Source: http://www.jonathanedwards.com/sermons/warnings/sinners.htm

walks on slippery ground needs nothing but his own weight to throw him down.

4. That the reason why they are not fallen already and do not fall now is only that God's appointed time is not come. For it is said, that when that due time, or appointed time comes, **their foot shall slide.** Then they shall be left to fall, as they are inclined by their own weight. God will not hold them up in these slippery places any longer, but will let them go; and then, at that very instant, they shall fall into destruction; as he that stands on such slippery declining ground, on the edge of a pit, he cannot stand alone, when he is let go he immediately falls and is lost.

The observation from the words that I would now insist upon is this.—"There is nothing that keeps wicked men at any one moment out of hell, but the mere pleasure of God."—By the **mere** pleasure of God, I mean his **sovereign** pleasure, his arbitrary will, restrained by no obligation, hindered by no manner of difficulty, any more than if nothing else but God's mere will had in the least degree, or in any respect whatsoever, any hand in the preservation of wicked men one moment.

★ ★ ★

The bow of God's wrath is bent, and the arrow made ready on the string, and justice bends the arrow at your heart, and strains the bow, and it is nothing but the mere pleasure of God, and that of an angry God, without any promise or obligation at all, that keeps the arrow one moment from being made drunk with your blood. Thus all you that never passed under a great change of heart, by the mighty power of the Spirit of God upon your souls; all you that were never born again, and made new creatures, and raised from being dead in sin, to a state of new, and before altogether unexperienced light and life, are in the hands of an angry God. However you may have reformed your life in many things, and may have had religious affections, and may keep up a form of religion in your families and closets, and in the house of God, it is nothing but his mere pleasure that keeps you from being this moment swallowed up in everlasting destruction. However unconvinced you may now be of the truth of what you hear, by and by you will be fully convinced of it. Those that are gone from being in the like circumstances with you, see that it was so with them; for destruction came suddenly upon most of them; when they expected nothing of it, and while they were saying, Peace and safety: now they see, that those things on which they depended for peace and safety, were nothing but thin air and empty shadows.

The God that holds you over the pit of hell, much as one holds a spider, or some loathsome insect over the fire, abhors you, and is dreadfully provoked: his wrath towards you burns like fire; he looks upon you as worthy of nothing else, but to be cast into the fire; he is of purer eyes than to bear to have you in his sight; you are ten thousand times more abominable in his eyes, than the most hateful venomous serpent is in ours. You have offended him infinitely more than ever a stubborn rebel did his prince; and yet it is nothing but his hand that holds you from falling into the fire every moment. It is to be ascribed to nothing else, that you did not go to hell the last night; that you was suffered to awake again in this world, after you closed your eyes to sleep. And there is no other reason to be given, why you have not dropped into hell since you arose in the morning, but that God's hand has held you up. There is no other reason to be given why you have not gone to hell, since you have sat here in the house of God, provoking his pure eyes by your sinful wicked manner of attending his solemn worship. Yea, there is nothing else that is to be given as a reason why you do not this very moment drop down into hell.

O sinner! Consider the fearful danger you are in: it is a great furnace of wrath, a wide and bottomless pit, full of the fire of wrath, that you are held over in the hand of that God, whose wrath is provoked and incensed as much against you, as against many of the damned in hell. You hang by a slender thread, with the flames of divine wrath flashing about it, and ready every moment to singe it, and burn it asunder; and you have no interest in any Mediator, and nothing to lay hold of to save yourself, nothing to keep off the flames of wrath, nothing of your own, nothing that you ever have done, nothing that you can do, to induce God to spare you one moment.

★ ★ ★

How dreadful is the state of those that are daily and hourly in the danger of this great wrath and infinite misery! But this is the dismal case of every soul in this congregation that has not been born again, however moral and strict, sober and religious, they may otherwise be. Oh that you would consider it, whether you be young or old! There is reason to think, that there are many in this congregation now hearing this discourse, that will actually be the subjects of this very misery to all eternity. We know not who they are, or in what seats they sit, or what thoughts they now have. It may be they are now at ease, and hear all these things without much disturbance, and are now flattering themselves that they are not the persons, promising themselves that they shall escape. If we knew that there was one person, and but one, in the whole congregation, that was to be the subject of this misery, what an awful thing would it be to think of! If we knew who it was, what an awful sight would it be to see such a person! How might all the rest of the congregation lift up a lamentable and bitter cry over him! But, alas! instead of one, how many is it likely will remember this discourse in hell? And it would be a wonder, if some that are now present should not be in hell in a very short time, even before this year is out. And it would be no wonder if some persons, that now sit here, in some seats of this meeting-house, in health, quiet and secure, should be there before tomorrow morning. Those of you that finally continue in a natural condition, that shall keep out of hell longest will be there in a little time! your damnation does not slumber; it will come swiftly, and, in all probability, very suddenly upon many of you. You have reason to wonder that you are not already in hell. It is doubtless the case of some whom you have seen and known, that never deserved hell more than you, and that heretofore appeared as likely to have been now alive as you. Their case is past all hope; they are crying in extreme misery and perfect despair; but here you are in the land of the living and in the house of God, and have an opportunity to obtain salvation. What would not those poor damned hopeless souls give for one day's opportunity such as you now enjoy!

And now you have an extraordinary opportunity, a day wherein Christ has thrown the door of mercy wide open, and stands in calling and crying with a loud voice to poor sinners; a day wherein many are flocking to him, and pressing into the kingdom of God. Many are daily coming from the east, west, north and south; many that were very lately in the same miserable condition that you are in, are now in a happy state, with their hearts filled with love to him who has loved them, and washed them from their sins in his own blood, and rejoicing in hope of the glory of God. How awful is it to be left behind at such a day! To see so many others feasting, while you are pining and perishing! To see so many rejoicing and singing for joy of heart, while you have cause to mourn for sorrow of heart, and howl for vexation of spirit! How can you rest one moment in such a condition? Are not your souls as precious as the souls of the people at Suffield, where they are flocking from day to day to Christ?

Are there not many here who have lived long in the world, and are not to this day born again? and so are aliens from the commonwealth of Israel, and have done nothing ever since they have lived, but treasure up wrath against the day of wrath? Oh, sirs, your case, in an especial manner, is extremely dangerous. Your guilt and hardness of heart is extremely great. Do you not see how generality persons of your years are passed over and left, in the present remarkable and wonderful dispensation of God's mercy? You had need to consider yourselves, and awake thoroughly out of sleep. You cannot bear the fierceness and wrath of the infinite God.—And you, young men, and young women, will you neglect this precious season which you now enjoy, when so many others of your age are renouncing all youthful vanities, and flocking to Christ? You especially have now an extraordinary opportunity; but if you neglect it, it will soon be with you as with those persons who spent all the precious days of youth in sin, and are now come to such a dreadful pass in blindness and hardness.—And you, children, who are unconverted, do not you know that you are going down to hell, to bear the dreadful wrath of that God, who is now angry with you every day and every night? Will you be content to be the children of the devil, when so many other children in the land are converted, and are become the holy and happy children of the King of kings?

And let every one that is yet out of Christ, and hanging over the pit of hell, whether they be old men and women, or middle aged, or young people, or little children, now hearken to the loud calls of God's word and providence. This acceptable year of the Lord, a day of such great favour to some, will doubtless be a day of as remarkable vengeance to others. Men's hearts harden, and their guilt increases apace at such a day as this, if they neglect their souls; and never was there so great danger of such persons being given up to hardness of heart and blindness of mind. God seems now to be hastily gathering in his elect in all parts of the land; and probably the greater part of adult persons that ever shall be saved, will be brought in now in a little time, and that it will be as it was on the great out-pouring of the Spirit upon the Jews in the apostles' days;

the election will obtain, and the rest will be blinded. If this should be the case with you, you will eternally curse this day, and will curse the day that ever you was born, to see such a season of the pouring out of God's Spirit, and will wish that you had died and gone to hell before you had seen it. Now undoubtedly it is, as it was in the days of John the Baptist, the axe is in an extraordinary manner laid at the root of the trees, that every tree which brings not forth good fruit, may be hewn down and cast into the fire.

Therefore, let every one that is out of Christ, now awake and fly from the wrath to come. The wrath of Almighty God is now undoubtedly hanging over a great part of this congregation. Let every one fly out of Sodom: "Haste and escape for your lives, look not behind you, escape to the mountain, lest you be consumed."

2.22

The Danger of an Unconverted Ministry (1742)

GILBERT TENNENT

My Brethren, we should mourn over those, that are destitute of faithful ministers, and sympathize with them. Our bowels should be moved with the most compassionate tenderness, over these dear fainting souls, that are as sheep having no shepherd; and that after the example of our blessed Lord.

Dear Sirs! We should also most earnestly pray for them, that the compassionate Saviour may preserve them, by his mighty power, through faith unto salvation; support their sinking spirits, under the melancholy uneasiness of a dead ministry; sanctify and sweeten to them the dry morsels they get under such blind men, when they have none better to repair to. . . .

And indeed, my Brethren, we should join our endeavours to our prayers. The most likely method to stock the church with a faithful ministry, in the present situation of things, the public academies being so much corrupted and abused generally, is to encourage private schools, or seminaries of learning, which are under the care of skillful and experienced Christians; in which those

Source: Gilbert Tennent, "The Danger of an Unconverted Ministry" (Boston, 1742).

only should be admitted, who upon strict examination, have in the judgment of a reasonable charity, the plain evidences of experimental religion. Pious and experienced youths, who have a good natural capacity, and great desires after the ministerial work, from good motives, might be sought for, and found up and down in the country, and put to private Schools of the Prophets; especially in such places where the public ones are not. This method, in my opinion, has a noble tendency, to build up the Church of God. . . . Don't think it much, if the Pharisees should be offended at such a proposal; . . . If they could help it, they wouldn't let one faithful man come into the ministry; and therefore their opposition is an encouraging sign. Let all the followers of the Lamb stand up and act for God against all opposers: Who is upon God's side?

The improvement of this subject remains. And

1. If it be so, that the case of those, who have no other or no better than Pharisee-teacher, is to be pitied: then what a scroll and scene of mourning and lamentation, and woe, is opened, because of the swarms of locusts, the crowds of Pharisees, that have as covetously as cruelly crept into the ministry, in this adulterous generation, who as nearly resemble the character given of the old Pharisees, as one crow's egg does another. It is true that some of the modern Pharisees have learned to prate a little more orthodoxly about the new birth than their predecessor Nicodemus, who are, in the meantime, as great strangers to the feeling experience of it, as he. They are blind who see not this to be the case of the body of the clergy of this generation. . . .

2. From what has been said, we may learn that such who are contented under a dead ministry have not in them the temper of that Saviour they profess. It's an awful sign that they are as blind as moles and as dead as stones, without any spiritual taste and relish. And alas! isn't this the case of multitudes? If they can get one that has the name of a minister, with a . . . black coat or gown to carry on a Sabbathday among them, although never so coldly and insuccessfully; if he is free from gross crimes in practice and takes good care to keep at a due distance from their consciences, and is never troubled about his insuccessfulness; O! think the poor fools, that is a fine man indeed; our minister is a prudent charitable man, he is not always harping upon terror, and sounding damnation in our ear, like some rash-headed preachers, who by their uncharitable methods, are ready to put poor people out of their wits, or to run them into despair. O! how terrible a thing is that despair! Ay, our minister, honest man, gives us good caution against it. Poor silly souls! . . .

3. We may learn the mercy and duty of those that enjoy a faithful ministry. Let such glorify God for so distinguishing a privilege and labor to walk worthy of it, to all well-pleasing; lest for their abuse thereof, they be exposed to a greater damnation.

4. If the ministry of natural men be as it has been represented, then it is both lawful and expedient to go from them to hear godly persons; yea, it's so far from being sinful to do this, that one who lives under a pious

minister of lesser gifts, after having honestly endeavored to get benefit by his ministry and yet gets a little or none, but does find real benefit and more benefit elsewhere; I say, he may lawfully go, and that frequently, where he gets most good to his precious soul. . . .

Is not the visible Church composed of persons of the most contrary characters? While some are sincere servants of God, are not many servants of Satan, under a religious mask? And have not these a fixed enmity against the other? How is it then possible that a harmony should subsist between such, till their nature be changed? Can Light dwell with Darkness? . . .

And let those who live under the ministry of dead men, whether they have got the form of religion or not, repair to the living, where they may be edified. Let who will, oppose it. . . . But though your neighbors growl against you and reproach you for doing your duty in seeking your soul's good, bear their unjust censures with Christian meekness and persevere.

THE FIRST AMERICAN "ENLIGHTENMENT"

True to the American characteristic of simultaneously holding two diametrically opposed opinions, of going in two different directions at the same time, along with the "Great Awakening" of the eighteenth century came an Intellectual "Enlightenment" which challenged the religious assumptions and practices of many if not most, Americans.

Two Americans who embodied the American version of the French Enlightenment were Benjamin Franklin and Thomas Jefferson. Both men were born into traditional religious communities, Franklin's Puritan, Jefferson's Anglican; both lived during the age of the fervent revivalists; both gained widespread popular acclaim for their contributions to the independence movement; yet both at some point abandoned traditional Christianity for the deism that appealed to the philosophers of Europe in that age.

Franklin expressed this intellectual approach to religion in his **"First Principles"** of 1728 and in his **"Plan For Achieving Moral Perfection"** of the 1730s. His **Letter to Ezra Stiles** of 1790, not long before he died, reflects both his faith in reason and his religious skepticism, combined with his irrepressible sense of humor.

Jefferson, so literate, sensitive, and reflective, was surprisingly undisciplined in his writing. His book-length works are few, his thought scattered through his various "notes" on topics and his letters to a variety of acquaintances. In his famous **"Syllabus of an Estimate of the Merits of the Doctrines of Jesus,"** which compared those doctrines with those of others, and in a variety of comments made in letters to several confidants, among them a **Letter to Doctor Banjamin Waterhouse,** he expressed the American Enlightenment's dismissal of traditional, simplistic religious opinions.

2.23

First Principles (1728)

BENJAMIN FRANKLIN

I BELIEVE there is one Supreme most perfect Being, Author and Father of the Gods themselves.

For I believe that Man is not the most perfect Being but One, rather that as there are many Degrees of Beings his Inferiors, so there are many Degrees of Beings superior to him.

Also, when I stretch my Imagination thro' and beyond our System of Planets, beyond the visible fix'd Stars themselves, into that Space that is every Way infinite, and conceive it fill'd with Suns like ours, each with a Chorus of Worlds for ever moving round him, then this little Ball on which we move, seems, even in my narrow Imagination, to be almost Nothing, and my self less than nothing, and of no sort of Consequence.

When I think thus, I imagine it great Vanity in me to suppose, that the *Supremely Perfect,* does in the least regard such an inconsiderable Nothing as Man. More especially, since it is impossible for me to have any positive clear Idea of that which is infinite and incomprehensible, I cannot conceive otherwise, than that He, *the Infinite Father,* expects or requires no Worship or Praise from us, but that he is even INFINITELY ABOVE IT.

But since there is in all Men something like a natural Principle which enclines them to DEVOTION or the Worship of some unseen Power;

And since Men are endued with Reason superior to all other Animals that we are in our World acquainted with;

Source: *Benjamin Franklin Papers* (New Haven: Yale University Press, 1959), I, 102–104.

Therefore I think it seems required of me, and my Duty, as a Man, to pay Divine Regards to SOMETHING.

I CONCEIVE then, that the INFINITE has created many Beings or Gods, vastly superior to Man, who can better conceive his Perfections than we, and return him a more rational and glorious Praise. As among Men, the Praise of the Ignorant or of Children, is not regarded by the ingenious Painter or Architect, who is rather honour'd and pleas'd with the Approbation of Wise men and Artists.

It may be that these created Gods, are immortal, or it may be that after many Ages, they are changed, and Others supply their Places.

Howbeit, I conceive that each of these is exceeding wise, and good, and very powerful; and that Each has made for himself, one glorious Sun, attended with a beautiful and admirable System of Planets.

It is that particular wise and good God, who is the Author and Owner of our System, that I propose for the Object of my Praise and Adoration.

For I conceive that he has in himself some of those Passions he has planted in us, and that, since he has given us Reason whereby we are capable of observing his Wisdom in the Creation, he is not above caring for us, being pleas'd with our Praise, and offended when we slight Him, or neglect his Glory.

I conceive for many Reasons that he is *a good Being,* and as I should be happy to have so wise, good and powerful a Being my Friend, let me consider in what Manner I shall make myself most acceptable to him.

Next to the Praise due, to his Wisdom, I believe he is pleased and delights in the Happiness of those he has created; and since without Virtue Man can have no Happiness in this World, I firmly believe he delights to see me Virtuous, because he is pleas'd when he sees me Happy.

And since he has created many Things which seem purely design'd for the Delight of Man, I believe he is not offended when he sees his Children solace themselves in any manner of pleasant Exercises and innocent Delights, and I think no Pleasure innocent that is to Man hurtful.

I *love* him therefore for his Goodness and I *adore* him for his Wisdom.

Let me then not fail to praise my God continually, for it is his Due, and it is all I can return for his many Favours and great Goodness to me; and let me resolve to be virtuous, that I may be happy, that I may please Him, who is delighted to see me happy. Amen.

2.24

Plan for Achieving Moral Perfection (1730s)

BENJAMIN FRANKLIN

1. Temperance.

   Eat not to dullness; drink not to elevation.

2. Silence.

   Speak not but what may benefit others or yourself avoid trifling conversation.

3. Order.

   Let all your things have their places; let each part of your business have its time.

4. Resolution.

   Resolve to perform what you ought; perform without fail what you resolve.

5. Frugality.

   Make no expense but to do good to others or yourself; i.e., waste nothing.

6. Industry.

   Lose no time; be always employ'd in something useful; cut off all unnecessary actions.

7. Sincerity.

   Use no hurtful deceit; think innocently and justly, and, if you speak, speak accordingly.

8. Justice.

   Wrong none by doing injuries, or omitting the benefits that are your duty.

9. Moderation.

   Avoid extreams; forbear resenting injuries so much as you think they deserve.

10. Cleanliness.

    Tolerate no uncleanliness in body, cloaths, or habitation.

Source: Norman Cousins, *In God We Trust* (New York: Harper, 1958).

11. Tranquillity.

Be not disturbed at trifles, or at accidents common or unavoidable.

12. Chastity.

Rarely use venery but for health or offspring, never to dulness, weakness, or the injury of your own or another's peace or reputation.

13. Humility.

Imitate Jesus and Socrates.

2.25

Letter to Ezra Stiles (1790)

BENJAMIN FRANKLIN

You desire to know something of my religion. It is the first time I have been questioned upon it. But I cannot take your curiosity amiss, and shall endeavor in a few words to gratify it. Here is my creed. I believe in one God, Creator of the Universe. That he governs it by his Providence. That he ought to be worshipped. That the most acceptable service we render to him is doing good to his other children. That the soul of man is immortal, and will be treated with justice in another life respecting its conduct in this. These I take to be the fundamental principles of all sound religion, and I regard them as you do in whatever sect I meet with them.

As to Jesus of Nazareth, my opinion of whom you particularly desire, I think the system of morals and his religion, as he left them to us, the best the world ever saw or is likely to see; but I apprehend it has received various corrupting changes, and I have, with most of the present dissenters in England, some doubts as to his divinity; though it is a question I do not dogmatize upon, having never studied it, and think it needless to busy myself with it now, when I expect soon an opportunity of knowing the truth with less trouble. I see no harm, however, in its being believed, if that belief has the good consequence, as probably it has, of making his doctrines more respected and better observed;

Note: Footnotes have been deleted from this reading—ED.

Source: *The Works of Benjamin Franklin.* (Chicago: Townsend, MacCouns, 1882). pp. 423–425.

especially as I do not perceive, that the Supreme take it amiss, by distinguishing the unbelievers in his government of the work with any peculiar marks of his displeasure.

I shall only add, respecting myself, that having experienced the goodness of that Being in conducting me prosperously through a long life, I have no doubt of its continuance in the next, though without the smallest conceit of meriting such goodness. My sentiments on this head you will see in the copy of an old letter enclosed, which I wrote in answer to one from a zealous religionist, whom I had relieved in a paralytic case by electricity, and who being afraid I should grow proud upon it, sent me his serious though rather impertinent caution, I send you also the copy of another letter, which will show something of my disposition relating to religion. With great and sincere esteem and affection, I am, your obliged old friend and most obedient humble servant

B. Franklin

2.26

Syllabus of an Estimate of the Merit of the Doctrines of Jesus, Compared with Those of Others (1820)

THOMAS JEFFERSON

In a comparative view of the Ethics of the enlightened nations of antiquity, of the Jews and of Jesus, no notice should be taken of the corruptions of reason among the ancients, to wit, the idolatry and superstition of the vulgar, nor of the corruptions of Christianity by the learned among its professors.

Let a just view be taken of the moral principles inculcated by the most esteemed of the sects of ancient philosophy or of their individuals; particularly Pythagoras, Socrates, Epicurus, Cicero, Epictetus, Seneca, Antoninus.

Source: Norman Cousins (ed.) "In God We Trust" (New York: Harper & Brothers, 1958), pp. 169–171.

Independence National Historical Park

Thomas Jefferson, third president of the United States

I. Philosophers.

1. Their precepts related chiefly to ourselves, and the government of those passions which, unrestrained, would disturb our tranquillity of mind. In this branch of philosophy they were really great.

2. In developing our duties to others, they were short and defective. They embraced, indeed, the circles of kindred and friends, and inculcated patriotism, or the love of our country in the aggregate, as a primary obligation: towards our neighbors and countrymen they taught justice, but scarcely viewed them as within the circle of benevolence. Still less have they inculcated peace, charity and love to our fellow men, or embraced with benevolence the whole family of mankind.

II. Jews.

1. Their system was Deism; that is, the belief in one only God. But their ideas of him and of his attributes were degrading and injurious.

2. Their Ethics were not only imperfect, but often irreconcilable with the sound dictates of reason and morality, as they respect intercourse with those around us; and repulsive and anti-social, as respecting other nations. They needed reformation, therefore, in an eminent degree.

III. Jesus.

> In this state of things among the Jews, Jesus appeared. His parentage
> was obscure; his condition poor; his education null; his natural
> endowments great; his life correct and innocent: he was meek, benev-
> olent, patient, firm, disinterested, and of the sublimest eloquence.

The disadvantages under which his doctrines appear are remarkable.

1. Like Socrates and Epictetus, he wrote nothing himself.

2. But he had not, like them, a Xenophon or an Arrian to write for him. I
   name not Plato, who only used the name of Socrates to cover the whim-
   sies of his own brain. On the contrary, all the learned of his country,
   entrenched in its power and riches, were opposed to him, lest his labors
   should undermine their advantages; and the committing to writing his
   life and doctrines fell on unlettered and ignorant men, who wrote, too,
   from memory, and not till long after the transactions had passed.

3. According to the ordinary fate of those who attempt to enlighten and
   reform mankind, he fell an early victim to the jealousy and combination
   of the altar and the throne, at about thirty-three years of age, his reason
   having not yet attained the *maximum* of its energy, nor the course of his
   preaching, which was but of three years at most, presented occasions for
   developing a complete system of morals.

4. Hence the doctrines he really delivered were defective as a whole, and
   fragments only of what he did deliver have come to us mutilated, mis-
   stated, and often unintelligible.

5. They have been still more disfigured by the corruptions of schismatizing
   followers, who have found an interest in sophisticating and perverting
   the simple doctrines he taught, by engrafting on them the mysticisms of
   a Grecian sophist, frittering them into subtleties, and obscuring them
   with jargon, until they have caused good men to reject the whole in
   disgust, and to view Jesus himself as an impostor.

Notwithstanding these disadvantages, a system of morals is presented to us
which, if filled up in the style and spirit of the rich fragments he left us, would
be the most perfect and sublime that has ever been taught by man.

The question of his being a member of the Godhead, or in direct communication with it, claimed for him by some of his followers and denied by
others, is foreign to the present view, which is merely an estimate of the intrinsic
merits of his doctrines.

1. He corrected the Deism of the Jews, confirming them in their belief of one
   only God, and giving them juster notions of His attributes and government.

2. His moral doctrines, relating to kindred and friends were more pure and
   perfect man those of the most correct of the philosophers, and greatly
   more so than those of the Jews; and they went far beyond both in incul-
   cating universal philanthropy, not only to kindred and friends, to neighbors and countrymen, but to all mankind, gathering all into one family

under the bonds of love, charity, peace, common wants and common aids. A development of this head will evince the peculiar superiority of the system of Jesus over all others.

3. The precepts of philosophy, and of the Hebrew code, laid hold of actions only. He pushed his scrutinies into the heart of man; erected his tribunal in the region of his thoughts, and purified the waters at the fountain head.

4. He taught, emphatically, the doctrines of a future state, which was either doubted or disbelieved by the Jews, and wielded it with efficacy as an important incentive, supplementary to the other motives to moral conduct.

2.27

Letter to Doctor Benjamin Waterhouse (1822)

THOMAS JEFFERSON

The doctrines of Jesus are simple, and tend all to the happiness of man.

1. That there is only one God, and He all perfect.
2. That there is a future state of rewards and punishment.
3. That to love God with all thy heart and thy neighbor as thyself, is the sum of religion.

These are the great points on which He endeavored to reform the religion of the Jews. But compare with these the demoralizing dogmas of Calvin.

1. That there are three Gods.
2. That good works, or the love of our neighbor, are nothing.
3. That faith is everything, and the more incomprehensible the proposition, the more merit in its faith.
4. That reason in religion is of unlawful use.

Source: Norman Cousins (ed.) "In God We Trust" (New York: Harper & Brothers, 1958), pp. 160–161.

5. That God, from the beginning, elected certain individuals to be saved, and certain others to be damned; and that no crimes of the former can damn them; no virtues of the latter save.

Now, which of these is the true and charitable Christian? He who believes and acts on the simple doctrines of Jesus? Or the impious dogmatists, as Athanasius and Calvin? Verily I say these are the false shepherds foretold as to enter not by the door into the sheepfold, but to climb up some other way. They are mere usurpers of the Christian name, teaching a counter-religion made up of the *deliria* of crazy imaginations, as foreign from Christianity as is that of Mahomet. Their blasphemies have driven thinking men into infidelity, who have too hastily rejected the supposed Author himself, with the horrors so falsely imputed to Him. Had the doctrines of Jesus been preached always as pure as they came from his lips, the whole civilized world would now have been Christian. I rejoice that in this blessed country of free inquiry and belief, which has surrendered its creed and conscience to neither kings nor priests, the genuine doctrine of one only God is reviving, and I trust that there is not a *young man* now living in the United States who will not die a Unitarian.

CHAPTER 3

✳

Birth of a Nation

The Struggle for American Independence

As late as 1750, the people living in the British colonies of North America seemed satisfied to be a part of what was still a rather modest British Empire. There was little talk among the transatlantic Englishmen of independence from the mother country. The Seven Years War (1756–1763), which in America was dubbed the French and Indian War, changed the picture entirely; and in 1775 the first shots were exchanged in the American War for Independence. In 1776, the Americans declared their independence, in 1781 they achieved it, and in 1783 they were recognized by the world as a new nation.

It is interesting and instructive to see the way Americans reacted to the coming of the war, the way they fought it, the way they used their success to establish the new nation, the way they worked to guarantee freedom of religious choice, and the way they diversified and flourished religiously after independence. It is a colorful saga.

RELIGIOUS GROUPS RESPOND
TO THE INDEPENDENCE MOVEMENT

Religious groups and their leaders reacted to the call for American independence in a variety of ways. Loyalty to England, reluctance to participate in any war, fervent support both of independence and the war that it provoked, all of their varied responses were based on their different histories, theologies, and self-interests.

Most Quakers and Anglicans were loyal to the English crown, grateful for its beneficences to them, and the **Quaker and Anglican Statements** that follow make it clear that they were opposed to the independence movement. The **Mennonite Statement** reflects the fact that as pacifists they were opposed to all wars, including one that might mean independence. Anglicans and Quakers declined in numbers and influence after independence because many Americans considered them Tories, while the Mennonites remained a small religious community.

The small but growing Baptist and Methodist churches, indeed most of the New Light denominations, supported the independence movement and the war it brought, as the letter by the pastor John Allen **On Liberty** and Samuel Sherwood's sermon **"The Church's Flight into the Wilderness"** demonstrate. Even Samuel Adams employed religious language when he vociferously defended the declaration of **"American Independence."** And during the war, at a *Te Deum* arranged for the Continental Congress in 1779, a **"Sermon"** delivered by the Catholic chaplain to the French legation expressed strong support for independence from Protestant England. New Light Protestants and Catholics, by their fervent patriotism, gained favor with Americans during and after the war for independence.

3.1

Quaker Statement (1774)

A nd as our forefathers were often led to commemorate these and the many instances of Divine Favour conferred on them, thro' the difficulties they encountered in settling in the wilderness, let us be like minded with them—and if after a long time of enjoying the fruits of their labours, and partaking of the blessings of peace and plenty, we should be restrained or deprived of some of our rights and privileges, let us carefully guard against being drawn into the vindication of them, or seeking redress by any measures which are not consistent with our religious profession and principles, nor with the christian patience manifested by your ancestors in such times of trial[.] [A]nd we fervently desire all may impartially consider whether we have manifested that firmness in our love to the cause of Truth, and universal righteousness which is required of us, and that we may unite in holy resolutions to seek the Lord in sincerity, and to wait upon Him daily for wisdom, to order our conduct hereafter in all things to his praise.

And beloved Friends, we beseech you in brotherly affection to remember, that as under Divine Providence we are indebted to the King and his royal ancestors, for the continued favour of enjoying our religious liberties, we are under deep obligation to manifest our loyalty and fidelity, and that we should discourage every attempt which may be made by any to excite disaffection or disrespect to him, and particularly to manifest our dislike of all such writings as are, or may be published of that tendency.

And as it hath ever been our practice since we were a people, frequently to advise all professing with us to be careful not to defraud the King of his customs or duties, nor to be concerned in dealing in goods unlawfully imported; we find it necessary now most earnestly to exhort that the same care may be continued with faithfulness and diligence, and that Friends keep clear of purchasing any such goods, either for sale or private use; that so we may not be any way instrumental in countenancing or promoting the iniquity, false swearing, and violence, which are common consequences of an unlawful and clandestine trade.

Source: *An Epistle from Our Yearly-Meeting, Held at Philadelphia* . . . (Quakers of Philadelphia, 1774) pp. 3–4.

3.2

Anglican Statement (1775)

My Lord,

We now sit down under deep affliction of mind to address your Lordship upon a subject, in which the very existence of our Church in America seems to be interested. It has long been our fervent Prayer to Almighty God, that the unhappy controversy between the Parent Country and these Colonies might be terminated upon Principles honourable and advantageous to both, without proceeding to the extremities of civil war and the horrors of Bloodshed. We have long lamented that such a spirit of Wisdom and Love could not mutually prevail, as might devise some liberal Plan for this benevolent Purpose; and we have spared no means in our power for advancing such a spirit so far as our private Influence and advice could extend. But as to public advice we have hitherto thought it our Duty to keep our Pulpits wholly clear from every thing bordering, on this contest, and to pursue that line of Reason and Moderation which became our Characters; equally avoiding whatever might irritate the Tempers of the people, or create a suspicion that we were opposed to the Interest of the Country in which we live.

But the Time is now come, my Lord, when even our silence would be misconstrued, and when we are called upon to take a more public part. The Continental Congress have recommended the 20th of next month as a day of Fasting, Prayer & Humiliation thro' all the Colonies. Our Congregations too of all Ranks have associated themselves, determined never to submit to the Parliamentary claim of taxing them at pleasure; and the Blood already spilt in maintaining this claim is unhappily alienating the affections of many from the Parent Country, and cementing them closer in the most fixed purpose of a Resistance, dreadful even in Contemplation.

Under these Circumstances our People call upon us, and think they have a right to our advice in the most public manner from the Pulpit. Should we refuse, our Principles would be misrepresented, and even our religious useful-ness destroyed among our People. And our complying may perhaps be inter-preted to our disadvantage in the Parent Country. Under these difficulties (which have been increased by the necessity some of our Brethren have appre-hended themselves under of quitting their Charges), and being at a great dis-tance from the advice of our Superiors, we had only our own Consciences and each other to consult, and have accordingly determined on that part, which the general good seem to require. We were the more willing to comply with

Source: W. S. Perry (ed.), *Historical Collectives Relating to the American Colonial Church* (New York: AMS Press, 1871[1969]), II, 470 ff.

the request of our Fellow Citizens, as we were sure their Respect for us was so great, that they did not even wish any thing from us inconsistent with our characters as Ministers of the Gospel of Peace. . . .

Tho' it had of late been difficult for us to advise, or even correspond as usual, with our Brethren the Clergy of New York, we find that they have likewise in their Turn officiated to their Provincial Congress now sitting there, as Mr. [Jacob] Duche did both this year & the last, at the opening of the Continental Congress.

Upon this fair and candid state of things, we hope your Lordship will think our conduct has been such as became us; and we pray that we may be considered as among His Majesty's most dutiful & loyal subjects in this and every other Transaction of our Lives. Would to God that we could become mediators for the Settlement of the unnatural Controversy that now distracts a once happy Empire. All that we can do is to pray for such a Settlement, and to pursue those Principles of Moderation and Reason which your Lordship has always recommended to us.

3.3

Mennonite Statement (1775)

In the first place we acknowledge us indebted to the most high God, who created Heaven and Earth, the only good Being to thank him for all His great Goodness and Manifold Mercies and Love through our Savior Jesus Christ who is come to save the souls of Men, having all Power in Heaven and on Earth. Further we find ourselves indebted to be thankful to our late worthy assembly for their giving so good an Advice in these troublesome Times to all Ranks of People in Pennsylvania, particularly in allowing those, who, by the Doctrine of our Savior, Jesus Christ, are persuaded in their consciences to love their enemies, and not to resist Evil, to enjoy the Liberty of their Consciences for which, as also for all the good things we enjoy under their Care, we heartily thank that worthy Body of Assembly and all high and low in office who have advised to such a peaceful measure hoping and confiding that they and all others entrusted with Power in this hitherto blessed Province, may be moved by the same spirit of Grace, which animated the first Founder of this province, our late worthy Proprietor William Penn to grant Liberty of Conscience to all its inhabitants that they may in the great and memorable Day of Judgment be

Source: C. H. Smith, *The Mennonite Immigration to Pennsylvania in the Eighteenth Century* (Norristown, PA: Norristown Press, 1929) pp. 285–286.

put on the right Hand of that just Judge, who judgeth without Respect of Person and hear these blessed Words, "Come ye blessed of my Father, inherit the kingdom prepared for you, etc., what ye have done unto one of the least of these my Brethren ye have done unto me," among which number (i.e., the least of Christ's Brethren) we by his Grace hope to be ranked; and every Lenity and Favor shown to such tender conscience, although weak followers of this our blessed Saviour will not be forgotten by him in that great Day.

The Advice to those who do not find Freedom of Conscience to take up Arm that they ought to be helpful to those who are in Need and distressed Circumstances we receive with Cheerfulness towards all Men of what Station they may be—it being our principle to feed the Hungry and give the Thirsty Drink. We have dedicated ourselves to serve all Men in every Thing that can be helpful to the Preservation of Men's Lives but we find no Freedom in giving or doing, or assisting, in anything by which Men's Lives are destroyed or hurt. We beg the Patience of all those who believe we err on this point. We are always ready, according to Christ's command to Peter, to pay the Tribute, that we may offend no Man, and so we are willing to pay Taxes and so render unto Caesar those Things that are Caesar's, and to God those Things that are God's. Although we think ourselves very weak to give God his due Honour he being a Spirit and Life, and. we only Dust and Ashes. We are also willing to be subject to the higher Powers and give in the manner Paul directs us: for he beareth the Sword not in vain, for he is the Minister of God, a Revenger to execute wrath upon him that doeth Evil. This Testimony we lay down before our worthy Assembly and all other Persons in Government, letting them know we are thankful as above mentioned, and that we are not at Liberty in Conscience to take up Arms to conquer our Enemies but rather to pray to God, who has power in Heaven and Earth, for us and Them.

3.4

On Liberty (1772)

JOHN ALLEN

TO THE RIGHT HONORABLE

THE EARL OF DARTMOUTH

Liberty, my Lord, is the native right of the *Americans*; it is the blood-bought treasure of their Forefathers; and they have the same essential right to their *native laws* as they have to the air they breath in, or to the light of the morning when the sun rises: And therefore they who oppress the *Americans* must be as great enemies to the law of nature, as they who would be, if it were in their power, vail the light of the sun from the universe. My Lord, the *Americans* have a privilege [to] boast of above all the world: They never were in bondage to any man, therefore it is more for them to give up their Rights, than it would be for all *Europe* to give up their Liberties into the hands of the *Turks*. Consider what *English* tyranny their Forefathers fled from; what seas of distress they met with; what savages they fought with; what blood-bought treasures, as the dear inheritance of their lives, they have left to their children, and without any aid from the King of *England;* and yet after this, these free-born people must be counted Rebels, if they will not loose every right to Liberty, which their venerable Ancestors purchased at so great expence as to lose their lives in accomplishing; and shall not their descendants be strenuous to maintain inviolate those sacred Rights, which God and Nature have given them, to the latest posterity. O *America! America* let it never be said that you have deserted the Grand Cause, and submitted to *English* ministerial *tyranny*. . . .

The Parliament of *England* cannot justly make any laws to tax the *Americans;* for they are not the Representatives of *America;* and therefore they are no legislative power of *America.* The House of Lords cannot do it, for they are Peers of *England,* not of *America;* and if neither King, Lords, nor Commons have any right to oppress or destroy the Liberties of the *Americans,* why is it then that the *Americans* do not stand upon their own strength, and shew their

Source: Roger Bruns (ed.), *Am I Not a Man and A Brother. . . .* (New York: Chelsea House, 1977) pp. 258–260.

power and importance, when the life of life, and every Liberty that is dear to them is in danger?

Therefore, let me advise you with all the power of affection, with all the pathos of soul, (as one who esteems the full possession of Rights of the *Americans,* as the highest blessing of this life) to stand alarmed. See your danger—death is near—destruction is at the door. —Need I speak? Are not your harbours blockaded from you? Your castle secured by captives—your lives destroyed—revenues imposed upon you—taxation laid—military power oppressing—your Charter violated—your Governor pensioned—your constitution declining—your Liberties departing, and not content with this, they now attack the *life,* the soul and *capitol* of all your Liberties, to create your Judges, and make them independent upon you for office or support, and erect new Courts of Admiralty, to take away by violence, the husband from his family, his wife, his home, his friends. Such cruelty and tyranny ought ever to be held in the most hateful contempt, the same as you would *a banditti of slave-makers on the coast of* Africa.

Has not the voice of your Father's blood cried yet loud enough in your ears, "Ye Sons of *America* scorn to be Slaves?" Have you not heard the voice of blood in your streets, louder than that which reached Heaven, that cried for vengeance. That was, faith the Lord to *Cain,* the voice of thy brother's blood, but this is of many brethren. Therefore, if there be any vein, any nerve, any soul, any life, or spirit of Liberty in the Sons of *America,* shew your love for it; guard your freedom, prevent your chains; stand up as one man for your Liberty; for none but those, who set a just value upon this blessing are worthy to enjoy it. . . .

3.5

The Church's Flight into
the Wilderness (1776)

SAMUEL SHERWOOD

And to the woman were given two wings of a great eagle, that she might fly into the wilderness, into her place, where she is nourished for a time, and times, and half a time, from the face of the serpent. And the serpent cast out of his mouth water as a flood after the woman, that he might cause her to be carried away of the flood. And the earth helped the woman, and the earth opened her mouth, and swallowed up the flood which the dragon cast out of his mouth. And the dragon was wroth with the woman, and went to make war with the remnant of her seed, which keep the commandments of God, and have the testimony of Jesus Christ.

REV 12:14–17

We learn from what has been said, the true cause, as well as the deplorable effects of all dissentions and violent commotions amidst the Christian states and kingdoms of the world; which, like terrible earthquakes, to which they are compared, often shake them from the centre, and convulse them to death and ruin. If we trace them up to their time, source, and origin, we shall presently find, by the help of scripture-light, they all proceed from the inveterate envy and malice which the dragon has against the woman, and the war and contest he is carrying on against her, and her seed. This is plainly held forth in these prophecies of St. John, and is the grand subject of them.

It has, from the beginning, been the constant aim and design of the dragon, sometimes called the beast, and the serpent, satan, and the devil, to erect a scheme of absolute despotism and tyranny on earth, and involve all mankind in slavery and bondage; and so prevent their having that liberty and freedom which the Son of God came from heaven to procure for, and bestow on them; that he might keep them in a state of servile subjection to himself. He has been and still is the chief counsellor and directing agent in all the dark plots of oppression and persecution against God's church, to effect her destruction; that his own wicked scheme of tyranny might have a full establishment on earth, and bear down all before it.

★ ★ ★

Source: *Gospel Plow*, http://users.frii.com/gosplow/sherwood

This dragon, the great enemy of God, and of his church, whatever shape or form he has assumed, whether that of the spotted leopard, with the feet of a bear, and the mouth of a lion; whether his horns have been ten or only two, like a lamb or goat, giving life unto the image of the beast; yet he has in every appearance, when he had opportunity, discovered the like fierceness and cruelty of temper, thirsting for the blood of the saints. When his shape and form has wore a milder aspect, he has yet spoke as a dragon; and when times would allow of it, exercised all the power of the first beast, causing the earth, and them that dwell therein, to worship him; giving forth tyrannical mandates and decrees, that as many as would not worship the image of the beast, should be killed: Gathering all into his service, both small and great, rich and poor, free and bond, slaves, and savages, catholics and barbarians, to accomplish at any rate, his black and dark designs; passing the most vigorous acts, and severe edicts against those who refused compliance; enacting by his omnipotent power, that they should not buy nor sell, nor carry on any trade or commerce by land or sea.

Now, the administration seems here described, that has for a number of years, been so grievous and distressing to these colonies in America, claiming an absolute power and authority to make laws, binding in all cases whatever, without check or controul from any; which has proceeded in the exercise of this despotic, arbitrary power, to deprive one of them, of their most essential and chartered privileges; sent over fleets and armies to enforce their cruel, tyrannical edicts, which have involved us in all the calamities and horrors of a civil war; which have destroyed many useful lives, burnt two of our flourishing towns, captured many of our vessels that fell in their way, prohibited and destroyed our fishery and trade, forbidding us to buy or sell, and taken in a hostile manner, in a way of piracy and robbery our interest and property, and threaten us with general destruction, for no other reason than that we will not surrender our liberties, properties and privileges, and become abject vassals and slaves to despotic and arbitrary power.

★ ★ ★

It must be confessed, that the trials, afflictions and distresses of the church have been very great; but these have been as a purifying furnace, to cleanse her from dross and corruption, and to make her shine brighter in all the graces and virtues of Christianity. Her enemies and adversaries, in all their furious attacks and malicious encounters have never gained any considerable and lasting advantage to themselves; but generally have come off with loss, disappointment and shame; and had their own weapons, and the blows they have struck, retorted back on them, with redoubled force and vengeance. God promises to give power to his faithful witnesses and servants, "*And if any man will hurt them, fire proceedeth out of their mouth, and devoureth their enemies. And if any man will hurt them, he must in this manner be killed*" Rev. xi. 3, 5. If the enemies of the church, in the wars they set on foot, take any of her members captive, they themselves shall go into captivity; and he that killeth them with the sword, must be killed with the sword.

Agreeable to the great law of retaliation, which is wisely adopted at this day, by the honourable Continental Congress; and the execution of it in full, is warranted and justified by this, and other passages of sacred writ. Those that have undertaken to distress and persecute the woman and her seed, the faithful servants of Christ, have ever found the enterprize dangerous and ruinous to themselves. When the wicked persecuting tyrants of the earth, appear to have great power and strength, some of a selfish and timerous turn of mind, may inadvertantly think it safest to pay worship and allegiance to them, and reccive their mark, and seek shelter and protection under their wings, from the impending storm: But they are most artfully deluded and mistaken. "*The same,*" says the apostle, Rev. xiv. 10, "*shall drink of the wine of the wrath of God, which is poured out without mixture, into the cup of his indignation. And he shall be tormented with fire and brimstone, in the presence of the holy angels, and in the presence of the Lamb; and the smoke of their torment ascendeth up for ever and ever, and they have no rest day nor night.*"

★ ★ ★

Liberty has been planted here; and the more it is attacked, the more it grows and flourishes. The time is coming and hastening on, when Babylon the great shall fall to rise no more; when all wicked tyrant and oppressors shall be destroyed for ever. These violent attacks upon the woman in the wilderness, may possibly be some of the last efforts, and dying struggles of the man of sin. These commotions and convulsions in the British empire, may be leading to the fulfilment of such prophecies as relate to the downfall and overthrow, and to the future glory and prosperity of Christ's church.

It will soon be said and acknowledged, that the kingdoms of this world, are become the kingdoms of our Lord, and of his Christ. The vial of God's wrath begins to be poured out on his enemies and adversaries; and there is falling on them a noisome and grievous sore. And to such as have shed the blood of saints and prophets, to them, blood will be given to drink; for they are worthy. And they will gnaw their tongues of falsehood and deceit for pain; and have the cup of the wine of the fierceness of her wrath; and be rewarded double. The Lamb shall overcome them, for he is Lord of Lords, and King of Kings; and they that are with him, are called, and chosen, and faithful.

May the Lord shorten the days of tribulation, and appear in his glory, to build up Zion; that his knowledge might cover the earth, as the waters do the seas; that wars and tumults may cease thro' the world, and the wolf and the lamb lie down together, and nothing hurt or destroy throughout his holy mountain.

Amen

3.6

American Independence (1776)

SAMUEL ADAMS

Countrymen and brethren: I would gladly have declined an honor to which I find myself unequal. I have not the calmness and impartiality which the infinite importance of the occasion demands. I will not deny the charge of my enemies, that resentment for the accumulated injuries of our country and an ardor for her glory . . . may deprive me of that accuracy of judgment and expression which men of cooler passions may possess. Let me beseech you then, to hear me with caution, to examine without prejudice, and to correct the mistakes into which I may be hurried by my zeal. . . .

Our forefathers threw off the yoke of Popery in religion; for you is reserved the honor of leveling the popery of politics. . . . This day, I trust, the reign of political protestantism will commence. We have explored the temple of royalty, and found that the idol we have bowed down to, has eyes which see not, ears that hear not our prayers, and a heart like the nether millstone. We have this day restored the Sovereign, to whom alone men ought to be obedient. He reigns in Heaven, and with a propitious eye beholds his subjects assuming that freedom of thought, and dignity of self-direction which he bestowed on them. . . .

We are now on this continent to the astonishment of the world three millions of souls united in one common cause. We have large armies, well disciplined and appointed, with commanders inferior to none in military skill, and superior in activity and zeal We are furnished with arsenals and stores beyond our most sanguine expectations, and foreign nations are waiting to crown our success by their alliances. There are instances of, I would say, an almost astonishing Providence in our favor; our success has staggered our enemies, and almost given faith to infidels; so that we may truly say it is not our own arm which has saved us.

The hand of heaven appears to have led us on to be, perhaps, humble instruments and means in the great Providential dispensation which is completing. We have fled from the political Sodom; let us not look back, lest we perish and become a monument of infamy and derision to the world! . . .

And, brethren and fellow-countrymen, if it was ever granted to mortals to trace the designs of Providence, and interpret its manifestations in favor of their cause, we may, with humility of soul, cry out, Not unto us, not unto us,

Source: Frank Moore (ed.), *American Eloquence* (New York: D. Appleton & Co, 1876) pp. 324–330.

but to thy Name be the praise. The confusion of the devices among our enemies, and the rage of the elements against them, have done almost as much
towards our success as either our councils or our arms.

The time at which this attempt on our liberties was made, when we were
ripened into maturity, had acquired a knowledge of war, and were free from
the incursions of enemies in this country, the gradual advances, of our oppressors enabling us to prepare for our defence, the unusual fertility of our lands
and clemency of the seasons, the success which at first attended our feeble
arms, producing unanimity among our friends and reducing our internal foes
to acquiescense—these are all strong and palpable marks and assurances, that
Providence is yet gracious unto Zion, that it will turn away the captivity of
Jacob.

Our glorious reformers, when they broke through the fetters of superstition, effected more than could be expected from an age so darkened. But they
left much to be done by their posterity. They lopped off, indeed, some of the
branches of popery, but they left the root and stock when they left us under
the domination of human systems and decisions, usurping the infallibility
which can be attributed to Revelation alone. They dethroned one usurper
only to raise up another; they refused allegiance to the Pope, only to place the
civil magistrate in the throne of Christ, vested with authority to enact laws,
and inflict penalties in his kingdom. And if we now cast our eyes over the
nations of the earth we shall find, that instead of possessing the pure religion of
the gospel, they may be divided either into infidels who deny the truth, or
politicians who make religion a stalking horse for their ambition, or professors,
who walk in the trammels of orthodoxy, and are more attentive to traditions
and ordinances of men than to the oracles of truth.

Thus by the beneficence of Providence, we shall behold our empire arising, founded on justice and the voluntary consent of the people, and giving
full scope to the exercise of those faculties and rights which most ennoble our
species. Besides the advantages of liberty and the most equal constitution,
heaven has given us a country with every variety of climate and soil, pouring
forth in abundance whatever is necessary for the support, comfort, and strength
of a nation. Within our own borders we possess all the means of sustenance,
defence, and commerce; at the same time, these advantages are so distributed
among the different States of this continent, as if nature had in view to proclaim to us—be united among yourselves, and you will want nothing from the
rest of the world.

3.7

Sermon (1779)

SERAPHIN BANDOT

Gentlemen: We are assembled to celebrate the anniversary of that day which Providence had marked in his Eternal Decrees, to become the epoch of liberty and independence to thirteen United States of America. That Being, whose Almighty hand holds all existence beneath its dominion, undoubtedly produces in the depths of His wisdom, those great events which astonish the universe, and of which the most presumptuous, though instrumental in accomplishing them, dare not attribute to themselves the merit. But the finger of God is still more peculiarly evident in that happy, that glorious revolution, which calls forth this day's festivity. He hath struck the oppressors of a people free and peaceable, with the spirit of delusion which renders the wicked artificers of their own proper misfortunes. Permit me, my dear brethren, citizens of the United States, to address you on this occasion. It is that God, that all-powerful God who hath directed your steps, when you knew not where to apply for counsel: who, when you were without arms, fought for you with the sword of Justice; who, when you were in adversity, poured into your hearts the spirit of courage, of wisdom and of fortitude, and who hath at length raised up for your support a youthful sovereign, whose virtues bless and adorn a sensible, a faithful, and a generous nation. This nation has blended her interests with your interests, and her sentiments with yours. She participates in all your joys, and this day unites her voice to yours, at the foot of the altars of the Eternal God, to celebrate that glorious revolution, which has placed the sons of America among the free and independent nations of the earth.

We have nothing now to apprehend but the anger of Heaven, or that the measure of our guilt should exceed His mercy. Let us then prostrate ourselves at the feet of the immortal God who holds the fate of empires in His hands and raises them up at His pleasure, or breaks them down to dust. Let us conjure him to enlighten our enemies, and to dispose their hearts to enjoy that tranquillity and happiness which the revolution we now celebrate has established for a great part of the human race. Let us implore him to conduct us by that way which His providence has marked out for a union at so desirable an end. Let us offer unto him hearts imbued with sentiments of respect, consecrated by religion, by humanity, and by patriotism. Never is the august ministry of His altars more acceptable to His Divine Majesty than when it lays at His feet

Source: John Gilmary Shea, *History of the Catholic Church in the United States: 1763–1815* (Akron, OH: D. H. McBride & Co., 1888), Vol. 2, pp. 175–176.

homages, offerings and vows, so pure, so worthy the common parent of mankind. God will not reject our joy, for He is the author of it: nor will He reject our prayers, for they ask but the full accomplishment of the decrees He hath manifested. Filled with this spirit let us, in concert with each other, raise our hearts to the Eternal. Let us implore His infinite mercy to be pleased to inspire the rulers of both nations with the wisdom and force necessary to perfect what it hath begun. Let us, in a word, unite our voices to beseech Him to dispense His blessings upon the councils and the arms of the allies, and that we may soon enjoy the sweets of a peace which will cement the union, and establish the prosperity of the two empires. It is with this view that we shall cause that canticle to be performed which the custom of the Catholic Church hath consecrated to be at once a testimonial of public joy, a thanksgiving for benefits received from Heaven, and a prayer for the continuance of its mercies.

ESTABLISHING THE RIGHT
OF RELIGIOUS CHOICE

One of the most significant achievements in the formation of the nation during the war for independence was the assurance Americans sought and gained for the right of religious choice. The unestablished denominations had been calling for religious liberty for many years, as is evident in **"An Appeal to the Public for Religious Liberty,"** delivered by the Baptist leader Isaac Backus before the Constitutional Convention of 1787.

The right of religious choice was a cause dear to the heart of Thomas Jefferson who, while Governor of Virginia in 1779, penned his famous **"Virginia Statute for Religious Freedom,"** which was passed seven years later. In 1785, James Madison's defense of this ideal, **"Memorial and Remonstrance,"** helped block an attempt to create a state church in Virginia. The next year, Virginia at long last passed Jefferson's statute. Madison also worked for the passage of the First Amendment to the Constitution, which guaranteed that the federal government would neither establish a state religion or deny the free exercise of any religion.

The first president, George Washington, answered many letters from many different concerned denominations, giving them **Assurances** of his regard for the rights of religious freedom as guaranteed by the U.S. Constitution. His **Response** to a letter from a Jewish congregation in Rhode Island is especially enlightening.

The third president, Thomas Jefferson, believed that his authorship of the Virginia Statute for Religious Liberty was one of the three greatest achievements of his life, along with writing the Declaration of Independence and founding the University of Virginia. He did not mention being President of the United States. In a famous **Reply** to the Danbury, Connecticut, Association of Baptists, he gave his full support to the cause of religious choice and used the phrase "wall of separation" that became the mantra of Americans dedicated to the separation of church and state.

3.8

An Appeal to the Public for Religious Liberty (1773)

ISAAC BACKUS

I t is needful to observe that God has appointed two kinds of government in the world which are distinct in their nature and ought never to be confounded together—one of which is called civil and the other ecclesiastical government. And though we shall not attempt a full explanation of them, some essential points of difference between them are necessary to be mentioned in order truly to open our grievances.

SECTION I

Some essential points of difference between civil and ecclesiastical government.

All acts of execution of power in the civil state are to be performed in the name of the king or state they belong to, while all our religious acts are to be done in the name of the Lord Jesus, and so are to be performed heartily as to the Lord and not unto men. . . . It is often pleaded that magistrates ought to do their duty in religious as well as civil affairs. That is readily granted; but what is their duty therein? Surely it is to bow to the name of Jesus and to serve him with holy reverence; and if they do to the contrary they may expect to perish from the

Source: Isaac Backus, *An Appeal to the Public for Religious Liberty* (Boston, 1773).

way. . . . But where is the officer that will dare to come in the name of the Lord to demand, and forcibly to take, a tax which was imposed by the civil state? Can any man in the light of truth maintain his character as minister of Christ, if he is not contented with all that Christ's name and influence will procure for him, but will have recourse to the kings of the earth to force money from the people to support them under the name of an ambassador of the God of heaven? . . .

In all civil governments some are appointed to judge for others and have power to compel others to submit to their judgment, but our Lord has most plainly forbidden us either to assume or submit to any such thing in religion. . . . He declares that the cause of his coming into the world was to bear "witness unto the truth," and says he, "Everyone that is of the truth heareth my voice." This is the nature of his kingdom which he says "is not of this world" and gives that as the reason why his servants should not fight or defend him with sword. . . . And it appears to us that the true difference and exact line between ecclesiastical and civil government is this: that the church is armed with light and truth to pull down the strongholds of iniquity and to gain souls to Christ and his church, to be governed by his rules therein, and again to exclude those from their communion who will not be governed; while the state is armed with the sword to guard the peace and the civil rights of all persons and societies and to punish those who violate the same. And where these two kinds of government and the weapons which belong to them are well distinguished and improved according to the true nature and end of their institution, the effects are happy, and they do not at all interfere with each other; but where they have been confounded together, no tongue nor pen can fully describe the mischiefs that have ensued. . . .

SECTION II

A brief view of how civil and ecclesiastical affairs are blended together among us to the depriving of many people of that liberty of conscience which he has given them. . . . We view it to be our incumbent duty "to render unto Caesar" the things that are his but that it is of as much more importance not to render unto him anything that belongs only to God, who is to be obeyed rather than man. And as it is evident to us that God always claimed it as his sole prerogative to determine by his own laws what his worship shall be, who shall minister in it, and how they shall be supported: so it is evident that their prerogative has been, and still is, encroached upon in our land. For,

1. Our legislatures claim power to compel every town and parish within their jurisdiction to set up and maintain a pedobaptist worship among them, although it is well known that infant baptism is never expressed in the Bible. . . .

2. Our ascended Lord gives "gifts unto men" in a sovereign way as seems good to him and he requires "every man, as he has received the gift, even

so to minister the same; . . ." But the Massachusetts legislature, while they claim a power to compel each parish to settle a minister, have also determined that he must be one who has either an academical degree or a testimonial in his favor from a majority of the ministers in the country where the parish lies. So that let Christ give a man ever so great gifts, yet hereby these ministers derive a noble power from the state to forbid the improvement of the same if he follows not their schemes. . . .

3. Though the Lord hath "ordained that they which preach the gospel shall live by the gospel" or by the free "communications to them" which his gospel will produce . . . yet the ministers of our Lord have chosen to "live by the law"; and as a reason therefor one of their most noted writers [Cotton Mather], instead of producing any truth of God, recites the tradition of a man who said, "Ministers of the gospel would have a poor time of it, if they must rely on a free contribution of the people for their maintenance." And he says, ". . . it is enacted that there shall be a public worship of God in every plantation; that the person elected by the majority of the inhabitants shall be so, shall be looked upon as the minister of the place; that the salary for him, which they shall agree upon, shall be levied by a rate upon all inhabitants. In consequence of this, the minister thus chosen by the people is (not only Christ's but also) in reality the King's minister; and the salary raised for him is raised in the King's name."

Now who can hear Christ declare that his kindgom is "not of this world," and yet believe that this blending of the church and state together can be pleasing to him? For though their laws call them "orthodox ministers," yet the grand test of orthodoxy is the major vote of the people, be they saints or sinners, believers or unbelievers. . . .

Hence their ministers and churches must become subject to the court and the majority of the parish in order to have their salary raised in the "king's name." But how are either of them in the meantime subject to the authority of Christ in his church? . . . for though there is a show of equity in allowing every society to choose its own minister, yet let them be ever so unanimous for one who is of a different mode from the court, their choice is not allowed. . . .

Another argument which these ministers often mention is the apostolic direction to us to pray for all that are in authority that we may lead a quiet and peaceable life in all godliness and honesty. But do they pray and act according to that direction? . . . when it comes to be calmly represented that religion is a "voluntary obedience unto God" which, therefore, force cannot promote, how soon do they shift the scene and tell us that religious liberty is fully allowed to us, only the state have in their wisdom thought fit to tax all the inhabitants to support an order of men for the good of civil society. A little while ago it was for religion, and many have declared that without it we should soon have no religion left among us; but now tis to maintain civility. Though, by the way, it is well known that no men in the land have done more to promote uncivil treatment of dissenters from themselves than some of these pretended ministers of civility have done. In 1644 the court at Boston passed an act to punish men with banishment if they opposed infant baptism or departed from any of their congregations if it was going to be administered. And after they acted upon this law, one of their chief magistrates observed that such methods tended to make hypocrites. To which a noted minister replied, That if it did so, yet such were better than profane persons, because, said he, "hypocrites give God part of his due, the outward man, but the profane person giveth God neither outward nor inward man." By which it seems that in that day they were zealous to have the outward man, if no more, given to God; but now that conduct is condemned as persecution by their children, who profess to allow us full liberty of conscience because they do not hinder our giving our inward man to God, only claim a power to seize our outward man to get money for themselves. And though many of us have expended ten or twenty times as much in setting up and supporting that worship which we believe to be right as it would have cost us to have continued in the fashionable way, yet we are often accused of being covetous for dissenting from that way and refusing to pay more money out of our little incomes to uphold men from whom we receive no benefit but rather abuse. How far is this from leading "a peaceable life," either of godliness or honesty!

3.9

Virginia Statute for
Religious Freedom (1779)

THOMAS JEFFERSON

ell aware that the opinions and belief of men depend not on their own will, but follow involuntarily the evidence proposed to their minds; that Almighty God hath created the mind free, and manifested his supreme will that free it shall remain by making it altogether insusceptible of restraint; that all attempts to influence it by temporal punishments, or burthens, or by civil incapacitations, tend only to beget habits of hypocrisy and meanness, and are a departure from the plan of the holy author of our religion, who being lord both of body and mind, yet chose not to propagate it by coercions on either, as

Source: Julian Boyd (ed.), *Papers of Thomas Jefferson* (Princeton, NJ: Princeton University Press, 1950), II, 545–547.

was in his Almighty power to do, *but to extend it by its influence on reason alone;* that the impious presumption of legislators and rulers, civil as well as ecclesiastical, who, being themselves but fallible and uninspired men, have assumed dominion over the faith of others, setting up their own opinions and modes of thinking as the only true and infallible, and as such endeavoring to impose them on others, hath established and maintained false religions over the greatest part of the world and through all time: That to compel a man to furnish contributions of money for the propagation of opinions which he disbelieves *and abhors,* is sinful and tyrannical; that even the forcing him to support this or that teacher of his own religious persuasion, is depriving him of the comfortable liberty of giving his contributions to the particular pastor whose morals he would make his pattern, and whose powers he feels most persuasive to righteousness; and is withdrawing from the ministry those temporary rewards, which proceeding from an approbation of their personal conduct, are an additional incitement to earnest and unremitting labours for the instruction of mankind; that our civil rights have no dependance on our religious opinions, any more than our opinions in physics or geometry; that therefore the proscribing any citizen as unworthy the public confidence by laying upon him an incapacity of being called to offices of trust and emolument, unless he profess or renounce this or that religious opinion, is depriving him injuriously of those privileges and advantages to which, in common with his fellow citizens, he has a natural right; that it tends also to corrupt the principles of that *very* religion it is meant to encourage, by bribing, with a monopoly of worldly honours and emoluments, those who will externally profess and conform to it; that though indeed these are criminal who do not withstand such temptation, yet neither are those innocent who lay the bait in their way; *that the opinions of men are not the object of civil government, nor under its jurisdiction;* that to suffer the civil magistrate to intrude his powers into the field of opinion and to restrain the profession or propagation of principles on supposition of their ill tendency is a dangerous falacy, which at once destroys all religious liberty, because he being of course judge of that tendency will make his opinions the rule of judgment, and approve or condemn the sentiments of others only as they shall square with or differ from his own; that it is time enough for the rightful purposes of civil government for its officers to interfere when principles break out into overt acts against peace and good order; and finally, that truth is great and will prevail if left to herself; that she is the proper and sufficient antagonist to error, and has nothing to fear from the conflict unless by human interposition disarmed of her natural weapons, free argument and debate; errors ceasing to be dangerous when it is permitted freely to contradict them.

We the General Assembly of Virginia do enact that no man shall be compelled to frequent or support any religious worship, place, or ministry whatsoever, nor shall be enforced, restrained, molested, or burthened in his body or goods, nor shall otherwise suffer, on account of his religious opinions or belief; but that all men shall be free to profess, and by argument to maintain, their opinions in matters of religion, and that the same shall in no wise diminish, enlarge, or affect their civil capacities.

And though we well know that this Assembly, elected by the people for the ordinary purposes of legislation only, have no power to restrain the acts of succeeding Assemblies, constituted with powers equal to our own, and that therefore to declare this act irrevocable would be of no effect in law; yet we are free to declare, and do declare, that the rights hereby asserted are of the natural rights of mankind, and that if any act shall be hereafter passed to repeal the present or to narrow its operation, such act will be an infringement of natural right.

3.10

Memorial and Remonstrance (1785)

JAMES MADISON

We the subscribers, citizens of the said Commonwealth, having taken into serious consideration, a Bill printed by order of the last Session of General Assembly, entitled "A Bill establishing a provision for Teachers of the Christian Religion," and conceiving that the same if finally armed with the sanctions of a law, will be a dangerous abuse of power, are bound as faithful members of a free State to remonstrate against it, and to declare the reasons by which we are determined. We remonstrate against the said Bill,

1. Because we hold it for a fundamental and undeniable truth, "that Religion or the duty which we owe to our Creator and the manner of discharging it, can be directed only by reason and conviction, not by force or violence." The Religion then of every man must be left to the conviction and conscience of every man; and it is the right of every man to exercise it as these may dictate. This right is in its nature an unalienable right. It is unalienable, because the opinions of men, depending only on the evidence contemplated by their own minds cannot follow the dictates of other men: It is unalienable also, because what is here a right towards men, is a duty towards the Creator. It is the duty of every man to render to the Creator such homage and such only as he believes to be

Source: *Papers of James Madison* (Chicago: University of Chicago Press, 1973), VIII, 298ff.

acceptable to him. This duty is precedent, both in order of time and in degree of obligation, to the claims of Civil Society. Before any man can be considered as a member of Civil Society, he must be considered as a subject of the Governour of the Universe: And if a member of Civil Society, who enters into any subordinate Association, must always do it with a reservation of his duty to the General Authority; much more must every man who becomes a member of any particular Civil Society, do it with a saving of his allegiance to the Universal Sovereign. We maintain therefore that in matters of Religion, no mans right is abridged by the institution of Civil Society and that Religion is wholly exempt from its cognizance. True it is, that no other rule exists, by which any question which may divide a Society, can be ultimately determined, but the will of the majority; but it is also true that the majority may trespass on the rights of the minority.

2. Because if Religion be exempt from the authority of the Society at large, still less can it be subject to that of the Legislative Body. The latter are but the creatures and vicegerents of the former. Their jurisdiction is both derivative and limited: it is limited with regard to the co-ordinate departments, more necessarily is it limited with regard to the constituents. The preservation of a free Government requires not merely, that the metes and bounds which separate each department of power be invariably maintained; but more especially that neither of them be suffered to overleap the great Barrier which defends the rights of the people. The Rulers who are guilty of such an encroachment, exceed the commission from which they derive their authority, and are Tyrants. The People who submit to it are governed by laws made neither by themselves nor by an authority derived from them, and are slaves.

★ ★ ★

15. Because finally, "the equal right of every citizen to the free exercise of his Religion according to the dictates of conscience" is held by the same tenure with all our other rights. If we recur to its origin, it is equally the gift of nature; if we weigh its importance, it cannot be less dear to us; if we consult the "Declaration of those rights which pertain to the good people of Virginia, as the basis and foundation of Government," it is enumerated with equal solemnity, or rather studied emphasis. Either then, we must say, that the Will of the Legislature is the only measure of their authority; and that in the plenitude of this authority, they may sweep away all our fundamental rights; or, that they are bound to leave this particular right untouched and sacred: Either we must say, that they may control the freedom of the press, may abolish the Trial by Jury, may swallow up the Executive and judiciary Powers of the State; nay that they may despoil us of our very right of suffrage, and erect themselves into an independent and hereditary Assembly or, we must say, that they have no authority to enact into law the Bill under consideration. We the Subscribers say, that

the General Assembly of this Commonwealth have no such authority:
And that no effort may be omitted on our part against so dangerous an
usurpation, we oppose to it, this remonstrance; earnestly praying, as we
are in duty bound, that the Supreme Lawgiver of the Universe, by illu-
minating those to whom it is addressed, may on the one hand, turn their
Councils from every act which would affront his holy prerogative, or
violate the trust committed to them: and on the other, guide them into
every measure which may be worthy of his [blessing, may re]dound to
their own praise, and may establish more firmly the liberties, the prosperity and the happiness of the Commonwealth.

3.11

Assurances of Religious Freedom (1789–1790)

GEORGE WASHINGTON

REPLY TO AN ADDRESS SENT BY THE GENERAL COMMITTEE OF THE UNITED BAPTIST CHURCHES IN VIRGINIA, MAY, 1789

If I could have entertained the slightest apprehension, that the constitution
framed in the convention, where I had the honor to preside, might possibly
endanger the religious rights of any ecclesiastical society, certainly I would never
have placed my signature to it; and if I could now conceive that the general government might ever be so administered as to render the liberty of conscience inse-
cure, I beg you will be persuaded, that no one would be more zealous than myself
to establish effectual barriers against the horrors of spiritual tyranny, and every
species of religious persecution. For you doubtless remember, that I have often

Source: Norman Cousins (ed.) "In God We Trust" (New York: Harper & Brothers, 1958) pp. 44ff.

expressed my sentiments that every man, conducting himself as a good citizen, and being accountable to God alone for his religious opinions, ought to be protected in worshipping the Deity according to the dictates of his own conscience.

★ ★ ★

REPLY TO AN ADDRESS SENT BY THE GENERAL ASSEMBLY OF PRESBYTERIAN CHURCHES IN THE UNITED STATES (ADDRESS DATED MAY 26, 1789; WASHINGTON'S REPLY UNDATED)

While I reiterate the professions of my dependence upon Heaven as the source of all public and private blessings; I will observe that the general prevalence of piety, philanthropy, honesty, industry and economy seems, in the ordinary course of human affairs, particularly necessary for advancing and confirming the happiness of our country. While all men within our territories are protected in worshipping the Deity according to the dictates of their consciences; it is rationally to be expected from them in return, that they will be emulous of evincing the sanctity of their professions by the innocence of their lives and the beneficence of their actions; for no man, who is profligate in his morals, or a bad member of the civil community, can possibly be a true Christian, or a credit to his own religious society.

I desire you to accept my acknowledgments for your laudable endeavors to render men sober, honest, and good Citizens, and the obedient subjects of a lawful government.

REPLY TO AN ADDRESS SENT BY THE RELIGIOUS SOCIETY CALLED QUAKERS FROM THEIR YEARLY MEETING FOR PENNSYLVANIA, NEW JERSEY, DELAWARE, AND THE WESTERN PARTS OF MARYLAND AND VIRGINIA, SEPTEMBER 28, 1789 (REPLY UNDATED)

Government being, among other purposes, instituted to protect the persons and consciences of men from oppression, it certainly is the duty of rulers, not only to abstain from it themselves, but according to their stations, to prevent it in others.

The liberty enjoyed by the people of these States, of worshipping Almighty God agreeably to their consciences, is not only among the choicest of their *blessings,* but also of their *rights.* While men perform their social duties faithfully, they do all that society or the state can with propriety demand or expect; and remain responsible only to their Maker for the religion, or modes of faith, which they may prefer or profess.

Your principles and conduct are well known to me; and it is doing the people called Quakers no more than justice to say, that (except their declining to share with others the burthen of the common defense) there is no denomination among us, who are more exemplary and useful citizens.

I assure you very explicitly, that in my opinion the conscientious scruples of all men should be treated with great delicacy and tenderness; and it is my wish and desire, that the laws may always be as extensively accommodated to them, as a due regard to the protection and essential interests of the nation may justify and permit.

REPLY TO A CONGRATULATORY ADDRESS BY A COMMITTEE OF ROMAN CATHOLICS WAITING UPON THE PRESIDENT, MARCH 15, 1790, ACCORDING TO THE MARYLAND *JOURNAL* AND BALTIMORE *ADVERTISER*

I feel that my conduct in War and in Peace has met with more general approbation than could reasonably have been expected; and I find myself disposed to consider that fortunate circumstance, in a great degree, resulting from the able support and extraordinary candor of my fellow-citizens of all denominations.

As mankind become more liberal, they will be more apt to allow, that all those who conduct themselves as worthy members of the community are equally entitled to the protection of civil government. I hope ever to see America among the foremost nations in examples of justice and liberality. And I presume, that your fellow-citizens will not forget the patriotic part which you took in the accomplishment of their revolution, and the establishment of their government; or the important assistance, which they received, from a Nation in which the Roman Catholic religion is professed. . . . May the members of your Society in America, animated alone by the pure spirit of Christianity, and still conducting themselves as the faithful subjects of our free government, enjoy every temporal and spiritual felicity.

3.12

Response
to Message from a Rhode Island
Jewish Congregation

GEORGE WASHINGTON

To the President of the United States of America
Newport Rhode Island, August 17th, 1790.

Sir,

Permit the children of the Stock of Abraham to approach you with the most cordial affection and esteem for your person & merits and to join with our fellow Citizens in welcoming you to New Port.

With pleasure we reflect on those days—those days of difficulty, & danger when the God of Israel, who delivered David from the peril of the sword, shielded your head in the day of battle: and we rejoice to think, that the same Spirit who rested in the Bosom of the greatly beloved Daniel enabling him to preside over the Provinces of the Babylonish Empire, rests and ever will rest upon you, enabling you to discharge the arduous duties of Chief Magistrate in these States.

Deprived as we heretofore have been of the invaluable rights of free Citizens, we now (with a deep sense of gratitude to the Almighty disposer of all events) behold a Government, erected by the Majesty of the People—a Government, which to bigotry gives no sanction, to persecution no assistance—but generously affording to All liberty of conscience, and immunities of Citizenship: deeming every one, of whatever Nation, tongue, or language, equal parts of the great governmental Machine:

This so ample and extensive Federal Union whose basis is Philanthropy, Mutual Confidence and Publick Virtue, we cannot but acknowledge to be the work of the Great God, who ruleth in the Armies Of Heaven and among the Inhabitants of the Earth, doing whatever seemeth him good.

For all the Blessings of civil and religious liberty which we enjoy under an equal and benign administration, we desir to send up our thanks to the Ancient of Days, the great preserver of Men—beseeching him, that the Angel who

Source: http://www.au.org/site/DocServer/Washingtons_letter_to_Truro_synagogue
pfd?docId = 146

conducted our forefathers through the wilderness into the promised land, may graciously conduct you through all the difficulties and dangers of this mortal life: and, when like Joshua full of days and full of honour, you are gathered to your Fathers, may you be admitted into the Heavenly Paradise to partake of the water of life, and the tree of immortality.

Done and Signed by Order of the Hebrew Congregation in Newport Rhode Island

MOSES SEIXAS, WARDEN

[Newport, R.I., 18 August 1790]

Gentlemen,

While I receive, with much satisfaction, your Address replete with expressions of affection and esteem; I rejoice in the opportunity of assuring you, that I shall always retain a grateful remembrance of the cordial welcome I experienced in my visit to Newport, from all classes of Citizens.

The reflection on the days of difficulty and danger which are past is rendered the more sweet, from a consciousness that they are succeeded by days of uncommon prosperity and security. If we have wisdom to make the best use of the advantages with which we are now favored, we cannot fail, under the just administration of a good Government, to become a great and a happy people.

The Citizens of the United States of America have a right to applaud themselves for having given to mankind examples of an enlarged and liberal policy: a policy worthy of imitation. All possess alike liberty of conscience and immunities of citizenship It is now no more that toleration is spoken of, as if it was by the indulgence of one class of people, that another enjoyed the exercise of their inherent natural rights. For happily the Government of the United States, which gives to bigotry no sanction, to persecution no assistance requires only that they who live under its protection should demean themselves as good citizens, in giving it on all occasions their effectual support.

It would be inconsistent with the frankness of my character not to avow that I am pleased with your favorable opinion of my Administration, and fervent wishes for my felicity. May the Children of the Stock of Abraham, who dwell in this land, continue to merit and enjoy the good will of the other Inhabitants; while every one shall sit in safety under his own vine and figtree, and there shall be none to make him afraid. May the father of all mercies scatter light and not darkness in our paths, and make us all in our several vocations useful here, and in his own due time and way everlastingly happy.

GO: WASHINGTON

3.13

On the Wall of Separation between Church and State (1802)

THOMAS JEFFERSON

LETTER TO JEFFERSON FROM DANBURY, CONNECTICUT BAPTIST ASSOCIATION, OCTOBER 7, 1801

Sir, Among the many millions in America and Europe who rejoice in your Election to office; we embrace the first opportunity which we have enjoyed in our collective capacity, since your Inauguration, to express our great satisfaction, in your appointment to the chief Magistracy in the United States; And though our mode of expression may be less courtly and pompous than what many others clothe their addresses with, we beg you, Sir to believe, that none are more sincere.

Our Sentiments are uniformly on the side of Religious Liberty—That Religion is at all times and places a matter between God and individuals—That no man ought to suffer in name, person, or effects on account of his religious Opinions—That the legitimate Power of civil government extends no further than to punish the man who works *ill to his neighbor*: But Sir our constitution of government is not specific. Our ancient of our government, at the time of our revolution; and such had been our Laws & usages, and such still are; that Religion is considered as the first object of Legislation; and therefore what religious privileges we enjoy (as a minor part of the State) we enjoy as favors granted, and not as inalienable rights: and these favors we receive at the expense of such degrading acknowledgements, as are inconsistent with the rights of freemen. It is not to be wondered at therefore; if those, who seek after power & gain under the pretense of *government & Religion* should reproach

Source: Andrew Lipscomb and Albert Bergh (eds.) *Writings of Thomas Jefferson* (Washington, DC: Thomas Jefferson Memorial Association of the United States, 1903) pp. 281–282.

their fellow men—should reproach their chief Magistrate, as an enemy of religion Law & good order because he will not, dare not assume the prerogatives of Jehovah and make Laws to govern the Kingdom of Christ.

Sir, we are sensible that the President of the United States, is not the national legislator, and also sensible that the national government cannot destroy the Laws of each State; but our hopes are strong that the sentiments of our beloved President, which have had such genial affect already, like the radiant beams of the Sun, will shine and prevail through all these States and all the world till Hierarchy and Tyranny be destroyed from the Earth. Sir, when we reflect on your past services, and see a glow of philanthropy and good will shining forth in a course of more than thirty years we have reason to believe that America's God has raised you up to fill the chair of State out of that good will which he bears to the Millions which you preside over. May God strengthen you for the arduous task which providence & the voice of the people have called you to sustain and support you in your Administration against all the predetermined opposition of those who wish to rise to wealth & importance on the poverty and subjection of the people.

And may the Lord preserve you safe from every evil and bring you at last to his Heavenly Kingdom through Jesus Christ our Glorious Mediator.

Signed in behalf of the Association.

NEHH DODGE

EPHRAM ROBBINS, THE COMMITTEE

STEPHEN S. NELSON

JEFFERSON'S REPLY, JANUARY 1, 1802

Gentlemen:

The affectionate sentiments of esteem and approbation which are so good to express towards me, on behalf of the Danbury Baptist Association, give me the highest satisfaction. My duties dictate a faithful and zealous pursuit of the interests of my constituents, and in proportion as they are persuaded of my fidelity to those duties, the discharge of them becomes more and more pleasing.

Believing with you that religion is a matter which lies solely between man and his God; that he owes account to none other for his faith or his worship; that the legislative powers of the government reach actions only, and not opinions, I contemplate with sovereign reverence that act of the whole American people which declared that their legislature should "make no law respecting an establishment of religion, or prohibiting the free exercise thereof," thus building a wall of separation between church and State. Adhering to this expression of the supreme will of the nation in behalf of the rights of conscience, I shall see with sincere satisfaction the progress of those sentiments which tend to restore man to all of his natural rights, convinced he has no natural right in opposition to his social duties.

I reciprocate your kind prayers for the protection and blessings of the common Father and Creator of man, and tender you and your religious association, assurances of my high respect and esteem.

THOMAS JEFFERSON

RELIGIOUS FRICTIONS AND FURTHER DIVERSIFICATION

With the guarantee of freedom of religious thought and practice, with the rapid growth of groups that had before independence been too small to notice, with further diversification of the American religious mosaic, came inevitable frictions and conflict. It is clear from the **Report to the Vatican** from Archbishop of Baltimore John Carroll in the late eighteenth century that the number, diffusion, and influence of American Catholics were rising. There were reactions to Catholic growth from the still overwhelmingly Protestant majority.

Samuel F. B. Morse, known for his invention of the telegraph code, tried to warn Protestants of the *Imminent Dangers* this increase in the Catholic population posed. Anti-Catholic fiction such as *Awful Disclosures* painted the Church in luridly malevolent colors. **Protestant Intolerance** was rife as anti-Catholic movements allied themselves with the Know-Nothing Party to demand Catholic exclusion.

Perhaps because they were not so numerous and burgeoning as Catholics, Unitarians did not attract as much publicity and opposition. Despite his Unitarianism, Jefferson was twice elected president. But as is obvious from William Ellery Channing's outline of the doctrines of **"Unitatarian Christianity,"** especially in its denial of the Trinity, Unitarianism also deviated from the Protestant orthodoxy that many, if not most, Americans believed was the backbone of the nation.

It is no wonder, with theological controversies and denominational conflicts swirling through the young nation in a scramble to make America conform to one or another religious pattern, that Native Americans found the efforts to make Christians of them a bit ridiculous. The Iroquois spokesman Red Jacket seemed to be poking fun at white America's religious battles when in 1820 he addressed a Boston Missionary Society, which wanted to evangelize his people in western New York, and explained that **"We Never Argue about Religion."**

3.14

Report
to the Vatican (1785)

JOHN CARROLL

ON THE NUMBER OF CATHOLICS
IN THE UNITED STATES

There are in Maryland about 15,800 Catholics; of these there are about 9,000 freemen, adults or over twelve years of age; children under that age, about 3,000; and about that number of slaves of all ages of African origin, called negroes. There are in Pennsylvania about 7,000, very few of whom are negroes, and the Catholics are less scattered and live nearer to each other. There are not more than 200 in Virginia who are visited four or five times a year by a priest. Many other Catholics are said to be scattered in that and other states, who are utterly deprived of all religious ministry. In the State of New York I hear there are at least 1,500. (Would that some spiritual succor could be afforded them!) They have recently, at their own expense, sent for a Franciscan Father from Ireland, and he is said to have the best testimonials as to his learning and life; he had arrived a little before I received the letters in which faculties were transmitted to me, communicable to my fellow-priests. I was for a time in doubt whether I could properly approve this priest for the administration of the sacraments. I have now, however, decided, especially as the feast of Easter is so near, to consider him as one of my fellow-priests, and to grant him faculties, and I trust that my decision will meet your approbation. As to the Catholics who are in the territory bordering on the river called Mississippi and in all that region which following that river extends to the Atlantic Ocean, and from it extends to the limits of Carolina, Virginia, and Pennsylvania—this tract of country contains, I hear, many Catholics, formerly Canadians, who speak French, and I fear that they are destitute of priests. Before I received your Eminence's letters there went to them a priest, German by birth, but who came last from France; he professes to belong to the Carmelite order; he was furnished with no sufficient testimonials that he was sent by his lawful superior. What he is doing and what

Source: Peter Guilday, *The Life & Times of John Carroll* (Westminster, MD: Newman Press, 1922[1954]) pp. 225–257.

is the condition of the Church in those parts, I expect soon to learn. The jurisdiction of the Bishop of Quebec formerly extended to some part of that region; but I do not know whether he wishes to exercise any authority there, now that all these parts are subject to the United States.

ON THE CONDITION, PIETY, AND DEFECTS, ETC., OF CATHOLICS

In Maryland a few of the leading more wealthy families still profess the Catholic faith introduced at the very foundation of the province by their ancestors. The greater part of them are planters and in Pennsylvania almost all are farmers, except the merchants and mechanics living in Philadelphia. As for piety, they are for the most part sufficiently assiduous in the exercises of religion and in frequenting the sacraments, but they lack that fervor, which frequent appeals to the sentiment of piety usually produce, as many congregations hear the word of God only once a month, and sometimes only once in two months. We are reduced to this by want of priests, by the distance of congregations from each other and by difficulty of travelling. This refers to Catholics born here, for the condition of the Catholics who in great numbers are flowing in here from different countries of Europe, is very different. For while there are few of our native Catholics who do not approach the sacraments of Penance and the Holy Eucharist, at least once a year, especially in Easter time, you can scarcely find any among the newcomers who discharge this duty to religion, and there is reason to fear that the example will be very pernicious especially in commercial towns. The abuses that have grown among Catholics are chiefly those, which result from unavoidable intercourse with non-Catholics, and the examples thence derived: namely more free intercourse between young people of opposite sexes than is compatible with chastity in mind and body; too great fondness for dances and similar amusements; and an incredible eagerness, especially in girls, for reading love stories which are brought over in great quantities from Europe. Then among other things, a general lack of care in instructing their children and especially the negro slaves in their religion, as these people are kept constantly at work, so that they rarely hear any instructions from the priest, unless they can spend a short time with one; and most of them are consequently very dull in faith and depraved in morals. It can scarcely be believed how much trouble and care they give the pastors of souls.

ON THE NUMBER OF THE PRIESTS, THEIR QUALIFICATIONS, CHARACTER AND MEANS OF SUPPORT

There are nineteen priests in Maryland and five in Pennsylvania. Of these two are more than seventy years old, and three others very near that age: and they are consequently almost entirely unfit to undergo the hardships, without which this Vineyard of the Lord cannot be cultivated. Of the remaining priests, some are in very bad health, and there is one recently approved by me for a few months only, that in the extreme want of priests I may give him a trial; for some doings were reported of him which made me averse to employing him. I will watch him carefully, and if anything occurs unworthy of priestly gravity I will recall the faculties granted, whatever inconvenience this may bring to many Catholics: for I am convinced that the Catholic faith will suffer less harm, if for a short time there is no priest at a place, than if living as we do among fellow-citizens of another religion, we admit to the discharge of the sacred ministry, I do not say bad priests, but incautious and imprudent priests. All the other clergymen lead a life full of labour, as each one attends congregations far apart, and has to be riding constantly and with great fatigue, especially to sick calls. Priests are maintained chiefly from the proceeds of the estates; elsewhere by the liberality of the Catholics. There is properly no ecclesiastical property here: for the property by which the priests are supported, is held in the names of individuals and transferred by will to devisees. This course was rendered necessary when the Catholic religion was cramped here by laws, and no remedy has yet been found for this difficulty, although we made an earnest effort last year. There is a college in Philadelphia, and it is proposed to establish two in Maryland, in which Catholics can be admitted, as well as others, as presidents, professors and pupils. We hope that some educated there will embrace the ecclesiastical state. We think accordingly of establishing a Seminary, in which they can be trained to the life and learning suited to that state.

3.15

Imminent Dangers (1835)

SAMUEL F. B. MORSE

I have set forth in a very brief and imperfect manner the evil, the great and increasing evil, that threatens our free institutions from *foreign interference*. Have I not shown that there is real cause for alarm? Let me recapitulate the facts in the case, and see if any one of them can be denied; and if not, I submit it to the calm decision of every American, whether he can still sleep in fancied security, while incendiaries are at work; and whether he is ready quietly to surrender his liberty, civil and religious, into the hands of foreign powers.

1. It is a fact, that in this age the subject of civil and religious liberty agitates in the most intense manner the various European governments.

2. It is a fact, that the influence of American free institutions in subverting European despotic institutions is greater now than it has ever been, from the fact of the greater maturity, and long-tried character, of the American form of government.

3. It is a fact, that Popery is opposed in its very nature to Democratic Republicanism; and it is, therefore, as a political system, as well as religious, opposed to civil and religious liberty, and consequently to our form of government.

4. It is a fact, that this truth, respecting the intrinsic character of Popery, has lately been clearly and demonstratively proved in public lectures, by one of the Austrian Cabinet, a devoted Roman Catholic, and with the evident design (as subsequent events show) of exciting the Austrian government to a great enterprise in support of absolute power.

5. It is a fact, that this Member of the Austrian Cabinet, in his lectures, designated and proscribed this country by name, as the "*great nursery of destructive principles; as the Revolutionary school for France and the rest of Europe,*" whose contagious example of Democratic liberty had given, and would still give, trouble to the rest of the world, unless the evil were abated.

6. It is a fact, that very shortly after the delivery of these lectures, a Society was organized in the Austrian capital, called the St. Leopold Foundation, for the purpose "of promoting the greater activity of Catholic Missions in America."

Source: Samuel F.B. Morse, *Imminent Dangers to the Free Institutions of the United States through Foreign Immigration* (New York: Arno Press, 1835) pp. 15–16.

7. It is a fact, that this Society is under the patronage of the Emperor of Austria, —has its central direction at Vienna, —is under the supervision of Prince Metternich, —that it is an extensive combination, embodying the civil, as well as ecclesiastical *officers,* not only of the *whole Austrian Empire,* but of the neighbouring Despotic States, —that it is actively at work, collecting moneys, and sending agents to this country, to carry into effect its designs.

8. It is a fact, that the agents of these foreign despots, are, for the most part, *Jesuits.*

9. It is a fact, that the effects of this society are already apparent in the otherwise unaccountable increase of Roman Catholic cathedrals, churches, colleges, convents, nunneries, [etc.], in every part of the country; in the sudden increase of Catholic emigration; in the increased clanishness of the Roman Catholics, and the boldness with which their leaders are experimenting on the character of the American people.

10. It is a fact, that an unaccountable disposition to riotous conduct has manifested itself within a few years, when exciting topics are publicly discussed, wholly at variance with the former peaceful, deliberative character of our people.

11. It is a fact, that a species of police, unknown to our laws, has repeatedly been put in requisition to keep the peace among a certain class of foreigners, who are Roman Catholics, viz., Priest-police.

12. It is a fact, that Roman Catholic Priests have interfered to influence our elections.

13. It is a fact, that politicians on both sides have propitiated these priests, to obtain the votes of their people.

14. It is a fact, that numerous Societies of Roman Catholics, particularly among the Irish foreigners, are organized in various parts of the country, under various names, and ostensibly for certain benevolent objects; that these societies are united together by correspondence, all which may be innocent and praiseworthy, but, viewed in connexion with the recent aspect of affairs, are at least suspicious.

15. It is a fact, that an attempt has been made to organize a military corps of Irishmen in New-York, to be called the O'Connel Guards; thus commencing a military organization of foreigners.

16. It is a fact, that the greater part of the foreigners in our population is composed of Roman Catholics.

Facts like these I have enumerated might be multiplied, but these are the most important, and quite sufficient to make every American settle the question with himself, whether there is, or is not, danger to the country from the present state of our Naturalization Laws. I have stated what I believe to be facts. If they are *not* facts, they will easily be disproved, and I most sincerely hope they will be disproved. If they are facts, and my inferences from them are wrong, I can be shown where I have erred, and an inference more rational, and more probable, involving less, or perhaps no, danger to the country, can be deduced from them, which deduction, when I see it, I will most cheerfully accept, as a full explanation of these most suspicious doings of Foreign Powers.

I have spoken in these numbers freely of a particular religious sect, the Roman Catholics, because from the nature of the case it was unavoidable; because the foreign political conspiracy is identified with that creed. With the *religious tenets* properly so called, of the Roman Catholic, I have not meddled. If foreign powers, hostile to the principles of this government, have combined to spread any religious creed, no matter of what denomination, that creed does by that very act become a subject of political interest to all citizens, and must and will be thoroughly scrutinized. We are compelled to examine it. We have no choice about it. If instead of combining to spread with the greatest activity the Catholic Religion throughout our country, the Monarchs of Europe had united to spread Presbyterianism, or Methodism, I presume, there are few who would not see at once the propriety and the necessity of looking most narrowly at the political bearings of the peculiar principles of these Sects, or of any other Protestant Sects: and members of any Protestant Sects too, would be the last to complain of the examination. I know not why the Roman Catholics in this land of scrutiny are to plead exclusive exemption from the same trial.

3.16

Anti-Catholicism: *Awful Disclosures* (1836)

MARIA MONK

She gave me another piece of information which excited other feelings in me, scarcely less dreadful. Infants were sometimes born in the convent: but they were always baptized and immediately strangled! This secured their everlasting happiness; for the baptism purified them from all sinfulness, and being sent out of the world before they had time to do any thing wrong, they were at once admitted into heaven. How happy, she exclaimed, are those

Source: *Awful Disclosures of Maria Monk* (New York: Howe & Bates, 1836) pp. 58–59, 124–125.

who secure immortal happiness to such little beings! Their little souls would thank those who kill their bodies, if they had it in their power!

Into what a place and among what society had I been admitted! How differently did a Convent now appear from what I had supposed it to be! The holy women I had always fancied the nuns to be, the venerable Lady Superior, what were they? And the priests of the Seminary adjoining, some of whom indeed I had had reason to think were base and profligate men, what were they all? I now learnt they were often admitted into the nunnery, and allowed to indulge in the greatest crimes, which they and others called virtues?

After having listened for some time to the Superior alone, a number of the nuns were admitted, and took a free part in the conversation. They concurred in every thing which she had told me, and repeated, without any signs of shame or compunction, things which criminated themselves. I must acknowledge the truth, and declare that all this had an effect upon my mind. I questioned whether I might not be in the wrong, and felt as if their reasoning might have some just foundation. I had been several years under the tuition of Catholics, and was ignorant of the Scriptures, and unaccustomed to the society, example, and conversation of Protestants; had not heard any appeal to the Bible as authority, but had been taught, both by precept and example, to receive as truth every thing said by the priests. I had not heard their authority questioned, nor any thing said of any other standard of faith but their declarations. I had long been familiar with the corrupt and licentious expressions which some of them use at confessions, and believed that other women were also. I had no standard of duty to refer to, and no judgment of my own which I knew how to use, or thought of using.

All around me insisted that my doubts proved only my own ignorance and sinfulness; that they knew by experience they would soon give place to true knowledge, and an advance in religion; and I felt something like indecision.

* * *

A number of nuns usually confessed on the same day, but only one could be admitted into the room at a time. They took their places just without the door, on their knees, and went through the preparation prescribed by the rules of confession; repeating certain prayers, which always occupy a considerable time. When one was ready, she rose from her knees, entered, and closed the door behind her; and no other one even dare touch the latch until she came out.

I shall not tell what was transacted at such times, under the pretence of confessing, and receiving absolution from sin: far more guilt was often incurred than pardoned; and crimes of a deep die were committed, while trifling irregularities, in childish ceremonies, were treated as serious offences. I cannot persuade myself to speak plainly on such a subject, as I must offend the virtuous ear. I can only say, that suspicion cannot do any injustice to the priests, because their sins cannot be exaggerated.

3.17

An Example of Protestant Intolerance (1840)

Whereas, the principles of the court of Rome are totally irreconcilable with the gospel of Christ; liberty of conscience; the rights of man; and with the constitution and laws of the United States of America.—And whereas, the influence of Romanism is rapidly extending throughout this Republic, endangering the peace and freedom of our country—Therefore, being anxious to preserve the ascendancy of "pure religion and undefiled," and to maintain and perpetuate the genuine truths of Protestantism unadulterated; with devout confidence in the sanction of the Great Head of the Church to aid our efforts in withstanding the "power and great authority of the Beast, and the strong delusion of the False Prophet," we do hereby agree to be governed by the following Constitution:

I. This Society shall be called "The American Society, to promote the principles of the Protestant Reformation."

II. To act as a Home Missionary society—to diffuse correct information concerning the distinctions between Protestantism and Popery—to arouse Protestants to a proper sense of their duty in reference to the Romanists—and to use all evangelical methods to convert the Papists to Christianity by Lectures, and the dissemination of suitable Tracts and standard books upon the Romish controversy.

III. Any person who subscribes to the principles of this Constitution, and who contributes in any way to the funds of this Society, may be a member, and shall be entitled to a vote at all public meetings.

IV. The officers of this Society shall be a President, Vice-Presidents, a Treasurer, a Foreign Secretary, a Corresponding, and a Recording Secretary,—all to be elected by members of this Society.

V. This Society shall annually elect an Executive Committee of twenty gentlemen residing in New York city, and its vicinity, five of whom shall be a quorum, to do business, provided the President, or some one of the officers be one of them present. They shall enact their own bye [sic] laws, fill vacancies in their body, employ agents, and fix their compensation, appropriate the funds, call special meetings of the Society, and zealously endeavor to accomplish the object of the institution.

Source: Ray Billington, *The Protestant Crusade 1800–1860*. (New York: MacMillan & Co, 1938) pp. 437–438.

VI.   Any Society or Association founded on the same principles, may become auxiliary to this Society; and the officers of each auxiliary Association shall, ex-officio, be entitled to deliberate at all meetings of the
Society, for the transaction of its affairs.

VII.   This constitution may be amended by a vote of two-thirds of all the
members present at any annual meeting of the Society, which shall be
held on the second Tuesday of May, and should it be prevented from
taking place at that time, all the officers elected at the former annual
meeting shall hold over until such meeting shall be duly called and held.

VIII.   Any person contributing the sum of twenty dollars, or more, to the
funds of the Society, shall be constituted a life member; and those who
have made donations, or otherwise rendered eminent service in the
cause, shall be entitled to honorary membership.

3.18

Unitarian Christianity (1819)

WILLIAM ELLERY CHANNING

1. In the first place, we believe in the doctrine of God's UNITY, or that
there is one God, and one only. To this truth we give infinite importance, and we feel ourselves bound to take heed, lest any man spoil us of
it by vain philosophy. The proposition, that there is one God, seems to us
exceedingly plain. We understand by it, that there is one being, one
mind, one person, one intelligent agent, and one only, to whom unde-
rived and infinite perfection and dominion belong. . . .

We object to the doctrine of the Trinity, that, whilst acknowledging
in words, it subverts in effect, the unity of God. According to this doctrine, there are three infinite and equal persons, possessing supreme divinity, called the Father, Son, and Holy Ghost. Each of these persons, as
described by theologians, has his own particular consciousness, will, and
perceptions. They love each other, converse with each other, and delight
in each other's society. They perform different parts in man's redemption,

Source: William Ellery Channing, "Unitarian Christianity" (Baltimore, 1819).

each having his appropriate office, and neither doing the work of the other. The Son is mediator and not the Father. The Father sends the Son, and is not himself sent; nor is he conscious, like the Son, of taking flesh. Here, then, we have three intelligent agents, possessed of different consciousnesses, different wills, and different perceptions, performing different acts, and sustaining different relations; and if these things do not imply and constitute three minds or beings, we are utterly at a loss to know how three minds or beings are to be formed. . . . When we attempt to conceive of three Gods, we can do nothing more than represent to ourselves three agents, distinguished from each other by similar marks and peculiarities to those which separate the persons of the Trinity; and when common Christians hear these persons spoken of as conversing with each other, loving each other, and performing different acts, how can they help regarding them as different beings, different minds?

   We do, then, with all earnestness, though without reproaching our brethren, protest against the irrational and unscriptural doctrine of the Trinity. "To us," as to the Apostle and the primitive Christians, "there is one God, even the Father." With Jesus, we worship the Father, as the only living and true God. We are astonished, that any man can read the New Testament, and avoid the conviction, that the Father alone is God. We hear our Saviour continually appropriating this character to the Father. We find the Father continually distinguished from Jesus by this title. "God sent his Son." "God anointed Jesus." Now, how singular and inexplicable is this phraseology, which fills the New Testament, if this title belong equally to Jesus, and if a principal object of this book is to reveal him as God, as partaking equally with the Father in supreme divinity! We challenge our opponents to adduce one passage in the New Testament, where the word God means three persons, where it is not limited to one person, and where, unless turned from its usual sense by the connexion, it does not mean the Father. . . .

2. Having thus given our views of the unity of God, I proceed in the second place to observe, that we believe in the unity of Jesus Christ. We believe that Jesus is one mind, one soul, one being, as truly one as we are, and equally distinct from the one God. We complain of the doctrine of the Trinity, that, not satisfied with making God three beings, it makes Jesus Christ two beings, and this introduces infinite confusion into our conceptions of his character. This corruption of Christianity, alike repugnant to common sense and to the general strain of Scripture, is a remarkable proof of the power of a false philosophy in disfiguring the simple truth of Jesus.

   According to this doctrine, Jesus Christ, instead of being one mind, one conscious intelligent principle, whom we can understand, consists of two souls, two minds; the one divine, the other human; the one weak, the other almighty; the one ignorant, the other omniscient. Now we maintain, that this is to make Christ two beings. To denominate him one person, one being, and yet to suppose him made up of two minds, infinitely different from each other, is to abuse and confound language, and to throw darkness over all our conceptions of intelligent natures. According to the common doctrine, each of these two minds in Christ has its own consciousness, its own will, its own perceptions. They have, in fact, no common properties. The divine mind feels none of the wants and sorrows of the human, and the human is infinitely removed from the perfection and happiness of the divine. Can you conceive of two beings in the universe more distinct? We have always thought that one person was constituted and distinguished by one consciousness. The doctrine, that one and the same person should have two consciousnesses, two wills, two souls, infinitely different from each other, this we think an enormous tax on human credulity.

We say, that if a doctrine, so strange, so difficult, so remote from all previous conceptions of men, be indeed a part and an essential part of revelation, it must be taught with great distinctness, and we ask our brethren to point to some plain, direct passage, where Christ is said to be composed of two minds infinitely different, yet constituting one person. We find none. . . .

★ ★ ★

I have thus given the distinguishing views of those Christians in whose names I have spoken. We have embraced this system, not hastily or lightly, but after much deliberation; and we hold it fast, not merely because we believe it to be true, but because we regard it as purifying truth, as a doctrine according to godliness, as able to "work mightily" and to "bring forth fruit" in them who believe. That we wish to spread it, we have no desire to conceal; but we think, that we wish its diffusion, because we regard it as more friendly to practical piety and pure morals than the opposite doctrines, because it gives clearer and nobler views of duty, and stronger motives to its performance, because it recommends religion at once to the understanding and the heart, because it asserts the lovely and venerable attributes of God, because it tends to restore the benevolent spirit of Jesus to his divided and afflicted church, and because it cuts off every hope of God's favor, except that which springs from practical conformity to the life and precepts of Christ. We see nothing in our views to give offence, save their purity, and it is their purity, which makes us seek and hope their extension through the world.

3.19

We Never Argue about
Religion (1820)

RED JACKET

Friend and Brother! It was the will of the Great Spirit that we should meet together this day. He orders all things, and he has given us a fine day for our council. He has taken his garment from before the sun, and caused it to shine with brightness upon us. Our eyes are opened that we see clearly. Our ears are unstopped that we have been able to hear distinctly the words you have spoken. For all these favors we thank the Great Spirit, and him only. . . .

Brother! Continue to listen. You say that you are sent to instruct us how to worship the Great Spirit agreeably to his mind; and if we do not take hold of the religion which you white people teach, we shall be unhappy hereafter. You say that you are right and we are lost. How do we know this to be true? We understand that your religion is written in a book. If it was intended for us as well as for you, why has not the Great Spirit given it to us; and not only to us, but why did he not give to our forefathers the knowledge of that book, with the means of understanding it rightly? We only know what you tell us about it. How shall we know when to believe, being so often deceived by the white people?

Brother! You say there is but one way to worship and serve the Great Spirit. If there is but one religion, why do you white people differ so much about it? Why do not all agree, as you can all read the book?

Brother! We do not understand these things. We are told that your religion was given to your forefathers, and has been handed down from father to son. We also have a religion which was given to our forefathers, and has been handed down to us their children. We worship that way. It teacheth us to be thankful for all the favors we receive, to love each other, and to be united. We never quarrel about religion.

Source: Peter Nabokov, *Native American Testimony* (New York: Viking, 1991) p. 58.

CHAPTER 4

✳

A New Nation

Religious Growing Pains
and Pleasures

With independence acknowleged by the world community in 1783, and with a stronger Constitution adopted in 1788, the United States was indeed a new nation on the world scene. Religion, which played such a large part in colonial life, then took on a new role in shaping not just a people but an entire nation. As the nation grew and developed, so did its religious personality; and the process brought both growing pains and pleasures.

The American religious personality developed along lines established in colonial times. It was pluralistic, sometimes contradictory, often confused, yet somehow all of the scattered, contentious parts were able to make contributions to the ongoing history of the country. Later observers noted that during its formative years, the American Republic was developing a "civil or political religion" alongside the various denominations.

THE SECOND "AWAKENING"

Within a quarter century after the new nation was born, religion in America was back to conditions it had known a century earlier when the first Great Awakening rekindled spiritual and ecclesiastical fires. Taking advantage of the freedom to worship freely (which often meant the freedom not to worship at all), and moving westward faster than organized religion could follow, Americans were by the early nineteenth century perhaps less statistically religious than they had been in the late eighteenth century. Once again came a revival.

"A Spiritual Letter," written by Methodist leader Francis Asbury at the end of the eighteenth century, reflects the first stirrings of the second awakening. Congregationalist Lyman Beecher's sermon, **"Temperance,"** demonstrates the way the revival stimulated religious people to work for moral reform, in this particular case to curtail the excessive use of alcohol. Presbyterian-turned-Congregationalist preacher Charles G. Finney's sermon **"What a Revival of Religion Is"** analyzed the revival and its implications for American spirituality and social development. Yet even some who participated in the revival had doubts about the efficacy of some of its characteristic outbursts of emotion. In his retrospective *Autobiography,* Methodist evangelist Peter Cartwright expressed skepticism about phenomona such as "the jerks" and other emotional excesses.

4.1

A Spiritual Letter (1790)

FRANCIS ASBURY

Most dear and tender friends:

Whose I am, and whom under God I desire to serve; to build you up in holiness and comfort hath been through grace my great ambition. This is that which I laboured for; this is that which I suffer for: and in short, the end of all my applications to you, and to God for you. How do your souls prosper? Are they in a thriving case? What progress do you make in sanctification? Both the house of *Saul* grow weaker and weaker, and the house of *David* stronger and stronger? Beloved, I am jealous of you with a godly jealousy, lest any of you should lose ground in these declining times: and therefore cannot but be often calling upon you to look to your standing, and to watch and hold fast, that no man take your crown. Ah! how surely shall you reap in the end, if you faint not! Take heed therefore that you lose not the things you have wrought, but as you have begun well, so go on in the strength of Christ, and give diligence to the full assurance of hope to the end.

Do you need motives? 1. *How much are you behind hand?* Oh, the fair advantages that we have lost! What time, what sabbaths, sermons, sacraments, are upon the matter lost! How much work have we yet to do! Are you sure of heaven yet? Are you fit to die yet? Surely they that are under so many great wants, had need to set upon some more thriving courses.

Secondly, *Consider what others have gained, whilst we, it may be, sit down by the loss:* Have we not met many vessels richly laden, while our souls are empty? Oh, the golden prizes that some have won! While we have folded the hands to sleep, have not many of our own standing in religion, left us far behind them?

Thirdly, *Consider you will all find little enough when you come to die:* The wife among the virgins has no oil to spare at the coming of the bridegroom; temptation and death will put all your graces to it. How much ado have many had at last to put into this harbour! *David* cried for respite till he had recovered a little more strength.

Fourthly, *Consider how short your time for gathering in probably is?* The Israelites gathered twice so much manna against the sabbath as they did at other times, because at that time there was no manna fell. Brethren, you know not how long you have to lay in for. Do you ask for marks, how you may know your souls to be in a thriving case?

First, If your appetites be more strong. Do you thirst after God and grace, more than heretofore? Do your cares for and desires after the world abate? And do you hunger and thirst after righteousness? Whereas you were wont to come with an ill-will to holy duties, do you now come to them as hungry stomach to its meat?

Secondly, If your pulses beat more even. Are you still off and on, hot and cold? Or is there a more even spun thread of holiness through your whole course? Do you make good the ground from which you were formerly beaten off?

Thirdly, If you do look more to the carrying on together the duties of both tables. Do you not only look to the keeping of your own vineyards, but do you lay out yourselves for the good of others? and are ye filled with zealous desires for their conversion and salvation? Do you manage your talk and your trade, by the rules of religion?

Do you eat and sleep by rule? Doth religion form and mould, and direct your carriage towards husbands, wives, parents, children, masters, servants? Do you grow more universally conscientious? Is piety more diffusive than ever with you? Doth it come more abroad with you, out of your closets, into your houses, your shops, your fields? Doth it journey with you, and buy and sell for you? Hath it the casting voice in all you do?

Fourthly, If the duties of religion be more delightful to you. Do you take more delight in the word than ever? Are you more in love with secret prayer, and more abundant in it? Cannot you be content with your ordinary seasons, but are ever and anon making extraordinary visits to heaven? And upon all occasions turning aside to talk with God in some short ejaculations? Are you often darting up your soul heavenwards? Is it meat and drink for you to do the will of God? Do you come off more freely with God, and answer his calls with more readiness of mind?

Fifthly, If you are more abundant in those duties which are most displeasing to the flesh. Are you more earnest in mortification? Are you more strict and severe than ever in the duty of daily self-examination, and holy meditation? Do you hold the reins harder upon the flesh than ever? Do you keep a stricter watch upon your appetites? Do you set a stronger guard upon your tongues? Have you a more jealous eye upon your hearts?

Sixthly, If you grow more vile in your own eyes. Do you grow more out of love with men's esteem, and set less by it? Are you not marvellous tender of being slighted? Can you rejoice to see others preferred before you? Can you heartily value and love them that think meanly of you?

Seventhly, If you grow more quick of sense, more sensible of divine influences, or withdrawing. Are you more afraid of sin than ever? Are your sins a greater pain to you than heretofore? Are your very infirmities your great afflictions? and the daily working of corruption a continued grief of mind to you?

I must conclude abruptly, commending you to God, and can only tell you that I am

Yours in the Lord Jesus,
F.A.

4.2

Temperance (1828)

LYMAN BEECHER

B ut of all the ways to hell, which the feet of deluded mortals tread, that of the intemperate is the most dreary and terrific. The demand for artificial stimulus to supply the deficiencies of healthful aliment, is like the rage of thirst, and the ravenous demand of famine. It is famine: for the artificial excitement has become as essential now to strength and cheerfulness, as simple nutrition once was. But nature, taught by habit to require what once she did

Source: http://occawlonline.pearsoned.com/bookbind/pubbooks/garratype_chapter10/
medialib/primarysources/_//_/.html

not need, demands gratification now with a decision inexorable as death, and to most men as irresistible. The denial is a living death. The stomach, the head, the heart, and arteries, and veins, and every muscle, and every nerve, feel the exhaustion, and the restless, unutterable wretchedness which puts out the light of life, and curtains the heavens, and carpets the earth with sackcloth. All these varieties of sinking nature, call upon the wretched man with trumpet tongue, to dispel this darkness, and raise the ebbing tide of life, by the application of the cause which produced these woes, and after a momentary alleviation will produce them again with deeper terrors, and more urgent importunity; for the repetition, at each time renders the darkness deeper, and the torments of self-denial more irresistible and intolerable.

At length, the excitability of nature flags, and stimulants of higher power, and in greater quantities, are required to rouse the impaired energies of life, until at length the whole process of dilatory murder, and worse than purgatorial suffering, having been passed over, the silver cord is loosed, the golden bowl is broken, the wheel at the cistern stops, and the dust returns to the earth as it was, and the spirit to God who gave it.

These sufferings, however, of animal nature, are not to be compared with the moral agonies which convulse the soul. It is an immortal being who sins, and suffers; and as his earthly house dissolves, he is approaching the judgment seat, in anticipation of a miserable eternity. He feels his captivity, and in anguish of spirit clanks his chains and cries for help. Conscience thunders, remorse goads, and as the gulf opens before him, he recoils, and trembles, and weeps, and prays, and resolves, and promises, and reforms, and "seeks it yet again,"—again resolves, and weeps, and prays, and "seeks it yet again!" Wretched man, he has placed himself in the hands of a giant, who never pities, and never relaxes his iron gripe. He may struggle, but he is in chains. He may cry for release, but it comes not; and lost! lost! may be inscribed upon the door posts of his dwelling.

In the mean time these paroxsyms of his dying moral nature decline, and a fearful apathy, the harbinger of spiritual death, comes on. His resolution fails, and his mental energy, and his vigorous enterprise; and nervous irritation and depression ensue. The social affections lose their fulness and tenderness, and conscience loses its power, and the heart its sensibility, until all that was once lovely and of good report, retires and leaves the wretch abandoned to the appetites of a ruined animal. In this deplorable condition, reputation expires, business falters and becomes perplexed, and temptations to drink multiply as inclination to do so increases, and the power of resistance declines. And now the vortex roars, and the struggling victim buffets the fiery wave with feebler stroke, and warning supplication, until despair flashes upon his soul, and with an outcry that pierces the heavens, he ceases to strive, and disappears. . . .

Upon national industry the effects of intemperance are manifest and mischievous.

The results of national industry depend on the amount of well-directed intellectual and physical power. But intemperance paralyses and prevents both these springs of human action.

In the inventory of national loss by intemperance, may be set down—the labor prevented by indolence, by debility, by sickness, by quarrels and litigation, by gambling and idleness, by mistakes and misdirected effort, by improvidence and wastefulness, and by the shortened date of human life and activity. Little wastes in great establishments, constantly occurring may defeat the energies of a mighty capital. But where the intellectual and muscular energies are raised to the working point daily by ardent spirits, until the agriculture, and commerce, and arts of a nation move on by the power of artificial stimulus, that moral power cannot be maintained, which will guaranty fidelity, and that physical power cannot be preserved and well directed, which will ensure national prosperity. The nation whose immense enterprise is thrust forward by the stimulus of ardent spirits, cannot ultimately escape debility and bankruptcy. . . .

The prospect of a destitute old age, or of a suffering family, no longer troubles the vicious portion of our community. They drink up their daily earnings, and bless God for the poor-house, and begin to look upon it as, of right, the drunkard's home, and contrive to arrive thither as early as idleness and excess will give them a passport to this sinecure of vice. Thus is the insatiable destroyer of industry marching through the land, rearing poor-houses, and augmenting taxation: night and day, with sleepless activity, squandering property, cutting the sinews of industry, undermining vigor, engendering disease, paralysing intellect, impairing moral principle, cutting short the date of life, and rolling up a national debt, invisible, but real and terrific as the debt of England: continually transferring larger and larger bodies of men, from the class of contributors to the national income, to the class of worthless consumers. . . .

The effects of intemperance upon civil liberty may not be lightly passed over.

It is admitted that intelligence and virtue are the pillars of republican institutions, and that the illumination of schools, and the moral power of religious institutions, are indispensable to produce this intelligence and virtue.

But who are found so uniformly in the ranks of irreligion as the intemperate? Who like these violate the Sabbath, and set their mouth against the heavens—neglecting the education of their families—and corrupting their morals? Almost the entire amount of national ignorance and crime is the offspring of intemperance. Throughout the land, the intemperate are hewing down the pillars, and undermining the foundations of our national edifice. Legions have besieged it, and upon every gate the battle-axe rings; and still the sentinels sleep.

Should the evil advance as it has done, the day is not far distant when the great body of the laboring classes of the community, the bones and sinews of the nation, will be contaminated; and when this is accomplished, the right of suffrage becomes the engine of self-destruction. For the laboring classes constitute an immense majority, and when these are perverted by intemperance, ambition needs no better implements with which to dig the grave of our liberties, and entomb our glory.

Such is the influence of interest, ambition, fear, and indolence, that one violent partisan, with a handful of disciplined troops, may overrule the influence of five hundred temperate men, who act without concert. Already is the disposition to temporize, to tolerate, and even to court the intemperate, too apparent, on account of the apprehended retribution of their perverted suffrage. The whole power of law, through the nation, sleeps in the statute book, and until public sentiment is roused and concentrated, it may be doubted whether its execution is possible.

Where is the city, town, or village, in which the laws are not openly violated, and where is the magistracy that dares to carry into effect the laws against the vending or drinking of ardent spirits? Here then an aristocracy of bad influence has already risen up, which bids defiance to law, and threatens the extirpation of civil liberty. As intemperance increases, the power of taxation will come more and more into the hands of men of intemperate habits and desperate fortunes; of course the laws gradually will become subservient to the debtor, and less efficacious in protecting the rights of property. This will be a vital stab to liberty—to the security of which property is indispensable. For money is the sinew of war—and when those who hold the property of a nation cannot be protected in their rights, they will change the form of government, peaceably if they may, by violence if they must.

4.3

What a Revival of Religion Is (1835)

CHARLES G. FINNEY

eligion is the work of man. It is something for man to do. It consists in obeying God. It is man's duty. It is true, God induces him to do it. He influences him by his Spirit, because of his great wickedness and reluctance to obey. If it were not necessary for God to influence men—if men were disposed to obey God, there would be no occasion to pray, "O Lord, revive thy work." The ground of necessity for such a prayer is, that men are wholly indisposed to obey; and unless God interpose the influence of his Spirit, not a man on earth will ever obey the commands of God.

Source: Charles G. Finney, "What a Revival of Religion Is" (New York, 1835).

A "Revival of Religion" presupposes a declension. Almost all the religion in the world has been produced by revivals. God has found it necessary to take advantage of the excitability there is in mankind, to produce powerful excitements among them, before he can lead them to obey. Men are so sluggish, there are so many things to lead their minds off from religion, and to oppose the influence of the gospel, that it is necessary to raise an excitement among them, till the tide rises so high as to sweep away the opposing obstacles. They must be so excited that they will break over these counteracting influences, before they will obey God.

There is so little *principle* in the church, so little firmness and stability of purpose, that unless they are greatly excited, they will not obey God. They have so little knowledge, and their principles are so weak, that unless they are excited, they will go back from the path of duty, and do nothing to promote the glory of God. The state of the world is still such, and probably will be till the millennium is fully come, that religion must be mainly promoted by these excitements. How long and how often has the experiment been tried, to bring the church to act steadily for God, without these periodical excitements! Many good men have supposed, and still suppose, that the best way to promote religion, is to go along *uniformly*, and gather in the ungodly gradually, and without excitement. But however such reasoning may appear in the abstract, *facts* demonstrate its futility. If the church were far enough advanced in knowledge, and had stability of principle enough to *keep awake,* such a course would do; but the church is so little enlightened, and there are so many counteracting causes, that the church will not go steadily to work without a special excitement.

It is altogether improbable that religion will ever make progress among *heathen* nations except through the influence of revivals. The attempt is now making to do it by education, and other cautious and gradual improvements. But so long as the laws of mind remain what they are, it cannot be done in this way. There must be excitement sufficient to wake up the dormant moral powers, and roll back the tide of degradation and sin. And precisely so far as our own land approximates to heathenism, it is impossible for God or man to promote religion in such a state of things but by powerful excitements. This is evident from the fact that this has always been the way in which God has done it God does not create these excitements, and choose this method to promote religion for nothing, or without reason. Where mankind are so reluctant to obey God, they will not act until they are excited. For instance, how many there are who know that they ought to be religious, but they are afraid if they become pious they shall be laughed at by their companions. Many are wedded to idols, others are procastinating repentance, until they are settled in life, or until they have secured some favorite worldly interest. Such persons never will give up their false shame, or relinquish then ambitious schemes, till they are so excited that they cannot contain themselves any longer.

These remarks are designed only as an introduction to the discourse. I shall now proceed with the main design, to show,

    I. What a revival of religion is not;

    II. What it is; and

    III. The agencies employed in promoting it.

I. A REVIVAL OF RELIGION IS NOT A MIRACLE

1. A miracle has been generally defined to be, a Divine interference, setting aside or suspending the laws of nature. It is not a miracle, in this sense. All the laws of matter and mind remain in force. They are neither suspended nor set aside in a revival.

2. It is not a miracle according to another definition of the term miracle—*something above the powers of nature.* There is nothing in religion beyond the ordinary powers of nature. It consists entirely in the *right exercise* of the powers of nature. It is just that, and nothing else. When mankind becomes religious, they are not *enabled* to put forth exertions which they were unable before to put forth. They only exert the powers they had before in a different way, and use them for the glory of God.

3. It is not a miracle, or dependent on a miracle, in any sense. It is a purely philosophical result of the right use of the constituted means—as much as any other effect produced by the application of means. There may be a miracle among its antecedent causes, or there may not. The apostles employed miracles, simply as a means by which they arrested attention to their message, and established its Divine authority. But the miracle was not the revival. The miracle was one thing; the revival that followed it was quite another thing. The revivals in the apostles' days were connected with miracles, but they were not miracles.

I said that a revival is the result of the *right* use of the appropriate means. The means which God has enjoyed for the production of a revival, doubtless have a natural tendency to produce a revival. Otherwise God would not have enjoined them. But means will not produce a revival, we all know, without the blessing of God. No more will grain, when it is sowed, produce a crop without the blessing of God. It is impossible for us to say that there is not as direct an influence or agency from God, to produce a crop of grain, as there is to produce a revival. What are the laws of nature, according to which, it is supposed, that grain yields a crop? They are nothing but the constituted manner of the operations of God. In the Bible, the word of God is compared to grain, and preaching is compared to sowing seed, and the results to the springing up and growth of the crop. And the result is just as philosophical in the one case, as in the other, and is as naturally connected with the cause.

II. I AM TO SHOW WHAT A REVIVAL IS

It presupposes that the church is sunk down in a backslidden state, and a revival consists in the return of the church from her backslidings, and in the conversion of sinners.

1. A revival always includes conviction of sin on the part of the church. Backslidden professors cannot wake up and begin right away in the service of

God, without deep searchings of heart. The fountains of sin need to be broken up. In a true revival, Christians are always brought under such convictions; they see their sins in such a light, that often they find it impossible to maintain a hope of their acceptance with God. It does not always go to that extent; but there are always, in a genuine revival, deep convictions of sin, and often cases of abandoning all hope.

2. Backslidden Christians will be brought to repentance. A revival is nothing else than a new beginning of obedience to God. Just as in the case of a converted sinner, the first step is a deep repentance, a breaking down of heart, a getting down into the dust before God, with deep humility, and forsaking of sin.

3. Christians will have their faith renewed. While they are in their backslidden state they are blind to the state of sinners. Their hearts are as hard as marble. The truths of the Bible only appear like a dream. They admit it to be all true; their conscience and their judgment assent to it; but their faith does not see it standing out in bold relief; in all the burning realities of eternity. But when they enter into a revival, they no longer will renew the love of God in their hearts. . . .

4. A revival breaks the power of the world and of sin over Christians. It brings them to such vantage ground that they get a fresh impulse towards heaven. They have a new foretaste of heaven, and new desires after union to God; and the charm of the world is broken, and the power of sin overcome.

5. When the churches are thus awakened and reformed, the reformation and salvation of sinners will follow, going through the same stages of conviction, repentance, and reformation. Their hearts will be broken down and changed. Very often the most abandoned profligates are among the subjects. Harlots, and drunkards, and infidels, and all sorts of abandoned characters, are awakened and converted. The worst part of human society are softened, and reclaimed, and made to appear as lovely specimens of the beauty of holiness.

III. I AM TO CONSIDER THE AGENCIES EMPLOYED IN CARRYING FORWARD A REVIVAL OF RELIGION

Ordinarily, there are three agents employed in the work of conversion, and one instrument. The agents are God—some person who brings the truth to bear on the mind,—and the sinner himself. The instrument is the truth. There are *always two* agents, God and the sinner, employed and active in every case of genuine conversion.

1. The agency of God is two-fold; by his Providence and by his Spirit.

(a.) By his providential government, he so arranges events as to bring the sinner's mind and the truth in contact. He brings the sinner where the truth reaches his ears or his eyes. It is often interesting to trace the manner in which God arranges events so as to bring this about, and how he sometimes makes everything seem to favor a revival. The state of the weather, and of the public health, and other circumstances concur to make every thing just right to favor the application of truth with the greatest possible efficacy. How he sometimes sends a minister along, just at the time he is wanted! How he brings out a particular truth, just at the particular time when the individual it is fitted to reach is in the way to hear!

(b.) God's special agency by his Holy Spirit. Having direct access to the mind, and knowing infinitely well the whole history and state of each individual sinner, he employs that truth which is best adapted to his particular case, and then sets it home with Divine power. He gives it such vividness, strength, and power, that the sinner quails and throws down his weapons of rebellion, and turns to the Lord. Under his influence, the truth burns and cuts its way like fire. He makes the truth stand out in such aspects, that it crushes the proudest man down with the weight of a mountain. . . .

2. The agency of men is commonly employed. Men are not mere *instruments* in the hands of God. Truth is the instrument. The preacher is a moral agent in the work; he acts; he is not a mere passive instrument; he is voluntary in promoting the conversion of sinners.

3. The agency of the sinner himself. The conversion of a sinner consists in his obeying the truth. It is therefore impossible it should take place without his agency, for it consists in *his* acting right. He is influenced to this by the agency of God, and by the agency of men. Men act on their fellow-men, not only by language, but by their looks, their tears, their daily deportment. See that impenitent man there, who has a pious wife. Her very looks, her tenderness, her solemn, compassionate dignity, softened and moulded into the image of Christ, are a sermon to him all the time. He has to turn his mind away, because it is such a reproach to him. He feels a sermon ringing in his ears all day long.

If Christians have deep feeling on the subject of religion themselves, they will produce deep feeling wherever they go. And if they are cold, or light and trifling, they inevitably destroy all deep feeling, even in awakened sinners.

The church is required to use the means for the conversion of sinners. Sinners cannot properly be said to use the means for their own conversion. The church uses the means. What sinners do is to submit to the truth, or to resist it. It is a mistake of sinners, to think they are using means for their own conversion. The whole drift of a revival, and every thing about it, is designed to present the truth *to* your mind, for your obedience or resistance.

4.4

Autobiography (1856)

PETER CARTWRIGHT

Just in the midst of our controversies on the subject of the powerful exercises among the people under preaching, a new exercise broke out among us, called the *jerks*, which was overwhelming in its effects upon the bodies and minds of the people. No matter whether they were saints or sinners, they would be taken under a warm song or sermon, and seized with a convulsive jerking all over, which they could not by any possibility avoid, and the more they resisted the more they jerked. If they would not strive against it and pray in good earnest, the jerking would usually abate. I have seen more than five hundred persons jerking at one time in my large congregations. Most usually persons taken with the jerks, to obtain relief, as they said, would rise up and dance. Some would run, but could not get away. Some would resist; on such the jerks were generally very severe.

To see those proud young gentlemen and young ladies, dressed in their silks, jewelry, and prunella, from top to toe, take the *jerks*, would often excite my risibilities. The first jerk or so, you would see their fine bonnets, caps, and combs fly; and so sudden would be the jerking of the head that their long loose hair would crack almost as loud as a wagoner's whip.

I always looked upon the jerks as a judgment sent from God, first, to bring sinners to repentance; and, secondly, to show professors that God could work with or without means, and that he could work over and above means, and do whatsoever seemeth him good, to the glory of his grace and salvation of the world.

There is no doubt in my mind that, with weak-minded, ignorant, and superstitious persons, there was a great deal of sympathetic feeling with a man that claimed to be under the influence of this jerking exercise; and yet, with many, it was perfectly involuntary. It was, on all occasions, my practice to recommend fervent prayer as a remedy, and it almost universally proved an effectual antidote.

There were many other strange and wild exercises into which the subjects of this revival fell; such, for instance, as what was called the running, jumping, barking exercise. The Methodist preachers generally preached against this extravagant wildness. I did it uniformly in my little ministrations, and sometimes gave great offense; but I feared no consequences when I felt my awful responsibilities to God. From these wild exercises, another great evil arose from the heated and wild imaginations of some. They professed to fall into trances

Source: *Autobiography of Peter Cartwright* (written 1856), copyright: Abingdon Press, 1956.

and see visions; they would fall at meetings and sometimes at home, and lay apparently powerless and motionless for days, sometimes for a week at a time, without food or drink; and when they came to, they professed to have seen heaven and hell, to have seen God, angels, the devil and the damned; they would prophesy, and, under the pretense of Divine inspiration, predict the time of the end of the world, and the ushering of the great millennium.

This was the most troublesome delusion of all; it made such an appeal to the ignorance, superstition, and credulity of all the people, even saint as well as sinner. I watched this matter with a vigilant eye. If I opposed it, I would have to meet the clamor of the multitude; and if any one opposed it, these very visionists would single him out, and denounce the dreadful judgments of God against him. They would even set the very day that God was to burn the world, like the self-deceived modern Millerites. They would prophesy, that if any one did oppose them, God would send fire down from heaven and consume him, like the blasphemous Shakers. They would proclaim that they could heal all manner of diseases, and raise the dead, just like the diabolical Mormons. They professed to have converse with spirits of the dead in heaven and hell, like the modern spirit rappers. Such a state of things I never saw before, and I hope in God I shall never see again.

THE SECOND "ENLIGHTENMENT"

Just as had happened a century before, the second "awakening" was accompanied by a second "enlightenment." Spiritual renewal and rational inquiry seemed once again to come hand in hand. And just as in the century before, the nineteenth-century enlightenment had much to say about the nature and status of the religion of the day.

Ralph Waldo Emerson was a minister who lost his church because he disagreed with his congregation on the practice of the Lord's Supper. In an 1838 address before the Harvard Divinity School, he issued the **"Manifesto"** of his new faith, which came to be called Transcendentalism. He further described it in the most famous of his essays, **"Self Reliance,"** written in 1841.

His young friend Henry David Thoreau, although never even in his early years an orthodox Christian, was the other great Transcendentalist. Both in the account of his experiment in living with Nature, *Walden,* and in the fascinating **Journal** he faithfully kept through his abbreviated life, he made clear how he felt about the subject.

Walt Whitman's great hymn to the Natural Man, **"Song of Myself,"** from his *Leaves of Grass* collection, completed the cycle in which the Second Enlightenment both reflected and challenged America's nineteenth-century religious revival.

4.5

Manifesto (1838)

RALPH WALDO EMERSON

Truly speaking it is not instruction, but provocation, that I can receive from another soul. What he announces, I must find true in me, or reject; and on his word, or as his second, be he who he may, I can accept nothing. On the contrary, the absence of this primary faith is the presence of degradation. As is the flood, so is the ebb. Let this faith depart, and the very words it spake and the things it made become false and hurtful. Then falls the church, the state, art, letters, life. The doctrine of the divine nature being forgotten, a sickness infects and dwarfs the constitution. Once man was all; now he is an appendage, a nuisance. And because the indwelling Supreme Spirit cannot wholly be got rid of, the doctrine of it suffers this perversion, that the divine nature is attributed to one or two persons, and denied to all the rest, and denied with fury. The doctrine of inspiration is lost; the base doctrine of the majority of voices usurps the place of the doctrine of the soul. Miracles, prophecy, poetry, the ideal life, the holy life, exist as ancient history merely; they are not in the belief, nor in the aspiration of society; but, when suggested, seem ridiculous. Life is comic or pitiful as soon as the high ends of being fade out of sight, and man becomes near-sighted, and can only attend to what addresses the senses....

Jesus Christ belonged to the true race of prophets. He saw with open eye the mystery of the soul. Drawn by its severe harmony, ravished with its beauty, he lived in it, and had his being there. Alone in all history he estimated the greatness of man. One man was true to what is in you and me. He saw that God incarnates himself in man, and evermore goes forth anew to take possession of his World. He said, in this jubilee of sublime emotion, "I am divine. Through me, God acts; through me, speaks. Would you see God, see me; or see thee, when thou also thinkest as I now think." But what a distortion did his doctrine and memory suffer in the same, in the next, and the following ages! There is no doctrine of the Reason which will bear to be taught by the Understanding. The understanding caught this high chant from the poet's lips, and said, in the next age, "This was Jehovah come down out of heaven. I will kill you, if you say he was a man." The idioms of his language and the figures of his rhetoric have usurped the place of his truth; and churches are not built

Source: Ralph Waldo Emerson, "An Address to the Harvard Divinity School, July 15, 1838," *Complete Works of Ralph Waldo Emerson* (Boston, 1903) pp. 127–151.

From the Collections of the Library of Congress

Ralph Waldo Emerson,
Transcendentalist

on his principles, but on his tropes. Christianity became a Mythus, as the poetic teaching of Greece and of Egypt, before. He spoke of miracles; for he felt that man's life was a miracle, and all that man doeth, and he knew that this daily miracle shines as the character ascends. But the word Miracle, as pronounced by Christian churches, gives a false impression; it is Monster. It is not one with the blowing clover and the falling rain.

He felt respect for Moses and the prophets, but no unfit tenderness at postponing their initial revelations to the hour and the man that now is; to the eternal revelation in the heart. Thus was he a true man. Having seen that the law in us is commanding, he would not suffer it to be commanded. Boldly, with hand, and heart, and life, he declared it was God. Thus is he, as I think, the only soul in history who has appreciated the worth of man.

1. In this point of view we become sensible of the first defect of historical Christianity. Historical Christianity has fallen into the error that corrupts all attempts to communicate religion. As it appears to us, and as it has appeared for ages, it is not the doctrine of the soul, but an exaggeration of the personal, the positive, the ritual. It has dwelt, it dwells, with noxious exaggeration about the *person* of Jesus. The soul knows no persons. It invites every man to expand to the full circle of the universe, and will have no preferences but those of spontaneous love. . . .

That is always best which gives me to myself. The sublime is excited in me by the great stoical doctrine, Obey thyself. That which shows God in me, fortifies me. That which shows God out of me, makes me a wart and a wen. There is no longer a necessary reason for my being. Already the long shadows of untimely oblivion creep over me, and I shall decrease forever. . . .

2. The second defect of the traditionary and limited way of using the mind of Christ is a consequence of the first; this, namely; that the Moral Nature, that Law of laws whose revelations introduce greatness—yea, God himself—into the open soul, is not explored as the fountain of the established teaching in society. Men have come to speak of the revelation as somewhat long ago given and done, as if God were dead. The injury to faith throttles the preacher; and the goodliest of institutions becomes an uncertain and inarticulate voice. . . .

The man on whom the soul descends, through whom the soul speaks, alone can teach. Courage, piety, love, wisdom, can teach; and every man can open his door to these angels, and they shall bring him the gift of tongues. But the man who aims to speak as books enable, as synods use, as the fashion guides, and as interest commands, babbles. Let him hush.

4.6

Self-Reliance (1841)

RALPH WALDO EMERSON

Whoso would be a man must be a nonconformist. He who would gather immortal palms must not be hindered by the name of goodness, but must explore if it be goodness. Nothing is at last sacred but the integrity of your own mind. Absolve you to yourself, and you shall have the suffrage of the world. I remember an answer which when quite young I was prompted to make to a valued adviser, who was wont to importune me with the dear old doctrines of the church. On my saying, What have I to do with the sacredness of traditions, if I live wholly from within? my friend suggested,—"But these impulses may be from below, not from above." I replied, "They do not seem to me to be such; but if I am the Devil's child, I will live

Source: Ralph Waldo Emerson, "Self-Reliance" *Essays* (New York: J. W. Lovell, 1884).

then from the Devil." No law can be sacred to me but that of my nature. Good and bad are but names very readily transferable to that or this; the only right is what is after my constitution, the only wrong what is against it.

★ ★ ★

The relations of the soul to the divine spirit are so pure, that it is profane to seek to interpose helps. It must be that when God speaketh he should communicate, not one thing, but all things; should fill the world with his voice; should scatter forth light, nature, time, souls, from the centre of the present thought; and new date and new create the whole. Whenever a mind is simple, and receives a divine wisdom, old things pass away,—means, teachers, texts, temples fall; it lives now, and absorbs past and future into the present hour. All things are made sacred by relation to it,—one as much as another. All things are dissolved to their centre by their cause, and, in the universal miracle, petty and particular miracles disappear. If, therefore, a man claims to know and speak of God, and carries you backward to the phraseology of some old mouldered nation in another country, in another world, believe him not. Is the acorn better than the oak which is its fulness and completion? Is the parent better than the child into whom he has cast his ripened being? Whence, then, this worship of the past? The centuries are conspirators against the sanity and authority of the soul. Time and space are but physiological colors which the eye makes, but the soul is light; where it is, is day; where it was, is night; and history is an impertinence and an injury, if it be any thing more than a cheerful apologue or parable of my being and becoming.

4.7

Walden (1854)

HENRY DAVID THOREAU

I believe that what so saddens the reformer is not his sympathy with his fellows in distress, but, though he be the holiest son of God, is his private ail. Let this be righted, let the spring come to him, the morning rise over his couch, and he will forsake his generous companions without apology.

Source: Henry David Thoreau, *Walden* (New York: Library of America Series, 1985) pp. 384–385, 394–395.

My excuse for not lecturing against the use of tobacco is, that I never chewed it; that is a penalty which reformed tobacco-chewers have to pay; though there are things enough I have chewed, which I could lecture against. If you should ever be betrayed into any of these philanthropies, do not let your left hand know what your right hand does, for it is not worth knowing. Rescue the drowning and tie your shoe-strings. Take your time, and set about some free labor.

Our manners have been corrupted by communication with the saints. Our hymn-books resound with a melodious cursing of God and enduring him forever. One would say that even the prophets and redeemers had rather consoled the fears than confirmed the hopes of man. There is nowhere recorded a simple and irrespressible satisfaction with the gift of life, any memorable praise of God. All health and success does me good, however far off and withdrawn it may appear; all disease and failure helps to make me sad and does me evil, however much sympathy it may have with me or I with it. If, then, we would indeed restore mankind by truly Indian, botanic, magnetic, or natural means, let us first be as simple and well as Nature ourselves, dispel the clouds which hang over our own brows, and take up a little life into our pores. Do not stay to be an overseer of the poor, but endeavor to become one of the worthies of the world.

I read in the Gulistan, or Flower Garden, of Sheik Sadi of Shiraz, that "They asked a wise man, saying; Of the many celebrated trees which the Most High God has created lofty and umbrageous, they call none azad, or free, excepting the cypress, which bears no fruit; what mystery is there in this? He replied; Each has its appropriate produce, and appointed season, during the continuance of which it is fresh and blooming, and during their absence dry and withered; to neither of which states is the cypress exposed, begin always flourishing; and of this nature are the azads, or religious independents.—Fix not thy heart on that which is transitory; for the Dijlah, or Tigris, will continue to flow through Bagdad after the race of caliphs is extinct: if thy hand has plenty, be liberal as the date tree; but if it affords nothing to give away, be an azad, or free man, like the cypress."

★ ★ ★

I went to the woods because I wished to live deliberately, to front only the essential facts of life, and see if I could not learn what it had to teach, and not, when I came to die, discover that I had not lived. I did not wish to live what was not life, living is so dear; nor did I wish to practise resignation, unless it was quite necessary. I wanted to live deep and suck out all the marrow of life, to live so sturdily and Spartan-like as to put to rout all that was not life, to cut a broad swath and shave close, to drive life into a corner, and reduce it to its lowest terms, and, if it proved to be mean, why then to get the whole and genuine meanness of it, and publish its meanness to the world; or if it were sublime, to know it by experience, and be able to give a true account of it in my next excursion. For most men, it appears to me, are in a strange uncertainty about it, whether it is of the devil or of God, and have *somewhat hastily* concluded that it is the chief end of man here to "glorify God and enjoy him forever."

4.8

Journal Entries

HENRY DAVID THOREAU

1841, April 4, Sunday

That cheap piece of tinkling brass which the farmer hangs about his cow's neck has been more to me than the tons of metal which are swung in the belfry.

★ ★ ★

1842, Feb. 20

I am amused to see from my window here how busily man has divided and staked off his domain. God must smile at his puny fences running hither and thither everywhere over the land.

★ ★ ★

1842, Dec. 29

These motions everywhere in nature must surely [be] the circulations of God. The flowing sail, the running stream, the waving tree, the roving wind—whence else their infinite health and freedom? I can see nothing so proper and holy as unrelaxed play and frolic in this bower God has built for us. The suspicion of sin never comes to this thought. Oh, if men felt this they would never build temples even of marble or diamond, but it would be sacrilege and prophane, but disport them forever in this paradise.

★ ★ ★

1850, date uncertain

The Hindoos are more serenely and thoughtfully religious than the . Hebrews. They have perhaps a purer, more independent and impersonal knowledge of God. Their religious books describe the first inquisitive and contemplative access to God; the Hebrew bible a conscientious return, a grosser and more personal repentance. Repentance is not a free and fair highway to God. A wise man will dispense with repentance. It is shocking and passionate. God prefers that you approach him thoughtful, not penitent, though you are the chief of sinners. It is only by forgetting yourself that you draw near to him.

Source: Henry David Thoreau, *The Heart of Thoreau's Journals*, ed. Odell Shepherd (New York: Dover Publications 1961).

Note: Footnotes have been deleted from this reading—ED.

I do not prefer one religion or philosophy to another. I have no sympathy with the bigotry and ignorance which make transient and partial and puerile distinctions between one man's faith or form of faith and another's— as Christian and heathen. I pray to be delivered from narrowness, partiality, exaggeration, bigotry. To the philosopher all sects, all nations, are alike. I like Brahma, Hari, Buddha, the Great Spirit, as well as God.

★ ★ ★

1851, Sept. 11
My profession is to be always on the alert to find God in nature, to know his lurking-places, to attend all the oratorios, the operas, in nature.

★ ★ ★

1857, May 3, Sunday
Up and down the town, men and boys that are under subjection are pol-ishing their shoes and brushing their go-to-meeting clothes. I, a descendant of Northmen who worshipped Thor, spend my time worshipping neither Thor nor Christ; a descendant of Northmen who sacrificed men and horses, sacri-fice neither men nor horses. I care not for Thor nor for the Jews. I sympathize not today with those who go to church in newest clothes and sit quietly in straight-backed pews. I sympathize rather with the boy who has none to look after him, who borrows a boat and paddle and in common clothes sets out to explore these temporary vernal lakes. I meet such a boy paddling along under a sunny bank, with bare feet and his pants rolled up above his knees, ready to leap into the water at a moment's warning. Better for him to read *Robinson Crusoe* than Baxter's *Saints' Rest*.

★ ★ ★

1858, Aug. 18
Last evening one of our neighbors, who has just completed a costly house and front yard, the most showy in the village, illuminated in honor of the Atlantic telegraph. I read in great letters before the house the sentence "Glory to God in the highest." But it seemed to me that that was not a sentiment to be illuminated, but to keep dark about. A simple and genuine sentiment of reverence would not emblazon these words as on a signboard in the streets; They were exploding countless crackers beneath it, and gay company, passing in and out, made it a kind of housewarming. I felt a kind of shame for [it], and was inclined to pass quickly by, the ideas of indecent exposure and cant being suggested. What is religion? That which is never spoken.

★ ★ ★

1858, Nov. 30
Neither England nor America have [*sic*] any right to laugh at that sentence in the rare book called *The Blazon of Gentry,* written by a zealous student of heraldry, which says after due investigation that "Christ was a gentleman, as to the flesh, by the part of his mother, . . . and might have borne coat-armor. The

apostles also were gentlemen of blood, and many of them descended from that worthy conqueror Judas Machabeus; but, through the tract of time, and persecution of wars, poverty oppressed the kindred and they were constrayned to servile workes." Whatever texts we may quote or commentaries we may write, when we consider the laws and customs of these two countries we cannot fail to perceive that the above sentence is perfectly of a piece with our practical commentary on the New Testament. The above is really a pertinent reason offered why Christianity should be embraced in England and America. Indeed, it is, accordingly, only what may be called "respectable Christianity" that is at all generally embraced in the two countries.

4.9

Song of Myself (1867)

WALT WHITMAN

Swiftly arose and spread around me
    the peace and knowledge that pass
    all the argument of the earth,
And I know that the hand of God
    is the promise of my own,
And I know that the spirit of God
    is the brother of my own,
And that all the men ever born are
    also my brothers, and the women
    my sisters and lovers,
And that a kelson of the creation is love,
And limitless are leaves stiff or
    drooping in the fields,
And brown ants in the little wells
    beneath them,
And mossy scabs of the worm fence,
    heap'd stones, elder, mullein
    and poke-weed.

★ ★ ★

Source: Walt Whitman, "Song of Myself," *Leaves of Grass* (Philadelphia: R. Welsh & Co, 1882) found at http://www.princeton.edu/ ~batke/log.026.html

I do not despise you priests, all time,
     the world over,
My faith is the greatest of faiths
     and the least of faiths,
Enclosing worship ancient and modern
     and all between ancient and modern,
Believing I shall come again upon
     the earth after five thousand years,
Waiting responses from oracles,
     honoring the gods, saluting the sun,
Making a fetich of the first rock or stump,
     powowing with sticks in the circle of obis,
Helping the llama or brahmin
     as he trims the lamps of the idols,
Dancing yet through the streets in
     a phallic procession, rapt and
     austere in the woods a gymnosophist,
Drinking mead from the skull-cup,
     to Shastas and Vedas admirant,
     minding the Koran,
Walking the teokallis, spotted with
     gore from the stone and knife,
     beating the serpent-skin drum,

Accepting the Gospels, accepting him
     that was crucified, knowing assuredly
     that he is divine,
To the mass kneeling or the puritan's prayer
     rising, or sitting patiently in a pew,
Ranting and frothing in my insane crisis,
     or waiting dead-like till my spirit
     arouses me,
Looking forth on pavement and land,
     or outside of pavement and land,
Belonging to the winders of
     the circuit of circuits.

One of that centripetal and centrifugal gang
     I turn and talk like a man leaving charges
     before a journey.

Down-hearted doubters dull and excluded,
Frivolous, sullen, moping, angry, affected,
     dishearten'd, atheistical,
I know every one of you, I know the sea of
     torment, doubt, despair and unbelief.

How the flukes splash!
How they contort rapid as lightning,
    with spasms and spouts of blood!
Be at peace bloody flukes of doubters
    and sullen mopers,
I take my place among you as much
    as among any,
The past is the push of you, me, all,
    precisely the same.
And what is yet untried and afterward
    is for you, me, all, precisely the same.

I do not know what is untried and afterward,
But I know it will in its turn prove sufficient,
    and cannot fail.

Each who passes is consider'd, each
    who stops is consider'd, not a single
    one can it fail.

It cannot fail the young man
    who died and was buried,
Nor the young woman who died
    and was put by his side,
Nor the little child that peep'd in at the door,
    and then drew back and was never seen again,
Nor the old man who has lived
    without purpose, and feels it with
    bitterness worse than gall,
Nor him in the poor house tubercled
    by rum and the bad disorder,
Nor the numberless slaughter'd and wreck'd,
    nor the brutish call'd the ordure of humanity
Nor the sacs merely floating with
    open mouths for food to slip in,
Nor any thing in the earth, or down
    in the oldest graves of the earth,
Nor any thing in the myriads of spheres,
    nor the myriads of myriads that
    inhabit them,
Nor the present, nor the least wisp
    that is known.

★ ★ ★

And I say to mankind, Be not curious
    about God,

For I am who am curious about each
    am not curious about God,
(No array of terms can say how much I am
    at peace about God and about death.)

I hear and behold God in every object,
    yet understand God not in the least,
Nor do I understand who there can
    be more wonderful than myself.

Why should I wish to see God better
    than this day?
I see something of God each hour of the
    twenty-four, and each moment then,
In the faces of men and women I see God,
    and in my own face in the glass,
I find letters from God dropt in the street,
    and every one is sign'd by God's name,
And I leave them where they are,
    for I know that wheresoe'er I go,
Others will punctually come
    for ever and ever.

PERFECTIONISM AND ITS UTOPIAN EXPERIMENTS

As one part of the American mind called for spiritual renewal and the other for intellectual independence, it is not surprising that some people adopted new and novel forms of religious expression and practice. Perfectionism found fertile soil in nineteenth century America, with its plethora of social problems and plentiful western lands.

President of Oberlin College Asa Mahan best summed up the assumptions and goals of the Christian Perfection movement in his 1839 work, *Scripture Doctrine of Christian Perfection,* just as many experimental communities, all of which dreamed of creating a better human environment, were beginning to be established. One such community, founded by the minister George Ripley at West Roxbury, Massachusetts, was dedicated to communal living and both spiritual and intellectual growth. In 1842 Elizabeth Peabody described its hopeful goals in an article, **"Commentary on Brook Farm,"** which appeared in Brook Farm's journal *The Dial*.

The preacher John Humphrey Noyse, a man convinced that he and his followers could reach perfection, culminated his search for followers when he founded a far more ambitious community at Oneida in New York in 1848. Like Ripley, Noyse believed in economic socialism, but unlike Ripley he also believed in sexual socialism. As early as 1839, in a **Letter** for his *Battle Axe* newspaper, he advocated the abolition of monogamous marriage. At Oneida, he instituted a program of "complex marriage," in which a number of men were married to a number of women. The theme of sexual liberation was made clear in his community's ***Hand Book*** on Free Love. Noyse's most thorough defense of Oneida's unusual sexual practices may be found in his analysis of socialist communities, ***Bible Communism.***

For various reasons—economic mismanagement, hostility of orthodox neighbors, historical forces beyond their control—most of the perfectionist utopian communities eventually failed. One that did not fail, and which continues to thrive today, was the religious community of Joseph Smith and his successor Brigham Young. Converts to Smith's "latter day" revelation are commonly known today as Mormons. Claiming divine sanction, profiting from a legacy of strong leadership, the Mormons adopted a system of polygamy, settled in the pristine region that became the state of Utah, and established a society that not only survived but flourished. Joseph Smith clearly articulated in his **Visions,** and in his commentaries on such things as **Plural Marriage,** the way God wanted his people to live. Brigham Young, when he dedicated the Salt Lake City Temple and expounded on **"The Necessity of Building Temples,"** placed the Mormons squarely within the tradition of Israel and Christ as the Latter Day Saints.

4.10

Scripture Doctrine of Christian Perfection (1839)

ASA MAHAN

To present this subject in a somewhat more distinct and expanded form, the attention to the reader is now invited to a few remarks upon I Thes. v. 23. "And the very God of peace sanctify you wholly: and I pray God your whole spirit and soul and body be preserved blameless unto the coming of our Lord Jesus Christ." . . . In short, the prayer of the apostle is, that all the powers and susceptibilities of our being may not only be purified from all that is unholy, but wholly sanctified and devoted to Christ, and forever preserved in that state. Now, the powers and susceptibilities of our nature are all comprehended in the following enumeration: the will, the intellect, and our mental and physical susceptibilities and propensities. The question to which the special attention of the reader is invited is this: When are we in a perfectly sanctified and blameless state, in respect to the action of all these powers and susceptibilities?

1. That we be in a perfectly sanctified and blameless state in regard to our wills, implies, that the action of all our voluntary powers be in entire conformity to the will of God; that every choice, every preference, and every volition, be controlled by a filial regard to the divine requisitions. The perpetual language of the heart must be, "Lord, what wilt thou have me do?"

2. That we "be preserved blameless" in regard to our intellect, does not imply that we never think of what is evil. If this were so, Christ was not blameless, because he thought of the temptations of Satan. Nor could the Christian repel what is evil, as he is required to do. To repel evil, the evil itself must be before the mind, as an object of thought.

   To be blameless in respect to the action of our intellectual powers, does imply, (1) That every thought of evil be instantly suppressed and repelled. (2) That they be constantly employed on the inquiry, what is the truth and will of God, and by what means we may best meet the demands of the great law of love. (3) That they be employed in the perpetual contemplation of "whatsoever things are true, whatsoever things are honest, whatsoever things are just, whatsoever things are pure, what-

Source: Asa Mahan, *Scripture Doctrine of Christian Perfection* (Boston, 1840) pp. 7–13.

soever things are lovely, whatsoever things are of good report; if there be any virtue, and if there be any praise," in thinking of these things also. When the intellectual powers are thus employed, they are certainly in a blameless state.

3. That our feelings and mental susceptibilities be preserved blameless, does not imply, that they are, at all times and circumstances, in the same intensity of excitement, or in the same identical state. This the powers and laws of our being forbid. Nor, in that case, could we obey the command, "Rejoice with those that do rejoice, and weep with those that weep." Nor does it imply that no feelings can exist in the mind, which, under the circumstances then present, it would be improper to indulge. A Christian, for example, may feel a very strong desire to speak for Christ under circumstances when it would be improper for him to speak. The feeling itself is proper. But we must be guided by wisdom from above in respect to the question, when and where we are to give utterance to our feelings.

   That our feelings and mental susceptibilities be in a blameless state, does imply, (1) That they all be held in perfect and perpetual subjection to the will of God. (2) That they be in perfect and perpetual harmony with the truth and will of God as apprehended by the intellect, and thus constituting a spotless mirror, through which there shall be a perfect reflection of whatsoever things are "true," "honest," "just," "pure," "lovely," and of "good report."

4. That our "bodies be preserved blameless," does not, of course, imply that they are free from fatigue, disease, or death. Nor does it imply that no desire be excited through our physical propensities, which, under existing circumstances, it would be unlawful to indulge. The feeling of hunger in Christ, under circumstances in which indulgence was not proper, was not sinful. The consent of the will to gratify the feeling, and not the feeling itself, renders us sinners.

   That we be preserved in a sanctified and blameless state in respect to our bodies, does imply, (1) That we endeavor to acquaint ourselves with all the laws of our physical constitution. (2) That in regard to food, drink, and dress, and in regard to the indulgence of all our appetites and physical propensities, there be a sacred and undeviating conformity to these laws. (3) That every unlawful desire be instantly suppressed, and that all our propensities be held in perfect subjection to the will of God. (4) That our bodies, with all our physical powers and propensities, be "presented to God as a living sacrifice, holy and acceptable," to be employed in his service.

Such is Christian Perfection. It is the consecration of our whole being to Christ, and the perpetual employment of all our powers in his service. It is the perfect assimilation of our entire character to that of Christ, having at all times, and under all circumstances, the "same mind that was also in Christ Jesus." It is, in the language of Mr. Wesley, "In one view, purity of intention, dedicating all the life to God. It is the giving God all the heart; it is one desire and design ruling all our tempers. It is devoting, not a part, but all our soul, body, and substance to God. In another view, it is all the mind that was in Christ Jesus, enabling us to walk as he walked. It is the circumcision of the heart from all filthiness, from all inward as well as outward pollution. It is the renewal of the heart in the whole image of God, the full likeness of him that created it. In yet another, it is loving God with all our heart, and our neighbor as ourselves."

4.11

Commentary on Brook Farm (1842)

ELIZABETH PEABODY

I n the last number of the Dial [October 1841] were some remarks, under the perhaps ambitious title, of "A Glimpse of Christ's Idea of Society;" in a note to which, it was intimated, that in this number, would be given an account of an attempt to realize in some degree this great Ideal, by a little company in the midst of us, as yet without name or visible existence. The attempt is made on a very small scale. A few individuals, who, unknown to each other, under different disciplines of life, reacting from different social evils, but aiming at the same object,—of being wholly true to their natures as men and women; have been made acquainted with one another, and have determined to become the Faculty of the Embryo University.

In order to live a religious and moral life worthy the name, they feel it is necessary to come out in some degree from the world, and to form themselves into a community of property, so far as to exclude competition and the ordinary rules of trade;—while they reserve sufficient private property, or the means of obtaining it, for all purposes of independence, and isolation at will. They have bought a farm, in order to make agriculture the basis of their life, it being the most direct and simple in relation to nature.

A true life, although it aims beyond the highest star, is redolent of the healthy earth. The perfume of clover lingers about it. The lowing of cattle is the natural bass to the melody of human voices.

Source: *The Dial* (Jan. 1842), [Reprint: Russell & Russell (New York, 1961)] pp. 361–363.

On the other hand, what absurdity can be imagined greater than the institution of cities? They originated not in love, but in war. It was war that drove men together in multitudes, and compelled them to stand so close, and build walls around them. This crowded condition produces wants of an unnatural character, which resulted in occupations that regenerated the evil, by creating artificial wants. Even when that thought of grief,

"I know, where'er I go
That there hath passed away a glory from the Earth,"

came to our first parents, as they saw the angel, with the flaming sword of self-consciousness, standing between them and the recovery of spontaneous Life and Joy, we cannot believe they could have anticipated a time would come, when the sensuous apprehension of Creation—the great symbol of God—would be taken away from their unfortunate children,—crowded together in such a manner as to shut out the free breath and the Universal Dome of Heaven, some opening their eyes in the dark cellars of the narrow, crowded streets of walled cities. How could they have believed in such a conspiracy against the soul, as to deprive it of the sun and sky, and glorious apparelled Earth!—The growth of cities, which were the embryo of nations hostile to each other, is a subject worthy the thoughts and pen of the philosophic historian. Perhaps nothing would stimulate courage to seek, and hope to attain social good, so much, as a profound history of the origin, in the mixed nature of man, and the exasperation by society, of the various organized Evils under which humanity groans. Is there anything, which exists in social or political life, contrary to the soul's Ideal? That thing is not eternal, but finite, saith the Pure Reason. It has a beginning, and so a history. What man has done, man may *undo*. "By man came death; by man also cometh the resurrection from the dead."

The plan of the Community, as an Economy, is in brief this; for all who have property to take stock, and receive a fixed interest thereon; then to keep house or board in commons, as they shall severally desire, at the cost of provisions purchased at wholesale, or raised on the farm; and for all to labor in community, and be paid at a certain rate an hour, choosing their own number of hours, and their own kind of work. With the results of this labor, and their interest, they are to pay their board, and also purchase whatever else they require at cost, at the warehouses of the Community, which are to be filled by the Community as such. To perfect this economy, in the course of time they must have all trades, and all modes of business carried on among themselves, from the lowest mechanical trade, which contributes to the health and comfort of life, to the finest art which adorns it with food or drapery for the mind.

All labor, whether bodily or intellectual, is to be paid at the same rate of wages; on the principle, that as the labor becomes merely bodily, it is a greater sacrifice to the individual laborer, to give his time to it; because time is desirable for the cultivation of the intellect, in exact proportion to ignorance. Besides, intellectual labor involves in itself higher pleasures, and is more its own reward, than bodily labor.

Another reason, for setting the same pecuniary value on every kind of labor, is, to give outward expression to the great truth, that all labor is sacred, when done for a common interest. Saints and philosophers already know this, but the childish world does not; and very decided measures must be taken to equalize labors, in the eyes of the young of the community, who are not beyond the moral influences of the world without them. The community will have nothing done within its precincts, but what is done by its own members, who stand all in social equality;—that the children may not "learn to expect one kind of service from Love and Goodwill, and another from the obligation of others to render it,"—a grievance of the common society stated, by one of the associated mothers, as destructive of the soul's simplicity. Consequently, as the Universal Education will involve all kinds of operation, necessary to the comforts and elegances of life, every associate, even if he be the digger of a ditch as his highest accomplishment, will be an instructer in that to the young members. Nor will this elevation of bodily labor be liable to lower the tone of manners and refinement in the community. The "children of light" are not altogether unwise in their generation. They have an invisible but all-powerful guard of principles. Minds incapable of refinement, will not be attracted into this association. It is an Ideal community, and only to the ideally inclined will it be attractive; but these are to be found in every rank of life, under every shadow of circumstance. Even among the diggers in the ditch are to be found some, who through religious cultivation, can look down, in meek superiority, upon the outwardly refined, and the book-learned.

4.12

Battle Axe Letter (1836)

JOHN HUMPHREY NOYSE

When the will of God is done on earth, as it is in heaven, there will be no marriage. The marriage supper of the Lamb is a feast at which every dish is free to every guest. Exclusiveness, jealousy, quarreling, have no place there, for the same reason as that which forbids the guests at a thanks giving-dinner to claim each his eaparate dish, and quarrel with the rest for his rights. In a holy community, there is no more reason why sexual intercourse should be restrained by law, than why eating and drinking should be—and there is as little occasion for shame in the one case as in the other. . . . The guests of the marriage supper may have each his favorite dish, each a dish of his own procuring, and that without the jealousy of exclusiveness. I call a certain woman my wife—she is yours, she is Christ's, and in him she is the bride of all saints. She is dear in the hand of a stranger, and according to my promise to her I rejoice. My claim upon her cuts directly across the marriage covenant of the world, and God knows the end.

4.13

Oneida Community's *Hand Book* on Free Love (1867)

"This terrible combination of two very good ideas—freedom and love—was first used by the writers of the Oneida Community about twenty-one years ago, and probably originated with them. It was however soon taken up by a very different class of speculators scattered about the country, and has come to be the name of a form of socialism with which we have but little affinity. Still it is sometimes applied to our Communities; and as we are certainly responsible for starting it into circulation, it seems to be our duty to tell what meaning we attach to it, and in what sense we are willing to accept it as a designation of our social system.

"The obvious and essential difference between marriage and licentious connections may be stated thus:

"Marriage is permanent union. Licentiousness deals in temporary flirtations.

"In marriage, Communism of property goes with Communism of persons. In licentiousness, love is paid for as hired labor.

"Marriage makes a man responsible for the consequnces of his acts of love to a woman. In licentiousness, a man imposes on a woman the heavy burdens of maternity, ruining perhaps her reputation and her health, and then goes his way without responsibility.

"Marriage provides for the maintenance and education of children. Licentiousness ignores children as nuisances, and leaves them to chance.

"Now in respect to every one of these points of difference between marriage and licentiousness, *we stand with marriage.* Free Love with us does *not* mean freedom to love to-day and leave to-morrow; nor freedom to take a woman's person and keep our property to ourselves; nor freedom to freight a woman with our

Source: *Hand Book of the Oneida Community* (Oneida, NY: 1867).

offspring and send her down stream without care or help; nor freedom to beget children and leave them to the street and the poor-house. Our Communities are *families*, as distinctly bounded and separated from promiscuous society as ordinary households. The tie that binds us together is as permanent and sacred, to say the least, as that of marriage, for it is our religion. We receive no members (except by deception or mistake), who do not give heart and hand to the family interest for life and forever. Community of property extends just as far as freedom of love. Every man's care and every dollar of the common property is pledged for the maintenance and protection of the women, and the education of the children of the Community. Bastardy, in any disastrous sense of the word, is simply impossible in such a social state. Whoever will take the trouble to follow our track from the beginning, will find no forsaken women or children by the way. In this respect we claim to be in advance of marriage and common civilization."

4.14

Bible Communism (1870)

JOHN HUMPHREY NOYSE

Chapter II.—*Showing that Marriage is not an institution of the Kingdom of Heaven, and must give place to Communism.*

> **Proposition 5.**—In the Kingdom of Heaven, the institution of marriage, which assigns the exclusive possession of one woman to one man, does not exist. Matt. 22: 23–30.
>
> 6.—In the Kingdom of Heaven the intimate union of life and interest, which in the world is limited to pairs, extends through the whole body of believers; i.e., complex marriage takes the place of simple. John 17: 21. Christ prayed that all believers might be one, even as he and the Father are one. His unity with the Father is defined in the words, "All mine are thine, and all thine are mine." Ver. 10. This perfect community of interests, then, will be the condition of all, when his prayer is answered. The universal unity of the members of Christ, is described in the same terms

Source: J. H. Noyse, *Bible Communism* (New York: AMS Press, 1973 [From 1870 publication]).

that are used to describe marriage unity. Compare 1 Cor. 12: 12–27, with Gen. 2: 24 See also 1 Cor. 6: 15–17, and Eph. 5: 30–32.

7.—The effects of the effusion of the Holy Spirit on the day of Pentecost, present a practical commentary on Christ's prayer for the unity of believers, and a sample of the tendency of heavenly influences, which fully confirm the foregoing proposition. "All that believed were together and had all things common; and sold their possessions and goods, and parted them to all, as every man had need." "The multitude of them that believed were of one heart and of one soul; neither said any of them that aught of the things which he possessed was his own; but they had all things common." Acts 2: 44, 45, and 4: 32. Here is unity like that of the Father and the Son: "All mine thine, and all thine mine."

8.—Admitting that the Community principle of the day of Pentecost, in its actual operation at that time, extended only to material goods, yet we affirm that there is no intrinsic difference between property in persons and property in things; and that the same spirit which abolished exclusiveness in regard to money, would abolish, if circumstances allowed full scope to it, exclusiveness in regard to women and children. Paul expressly places property in women and property in goods in the same category, and speaks of them together, as ready to be abolished by the advent of the Kingdom of Heaven. "The time," says he, "is short; it remaineth that they that have wives be as though they had none; and they that buy as though they possessed not; for the fashion of this world passeth away." 1 Cor. 7: 29–31.

9.—The abolishment of appropriation is involved in the very nature of a true relation to Christ in the gospel. This we prove thus: The possessive feeling which expresses itself by the possessive pronoun *mine,* is the same in essence when it relates to persons, as when it relates to money or any other property. Amativeness and acquisitiveness are only different channels of one stream. They converge as we trace them to their source. Grammar will help us to ascertain their common center; for the possessive pronoun *mine,* is derived from the personal pronoun *I;* and so the possessive feeling, whether amative or acquisitive, flows from the personal feeling, that is, it is a branch of egotism. Now egotism is abolished by the gospel relation to Christ. The grand mystery of the gospel is vital union with Christ; the merging of self in his life; the extinguishment of the pronoun *I* at the spiritual center. Thus Paul says, "I live, yet not I, but Christ liveth in me." The grand distinction between the Christian and the unbeliever, between heaven and the world, is, that in one reigns the We-spirit, and in the other the I-spirit. From *I* comes *mine,* and from the I-spirit comes exclusive appropriation of money, women, etc. From *we* comes *ours,* and from the We-spirit comes universal community of interests.

10.—The abolishment of exclusiveness is involved in the love-relation required between all believers by the express injunction of Christ and the apostles, and by the whole tenor of the New Testament. "The new commandment is, that we love one another," and that, not by pairs, as in the world, but *en masse*. We are required to love one another fervently. The fashion of the world forbids a man and woman who are otherwise appropriated, to love one another fervently. But if they obey Christ they must do this; and whoever would allow them to do this, and yet would forbid them (on any other ground than that of present expediency), to express their unity, would "strain at a gnat and swallow a camel;" for unity of hearts is as much more important than any external expression of it, as a camel is larger than a gnat.

11.—The abolishment of social restrictions is involved in the anti-legality of the gospel. It is incompatible with the state of perfected freedom toward which Paul's gospel of "grace without law" leads, that man should be allowed and required to love in all directions, and yet be forbidden to express love except in one direction. In fact Paul says, with direct reference to sexual intercourse—"All things are lawful for me, but all things are not expedient; all things are lawful for me, but I will not be brought under the power of any;" (1 Cor. 6: 12) thus placing the restrictions which were necessary in the transition period on the basis, not of law, but of expediency and the demands of spiritual freedom, and leaving it fairly to be inferred that in the final state, when hostile surroundings and powers of bondage cease, all restrictions also will cease.

12.—The abolishment of the marriage sytem is involved in Paul's doctrine of the end of ordinances. Marriage is one of the "ordinances of the worldly sanctuary." This is proved by the fact that it has no place in the resurrection. Paul expressly limits it to life in the flesh. Rom. 7: 2, 3. The assumption, therefore, that believers are dead to the world by the death of Christ (which authorized the abolishment of Jewish ordinances), legitimately makes an end of marriage, Col. 2: 20.

13.—The law of marriage is the same in kind with the Jewish law concerning meats and drinks and holy days, of which Paul said that they were "contrary to us, and were taken out of the way, being nailed to the cross." Col. 2: 14. The plea in favor of the worldly social system, that it is not arbitrary, but founded in nature, will not bear investigation. All experience testifies (the theory of the novels to the contrary notwithstanding), that sexual love is not naturally restricted to pairs. Second marriages are contrary to the one-love theory, and yet are often the happiest marriages. Men and women find universally (however the fact may be concealed), that their susceptibility to love is not burnt out by one honey-moon, or satisfied by one lover. On the contrary, the secret history of the human heart will bear out the assertion that it is capable of loving any number of times and any number of persons, and that the more it loves the more it can love. This is the law of nature, thrust out of sight and condemned by common consent, and yet secretly known to all.

14.—The law of marriage "worketh wrath." (1) It provokes to secret adultery, actual or of the heart. (2) It ties together unmatched natures. (3) It sunders matched natures. (4) It gives to sexual appetite only a scanty and monotonous allowance, and so produces the natural vices of poverty, contraction of taste and stinginess or jealousy. (5) It makes no provision for the sexual appetite at the very time when that appetite is the strongest. By the custom of the world, marriage, in the average of cases, takes place at about the age of twenty-four; whereas puberty commences at the age of fourteen. For ten years, therefore, and that in the very flush of life, the sexual appetite is starved. This law of society bears hardest on females, because they have less opportunity of choosing their time of marriage than men. This discrepancy between the marriage system and nature, is one of the principal sources of the peculiar diseases of women, of prostitution, masturbation, and licentiousness in general.

17.—The restoration of true relations between the sexes is a matter second in importance only to the reconciliation of man to God. The distinction of male and female is that which makes man the image of God, i. e., the image of the Father and the Son. Gen. 1: 27. The relation of male and female was the first social relation. Gen. 2: 22. It is therefore the root of all other social relations. The derangement of this relation was the first result of the original breach with God. Gen. 3: 7; comp. 2: 25. Adam and Eve were, at the beginning, in open, fearless, spiritual fellowship, first with God, and secondly, with each other. Their transgression produced two corresponding alienations, viz., first, an alienation from God, indicated by their fear of meeting him and their hiding themselves among the trees of the garden; and secondly, an alienation from each other, indicated by their shame at their nakedness and their hiding themselves from each other by clothing. These were the two great manifestations of original sin—the only manifestations presented to notice in the record of the apostacy. The first thing then to be done, in an attempt to redeem man and reörganize society, is to bring about reconciliation with God; and the second thing is to bring about a true union of the sexes. In other words, religion is the first subject of interest, and sexual morality the second, in the great enterprise of establishing the Kingdom of Heaven on earth.

19.—From what precedes, it is evident that any attempt to revolutionize sexual morality before settlement with God, is out of order. Holiness must go before free love. Bible Communists are not responsible for the proceedings of those who meddle with the sexual question, before they have laid the foundation of true faith and union with God.

20.—Dividing the sexual relation into two branches, the amative and propagative, the amative or love-relation is first in importance, as it is in the order of nature. God made woman because "he saw it was not good for man to be alone;" (Gen. 2: 18); i. e., for social, not primarily for propagative, purposes. Eve was called Adam's "help-meet." In the whole of the specific account of the creation of woman, she is regarded as his companion, and her maternal office is not brought into view. Gen. 2: 18–25. Amativeness was necessarily the first social affection developed in the garden of Eden. The second commandment of the eternal law of love, "Thou shalt love thy neighbor as thyself," had amativeness for its first channel; for Eve was at first Adam's only neighbor. Propagation and the affections connected with it, did not commence their operation during the period of innocence. After the fall God said to the woman, "I will greatly multiply thy sorrow and thy conception"; from which it is to be inferred that in the original state, conception would have been comparatively infrequent.

21.—The amative part of the sexual relation, separate from the propagative, is eminently favorable to life. It is not a source of life (as some would make it), but it is the first and best distributive of life. Adam and Eve, in their original state, derived their life from God. Gen. 2: 7. As God is a dual being, the Father and the Son, and man was made in his image, a dual life passed from God to man. Adam was the channel specially of the life of the Father, and Eve of the life of the Son. Amativeness was the natural agency of the distribution and mutual action of these two forms of life. In this primitive position of the sexes (which is their normal position in Christ), each reflects upon the other the love of God; each excites and develops the divine action in the other.

22.—The propagative part of the sexual relation is in its nature the expensive department. (1) While amativeness keeps the capital stock of life circulating between two, propagation introduces a third partner. (2) The propagative act is a drain on the life of man, and when habitual, produces disease. (3) The infirmities and vital expenses of woman during the long period of pregnancy, waste her constitution. (4) The awful agonies of child-birth heavily tax the life of woman. (5) The cares of the nursing period bear heavily on woman. (6) The cares of both parents, through the period of the childhood of their offspring, are many and burdensome. (7) The labor of man is greatly increased by the necessity of providing for children. A portion of these expenses would undoubtedly have been curtailed, if human nature had remained in its original integrity, and will be, when it is restored. But it is still self-evident that the birth of children, viewed either as a vital or a mechanical operation, is in its nature expensive; and the fact that multiplied conception was imposed as a curse, indicates that it was so regarded by the Creator.

Proposition 23.—The amative and propagative functions are distinct from each other, and may be separated practically. They are confounded in the world, both in the theories of physiologists and in universal practice. The amative function is regarded merely as a bait to the propagative, and is merged in it. But if amativeness is, as we have seen, the first and noblest of the social affections, and if the propagative part of the sexual relation was originally secondary, and became paramount by the subversion of order in the fall, we are bound to raise the amative office of the sexual organs into a distinct and paramount function.

4.15

Visions (1827)

JOSEPH SMITH

. . . I had actually seen a light, and in the midst of that light I saw two Personages, and they did in reality speak to me; and though I was hated and persecuted for saying that I had seen a vision, yet it was true; and while they were persecuting me, reviling me, and speaking all manner of evil against me falsely for so saying, I was led to say in my heart: Why persecute me for telling the truth? I have actually seen a vision; and who am I that I can withstand God, or why does the world think to make me deny what I have actually seen? For I had seen a vision; I knew it, and I knew that God knew it, and I could not deny it, neither dared I do it; at least I knew that by so doing I would offend God, and come under condemnation.

I had now got my mind satisfied so far as the sectarian world was concerned—that it was not my duty to join with any of them, but to continue as I was until further directed. I had found the testimony of James to be true—that a man who lacked wisdom might ask of God, and obtain, and not be upbraided.

MORONI'S VISIT

I continued to pursue my common vocations in life until the twenty-first of September, one thousand eight hundred and twenty-three, all the time suffering severe persecution at the hands of all classes of men, both religious and irreligious, because I continued to affirm that I had seen a vision.

During the space of time which intervened between the time I had the vision and the year eighteen hundred and twenty-three—having been forbidden to join any of the religious sects of the day, and being of very tender years, and persecuted by those who ought to have been my friends and to have treated me kindly, and if they supposed me to be deluded to have endeavored in a proper and affectionate manner to have reclaimed me—I was left to all kinds of temptations; and, mingling with all kinds of society, I frequently fell into many foolish errors, and displayed the weakness of youth, and the foibles of human nature; which, I am sorry to say, led me into divers temptations, offensive in the sight of

Source: *History of the Church of Jesus Christ of Latter Day Saints* (Salt Lake City, Ut:, Deseret Book Co, 1967) I, 3–75.

God. In making this confession, no one need suppose me guilty of any great or malignant sins. A disposition to commit such was never in my nature.

In consequence of these things, I often felt condemned for my weakness and imperfections; when, on the evening of the above-mentioned twenty-first of September, after I had retired to my bed for the night, I betook myself to prayer and supplication to Almighty God for forgiveness of all my sins and follies, and also for a manifestation to me, that I might know of my state and standing before him; for I had full confidence in obtaining a divine manifestation, as I previously had one.

While I was thus in the act of calling upon God, I discovered a light appearing in my room, which continued to increase until the room was lighter than at noonday, when immediately a personage appeared at my bedside, standing in the air, for his feet did not touch the floor.

He had on a loose robe of most exquisite whiteness. It was a whiteness beyond anything earthly I had ever seen; nor do I believe that any earthly thing could be made to appear so exceedingly white and brilliant. His hands were naked, and his arms also, a little above the wrists; so, also, were his feet naked, as were his legs, a little above the ankles. His head and neck were also bare. I could discover that he had no other clothing on but this robe, as it was open, so that I could see into his bosom.

Not only was his robe exceedingly white, but his whole person was glorious beyond description, and his countenance truly like lightning. The room was exceedingly light, but not so very bright as immediately around his person. When I first looked upon him, I was afraid; but the fear soon left me.

He called me by name, and said unto me that he was a messenger sent from the presence of God to me, and that his name was Moroni; that God had a work for me to do; and that my name should be had for good and evil among all nations, kindreds, and tongues, or that it should be good and evil spoken of among all people.

He said there was a book deposited, written upon gold plates, giving an account of the former inhabitants of this continent, and the source from whence they sprang. He also said that the fulness of the everlasting Gospel was contained in it, as delivered by the Savior to the ancient inhabitants.

Also, that there were two stones in silver bows—and these stones, fastened to a breastplate, constituted what is called the Urim and Thummim—deposited with the plates; and the possession and use of these stones were what constituted "seers" in ancient or former times; and that God had prepared them for the purpose of translating the book.

After telling me these things, he commenced quoting the prophecies of the Old Testament. He first quoted part of the third chapter of Malachi; and he quoted also the fourth or last chapter of the same prophecy, though with a little variation from the way it reads in our Bibles. Instead of quoting the first verse as it reads in our books, he quoted it thus:

For behold, the day cometh that shall burn as an oven, and all the proud, yea, and all that do wickedly shall burn as stubble; for they that come shall burn them, saith the Lord of Hosts, that it shall leave them neither root nor branch.

And again, he quoted the fifth verse thus: *Behold, I will reveal unto you the Priesthood, by the hand of Elijah the prophet, before the coming of the great and dreadful day of the Lord.*

He also quoted the next verse differently: *And he shall plant in the hearts of the children the promises made to the fathers, and the hearts of the children shall turn to their fathers. If it were not so, the whole earth would be utterly wasted at his coming.*

In addition to these, he quoted the eleventh chapter of Isaiah, saying that it was about to be fulfilled. He quoted also the third chapter of Acts, twenty-second and twenty-third verses, precisely as they stand in our New Testament. He said that that prophet was Christ; but the day had not yet come when "they who would not hear his voice should be cut off from among the people," but soon would come.

He also quoted the second chapter of Joel, from the twenty-eighth verse to the last. He also said that this was not yet fulfilled, but was soon to be. And he further stated that the fulness of the Gentiles was soon to come in. He quoted many other passages of scripture, and he offered many explanations which cannot be mentioned here.

Again, he told me, that when I got those plates of which he had spoken—for the time that they should be obtained was not yet fulfilled—I should not show them to any person; neither the breastplate with the Urim and Thummim; only to those to whom I should be commanded to show them; if I did I should be destroyed. While he was conversing with me about the plates, the vision was open to my mind that I could see the place where the plates were deposited, and that so clearly and distinctly that I knew the place again when I visited it.

After this communication, I saw the light in the room begin to gather immediately around the person of him who had been speaking to me, and it continued to do so until the room was again left dark, except just around him; when, instantly I saw, as it were, a conduit open right up into heaven, and he ascended till he entirely disappeared, and the room was left as it had been before this heavenly light had made its appearance.

I lay musing on the singularity of the scene, and marveling greatly at what had been told to me by this extraordinary messenger; when, in the midst of my meditation, I suddenly discovered that my room was again beginning to get lighted, and in an instant, as it were, the same heavenly messenger was again by my bedside.

He commenced, and again related the very same things which he had done at his first visit, without the least variation; which having done, he informed me of great judgments which were coming upon the earth, with great desolations by famine, sword, and pestilence; and that these grievous judgments would come on earth in this generation. Having related these things, he again ascended as he had done before.

By this time, so deep were the impressions made on my mind, that sleep had fled from my eyes, and I lay overwhelmed in astonishment at what I had both seen and heard. But what was my surprise when again I beheld the same messenger at my bedside, and heard him rehearse or repeat over again to me the same things as before; and added a caution to me, telling me that Satan would try to tempt me (in consequence of the indigent circumstances of my father's family), to get the plates for the purpose of getting rich. This he forbade me, saying that I must have no other object in view in getting the plates but to glorify God, and must not be influenced by any other motive than that of building his kingdom; otherwise I could not get them.

After this third visit, he again ascended into heaven as before, and I was again left to ponder on the strangeness of what I had just experienced; when almost immediately after the heavenly messenger had ascended from me for the third time, the cock crowed, and I found that day was approaching, so that our interviews must have occupied the whole of that night.

I shortly after arose from my bed, and, as usual, went to the necessary labors of the day; but, in attempting to work as at other times, I found my strength so exhausted as to render me entirely unable. My father, who was laboring along with me, discovered something to be wrong with me, and told me to go home. I started with the intention of going to the house; but, in attempting to cross the fence out of the field where we were, my strength entirely failed me, and I fell helpless on the ground, and for a time was quite unconscious of anything.

The first thing that I can recollect was a voice speaking unto me, calling me by name. I looked up, and beheld the same messenger standing over my head, surrounded by light as before. He then again related unto me all that he had related to me the previous night, and commanded me to go to my father and tell him of the vision and commandments which I had received.

I obeyed; I returned to my father in the field, and rehearsed the whole matter to him. He replied to me that it was of God, and told me to go and do as commanded by the messenger. I left the field, and went to the place where the messenger had told me the plates were deposited; and owing to the distinctness of the vision which I had had concerning it, I knew the place the instant that I arrived there.

THE SACRED RECORD

Convenient to the village of Manchester, Ontario County, New York, stands a hill of considerable size, and the most elevated of any in the neighborhood. On the west side of this hill, not far from the top, under a stone of considerable size, lay the plates, deposited in a stone box. This stone was thick and rounding in the middle on the upper side, and thinner towards the edges, so that the middle part of it was visible above the ground, but the edge all around was covered with earth.

Having removed the earth, I obtained a lever, which I got fixed under the edge of the stone, and with a little exertion raised it up. I looked in, and there indeed did I behold the plates, the Urim and Thummim, and the breastplate, as stated by the messenger. The box in which they lay was formed by laying stones together in some kind of cement. In the bottom of the box were laid two stones crossways of the box, and on these stones lay the plates and the other things with them.

4.16

On Plural Marriage (1843)

JOSEPH SMITH

Verily thus saith the Lord, unto you my servant Joseph, that inasmuch as you have enquired of my hand, to know and understand wherein I the Lord justified my servants, Abraham, Isaac, and Jacob; as also Moses, David, and Solomon, my servants, as touching the principle and doctrine of their having many wives, and concubines: Behold! and lo, I am the Lord thy God, and will answer thee as touching this matter: Therefore, prepare thy heart to receive and obey the instructions which I am about to give unto you; for all those, who have this law revealed unto them, must obey the same; for behold! I reveal unto you a new and an everlasting covenant. . . .

I am the Lord thy God, and will give unto thee the law of my Holy Priesthood, as was ordained by me, and my Father, before the world was. Abraham received all things, whatsoever he received, by revelation and commandment, by my word, saith the Lord, and hath entered into this exaltation, and sitteth upon his throne.

Abraham received promises concerning his seed, and of the fruit of his loins,—from whose loins ye are, viz., my servant Joseph,—which were to continue, so long as they were in the world; and as touching Abraham and his seed, out of the world, they should continue; both in the world and out of the world should they continue as innumerable as the stars, or, if ye were to count the sand upon the sea-shore, ye could not number them. This promise is yours, also, because ye are of Abraham, and the promise was made unto Abraham, and by this law are the continuation of the works of my Father, wherein he glorifieth himself. Go ye, therefore, and do the works of Abraham,—enter ye into my law, and ye shall be saved. But if ye enter not into my law, ye cannot receive the promises of my Father, which he made unto Abraham.

God commanded Abraham, and Sarah gave Hagar to Abraham, to wife. And why did she do it? Because this was the law, and from Hagar sprang many people. This, therefore, was fulfilling, among other things, the promises. Was Abraham, therefore, under condemnation? Verily, I say unto you, *Nay;* for I the Lord commanded it. Abraham was commanded to offer his son Isaac; nevertheless, it was written, thou shalt not kill. Abraham, however, did not refuse, and it was accounted unto him for righteousness.

Source: *Deseret News Extra*, September 14, 1852.

Abraham received concubines, and they bare him children, and it was accounted unto him for righteousness, because they were given unto him, and he abode in my law: as Isaac also, and Jacob did none other things [than] that which they were commanded; and because they did none other things than that which they were commanded, they have entered into their exaltation, according to the promises, and sit upon thrones; and are not angels, but are Gods. David also received many wives and concubines, as also Solomon, and Moses my servant; as also many others of my servants from the beginning of creation until this time; and in nothing did they sin, save in those things which they received not of me. . . .

Now as touching the law of the priesthood, there are many things pertaining thereunto. Verily, if a man be called of my Father, as was Aaron, by mine own voice, and by the voice of him that sent me, and I have endowed him with the keys of the power of this priesthood, if he do anything in my name, and according to my law, and by my word, he will not commit sin, and I will justify him. Let no one, therefore, set on my servant Joseph; for I will justify him; for he shall do the sacrifice which I require at his hands for his transgressions, saith the Lord your God.

And again, as pertaining to the law of the Priesthood;—if any man espouse a virgin, and desire to espouse another, and the first give her consent; and if he espouses the second, and they are virgins, and have vowed to no other man, then is he justified; he cannot commit adultery, for they are given unto him; for he cannot commit adultery with that, that belongeth unto him, and to none else: and if he have ten virgins given unto him by this law, he cannot commit adultery; for they belong to him; and they are given unto him;—therefore is he justified. But if one, or either of the ten virgins, after she is espoused, shall be with another man, she has committed adultery, and shall be destroyed; for they are given unto him to multiply and replenish the earth, according to my commandment, and to fulfil the promise which was given by my Father before the foundation of the world; and for their exaltation in the eternal worlds, that they may bear the souls of men; for herein is the work of my Father continued, that he may be glorified.

4.17

The Necessity of Building Temples (1853)

BRIGHAM YOUNG

The Ark containing the covenant—or the Ark of the Covenant in the days of Moses, containing the sacred records—was moved from place to place in a cart. And so sacred was that Ark, if a man stretched forth his hand to steady it, when the cart jostled, he was smitten, and died. And would to God that all who attempt to do the same in this day, figuratively speaking, might share the same fate. And they will share it sooner or later, if they do not keep their hands, and tongues too, in their proper places, and stop dictating the order of the Gods of the Eternal Worlds.

When the Ark of the Covenant rested, or when the children of Israel had an opportunity to rest (for they were mobbed and harassed somewhat like the Latter-day Saints), the Lord, through Moses, commanded a Tabernacle to be built, wherein should rest and be stationed, the Ark of the Covenant. And particular instructions were given by revelation to Moses, how every part of said Tabernacle should be constructed, even to the curtains—the number thereof, and of what they should be made; and the covering, and the wood for the boards, and for the bars, and the court, and the pins, and the vessels, and the furniture, and everything pertaining to the Tabernacle. Why did Moses need such a particular revelation to build a Tabernacle? Because he had never seen one, and did not know how to build it without revelation, without a pattern.

Thus the Ark of the Covenant continued until the days of David, King of Israel, standing or occupying a Tabernacle, or tent. But to David, God gave commandment that he should build Him a house, therein He, Himself, might dwell, or which He might visit, and in which He might commune with His servants when He pleased.

From the day the children of Israel were led out of Egypt to the days of Solomon, Jehovah had no resting place upon the earth (and for how long a period before that day, the history is unpublished) but walked in the tent or Tabernacle, before the Ark, as it seemed to Him to good, having no place to lay His head.

David was not permitted to build the house which he was commanded to build, because he was a "man of blood," that is, he was beset by enemies on every

Source: Mormon Official Website: http://www.journals. mormonfundamentalim.org/vol_02/refJDvol 2-2.html.

© Bettmann/Corbis

Brigham Young, second
founder of the Mormon
movement

hand, and had to spend his days in war and bloodshed to save Israel (much as the
Latter-day Saints have done, only he had the privilege to defend himself and
people from mobocrats and murderers, while we have hitherto been denied that
privilege) and, consequently, he had no time to build a house unto the Lord, but
commanded his son Solomon, who succeeded him on the throne, to erect the
Temple at Jerusalem, which God had required at his hands.

The pattern of this Temple, the length, and breadth, and height of the inner
and outer courts, with all the fixtures thereunto appertaining, were given to
Solomon by revelation, through the proper source. And why was this revela-
tion-pattern necessary? Because that Solomon had never built a Temple, and
did not know what was necessary in the arrangement of the different apart-
ments, any better than Moses did what was needed in the Tabernacle.

This Temple, called Solomon's Temple, because Solomon was the master
workman, was completed some time previous to the appearance of the Son of
Man on the earth, in the form of the babe of Bethlehem, and had been dedicated as the House of the Lord, and accepted as a finished work by the Father,
who commanded it to be built, that His Son might have a resting place on the
earth, when he should enter on his mission.

★ ★ ★

Soon after the ascension of Jesus, through mobocracy, martyrdom, and apostacy, the Church of Christ became extinct from the earth, the Man Child—the Holy Priesthood— was received up into heaven from whence it came, and we hear no more of it on the earth, until the Angels restored it to Joseph Smith, by whose ministry the Church of Jesus Christ was restored, re-organized on earth, twenty-three years ago this day, with the title of "Latter-day Saints" to distinguish them from the Former-day Saints.

Soon after, the Church, though our beloved Prophet Joseph, was commanded to build a Temple to the Most High, in Kirtland, Ohio, and this was the next House of the Lord we hear of on the earth, since the days of Solomon's Temple. Joseph not only received revelation and commandment to build a Temple, but he received a pattern also, as did Moses for the Tabernacle, and Solomon for his Temple; for without a pattern, he could not know what was wanting, having never seen one, and not having experienced its use.

★ ★ ★

Before these endowments could be given at Kirtland, the Saints had to flee before mobocracy. And, by toil and daily labor, they found places in Missouri, where they laid the corner stones of Temples, in Zion and her Stakes, and then had to retreat to Illinois, to save the lives of those who could get away alive from Missouri, where fell the Apostle David W. Patten, with many like associates, and where were imprisoned in loathsome dungeons, and fed on human flesh, Joseph and Hyrum, and many others. But before all this had transpired, the Temple at Kirtland had fallen into the hands of wicked men, and by them been polluted, like the Temple at Jerusalem, and consequently it was disowned by the Father and the Son.

At Nauvoo, Joseph dedicated another Temple, the third on record. He knew what was wanting, for he had previously given most of the prominent individuals then before him their endowment. He needed no revelation, then, of a thing he had long experienced, any more than those now do, who have experienced the same things. It is only where experience fails, that revelation is needed.

Before the Nauvoo Temple was completed, Joseph was murdered—murdered at sun light, under the protection of the most noble government that then existed, and that now exists, on our earth. Has his blood been atoned for? No! And why? A martyr's blood to true religion was never atoned for on our earth. No man, or nation of men, without the Priesthood, has power to make atonement for such sins. The souls of all such, since the days of Jesus, are "under the altar," and are crying to God day and night, for vengeance. And shall they cry in vain? God forbid! He has promised He will hear them in His own due time, and recompense a righteous reward.

But what of the Temple in Nauvoo? By the aid of sword in one hand, and trowel and hammer in the other, with fire arms at hand, and a strong band of police, and the blessings of heaven, the Saints, through hunger, and thirst, and weariness, and watchings, and prayings, so far completed the Temple, despite the devices of the mob, that many received a small portion of their endowment, but we know of no one who received it in its fulness. And then, to save the lives of all the Saints from cruel murder, we removed westward, and being led by the all-searching eye of the Great Jehovah, we arrived at this place.

★ ★ ★

But what are we here for, this day? To celebrate the birth day of our religion! To lay the foundation of a Temple to the Most High God, so that when His Son, our Elder Brother, shall again appear, he may have place where he can lay his head, and not only spend a night or a day, but find a place of peace, that he may stay till he can say, "I am satisfied."

Brethren, shall the Son of Man be satisfied with our proceedings this day? Shall he have a house on the earth which he can call his own? Shall he have place where he can lay his head, and rest over night, and tarry as long as he pleases, and be satisfied and pleased with his accommodations?

These are questions for you to answer. If you say yes, you have got to do the work, or it will not be done. We do not want any whiners about this Temple. If you cannot commence cheerfully, and go through the labor of the whole building cheerfully, start for California, and the quicker the better. Make you a golden calf, and worship it. If your care for the ordinances of salvation, for yourselves, your living, and dead, is not first and foremost in your hearts, in your actions, and in everything you possess, go! Pay your debts, if you have any, and go in peace, and prove to God and all His Saints that you are what you profess to be, by your acts—a God of Gods—and know more than He that made you.

But if you are what you profess to be, do your duty—stay with the Saints, pay your Tithing, and be prompt in paying, as you are in feeding your family; and the Temple, of which we have now laid the South-east Corner Stone, will arise in beauty and grandeur, in a manner and time which you have not hitherto known or contemplated.

The Saints of these valleys have grown in riches, and abundance of the comforts of life, in a manner hitherto unparalleled on the page of history, and if they will do by their Heavenly Father as He has done by them, soon will this Temple be inclosed. But if you go in for a speculation with passersby, as many have hitherto done, you will not live to see the Topstone of this Temple laid; and your labors and toils for yourselves and friends, dead and alive, will be worse than though you had had no existence.

We dedicate this, the South-east Corner Stone of this Temple, to the Most High God. May it remain in peace till it has done its work, and until He who has inspired our hearts to fulfil the prophecies of His holy Prophets, that the House of the Lord should be reared in the "Tops of the Mountains," shall be satisfied, and say, "It is enough." And may every tongue, pen, and weapon, that may rise against this or any other Corner Stone of this building, feel the wrath and scourging of an incensed God! May sinners in Zion be afraid, and fearfulness surprise the hypocrite, from this hour. And may all who do not feel to say Amen, go speedily to that long night of rest from which no sleeper will awake, till roused by the trump of the Second Resurrection.

NATIVE AMERICAN RELIGIOUS
REACTION TO WHITE ENCROACHMENT

As soon as White Americans had the freedom to do so, they began moving westward, across the mountains and into the land the British had reserved for Native Americans. Conflict was inevitable, and among the first resisters were the Shawnee military leader Tecumseh and his brother Tenskwatawa, who in his role as a religious leader was commonly called **"The Prophet."** Tenskwatawa told, in some of the most dramatic language ever used in American history, of his own recovery from the white man's curse of alcohol and his dream of restoring the land of North America to his people.

The Shawnee and other Native Americans lost their battle with the United States and were commanded to move farther west, out of the way of white settlement. Among the tribes affected by this order were the Kickapoo, who for many years resisted the forced evacuation. A religious leader also rose among them, and the **Spiritual Vision Of Kanakuk** reflects the anguish of an oppressed people, their desperate reliance on the Great Spirit for salvation, and their realization that they were at the mercy of the United States.

4.18

Shawnee: Tenskwatawa,
"The Prophet" (1823)

"My brothers! My sisters! I have
    been given a great power. I have
    been told by Our Creator to use this
    power to save you.

My name is Tenskwatawa (He–
    Who–Opens–The–Door). I have

Source: http://www.wovoca.com/prophecy-shawnee-tecumseh-tenskwatawa.htm

been shown how to open the door
that has shut us out from happiness.

I died and went to the World
Above, and saw it. I had done every
sin against my people and myself.
You knew me! I was a sinner, I was
a drunkard! I had another name
then. That name is so smeared with
the filth of my old sins that my
mouth will not utter it, for my
mouth is now pure! Tenskwatawa
has never spoken a lie or an
obscenity, and never will. I have
come back cleansed. I am as we
were in the Beginning! In me is a
shinning power!

In the Beginning, we were full of
this shining power, strong because
we were pure. We moved silently
through the woods. With a silent
arrow we killed the animals and ate
pure meat. In silence the fish swam
in pure rivers, and we caught them
in silence and ate them. In silence
our corn and beans and squashes
grew from the earth, and those we
ate. We drank only clear water,
after the milk of our mother's
breast.

I have heard that lost silence. You
have not heard it because you have
not been dead. Up under the roof of
the sky, there is that pure silence!
In the beginning, our people broke
that beautiful silence only to pray
to the Great Good Spirit, or to
speak wisely in council, or to say
kind words to our children and our
elders, or to give the war cry when
we avenged wrongs.

Our Creator put us on this wide,
rich land, and told us we were free

to go where the game was, where
the soil was good for planting. That
was our state of true happiness. We
did not have to beg for anything.
Our Creator had taught us how to
find and make everything we
needed, from trees and plants and
animals and stone. We lived in
bark, and we wore only the skins of
animals. Our Creator taught us how
to use fire, in living, and in sacred
ceremonies. She taught us how to
heal with barks and roots, and how
to make sweet foods with berries
and fruits, with papaws and the
water of the maple tree. Our
Creator gave us tobacco, and said,
Send your prayers up to me on its
fragrant smoke. Our Creator taught
us how to enjoy loving our mates,
and gave us laws to live by, so that
we would not bother each other, but
help each other. Our Creator sang
to us in the wind and the running
water, in the bird songs, in
children's laughter, and taught us
music. And we listened, and our
stomachs were never dirty and
never troubled us.

Thus were we created. Thus we
lived for a long time, proud and
happy. We had never eaten pig
meat, nor tasted the poison called
whiskey, nor worn wool from
sheep, nor struck fire or dug earth
with steel, nor cooked in iron, nor
hunted and fought with loud guns,
nor ever had diseases which soured
our blood or rotted our organs. We
were pure, so we were strong and
happy.

But, beyond the Great Sunrise
Water, there lived a people who
had iron, and those dirty and

unnatural things, who seethed with
diseases, who fought to death over
the names of their gods! They had
so crowded and befouled their own
island that they fled from it,
because excrement and carrion
were up to their knees. They came
to our island. Our Singers had
warned us that a pale people would
come across the Great Water and
try to destroy us, but we forgot. We
did not know they were evil, so we
welcomed them and fed them. We
taught them much of what Our
Grandmother had taught us, how to
hunt, grow corn and tobacco, find
good things in the forest. They saw
how much room we had, and
wanted it. They brought iron and
pigs and wool and rum and disease.
They came farther and drove us
over the mountains. Then when
they had filled up and dirtied our
old lands by the sea, they looked
over the mountains and saw this
Middle Ground, and we are old
enough to remember when they
started rushing into it. We
remember our villages on fire every
year and the crops slashed every
fall and the children hungry every
winter. All this you know.

For many years we traded furs to
the English or the French, for wool
blankets and guns and iron things,
for steel awls and needles and axes,
for mirrors, for pretty things made
of beads and silver. And for liquor.
This was foolish, but we did not
know it. We shut our ears to the
Great Good Spirit. We did not want
to hear that we were being foolish.

But now those things of the white
men have corrupted us, and made

us weak and needful. Our men forgot how to hunt without noisy guns. Our women don't want to make fire without steel, or cook without iron, or sew without metal awls and needles, or fish without steel hooks. Some look in those mirrors all the time, and no longer teach their daughters to make leather or render bear oil. We learned to need the white men's goods, and so now a People who never had to beg for anything must beg for everything!

Some of our women married white men, and made half-breeds. Many of us now crave liquor. He whose filthy name I will not speak, he who was I before, was one of the worst of those drunkards. There are drunkards in almost every family. You know how bad this is.

And so you see what has happened to us. We were fools to take all these things that weakened us. We did not need them then, but we believe we need them now. We turned our backs on the old ways. Instead of thanking Weshemoneto for all we used to have, we turned to the white men and asked them for more. So now we depend upon the very people who destroy us! This is our weakness! Our corruption! Our Creator scolded me, "If you had lived the way I taught you, the white men could never have got you under their foot!"

And that is why Our Creator purified me and sent me down to you full of the shining power, to make you what you were before!

As you sit before me I will tell you
the many rules Our Creator gave
me for you. I will tell you how I
went to the World Above. When I
tell you of the punishments I saw,
they will terrify you! But listen,
those punishments will be upon you
unless you follow me through the
door that I am opening for you!

No red man must ever drink liquor,
or he will go and have the hot lead
poured in his mouth! You know I
have been a slave to liquor since
first I tasted it. But never again will
I take any! If ever you saw me taste
it again, you would know that what
I tell you is false!

This also Our Creator told me:
No red man shall take more than
one wife in the future. No red man
shall run after women. If he is
single, let him take a wife, and lie
only with her.

If any wife behaves badly, her
husband may whip her. But then
they shall look each other in the
face and laugh together, and have
no more ill will.

Any red woman who is living with
a white man must return to her
people, and must leave her children
with the husband, so that all nations
will be pure in their blood.

★ ★ ★

And now listen, for here is the most
important message I bring you:
The Great Good Spirit will call me
from time to time and teach me
more to help you. Our Creator told
me that all red men who refuse to

obey these laws are bad people, or
witches, and must be put to death.
Anyone who does not wish to live
in a way that pleases Weshemoneto
must want instead to please
Matchemoneto, and such a person
must be a witch. Witches should be
killed, for they divide the People
and weaken their spirit.

Hear me, my People. All red men
will soon know these messages I
have brought. They are hungry for
guidance from heaven. I will tell
the people I see, and you will tell
those you see. But I warn you: Our
Creator thundered and said that
anyone who reveals these laws to
any white men will die at once, and
never be shown the right road!

The Great Good Spirit will appoint
a place to be our holy town, and at
that place I will call all red men to
come and share this shining power.
For the People in all tribes are
corrupt and miserable! In that holy
town we will pray every morning
and every night for the earth to be
fruitful, and the game and fish to be
plentiful again. We will no longer
do the frolic dances that excite lust
and make us silly. Instead, the
Great Good Spirit will teach me the
old dances we did before the
corruption, and from these dances
we will receive strength and
happiness!

Now I, Tenskwatawa, He-Opens-
the-Door, will go and be alone for a
while, to learn more of what we
must do. I have told you everything
I know, but soon I will know more.
You will go and tell what you have
learned here, but tell it to no white

man, or to anyone who would tell it
to a white man. Get rid of cats and
long-eared dogs! Make good bows!
Put out your fires made with steel,
and kindle an everlasting fire by
wood on wood. Turn your backs on
the whiskey sellers and the traders,
and do not listen to the Jesus
missonaries! Look among
yourselves for witches, and note
who they are, and they will be
judged soon. How will you know
witches? I will tell you: They will
be doing commerce with
Americans, and going to their
treaty councils, against the
warnings of Our Creator.

4.19

Kickapoo: The Spiritual Vision of Kanakuk (1830s)

My father, the Great Spirit has placed us all on this earth, he has given to our nation a piece of land. Why do you want to take it away and give us so much trouble? We ought to live in peace and happiness among ourselves and with you. I have come down to see you and have all explained.

My father the Great Spirit appeared to me; he saw my heart was in sorrow about our land; he told me not to give up the business, but go to my Great Father and he would listen to me. My father, when I talked to the Great Spirit, I saw the chiefs holding the land fast. He told me the life of our children was short and that the earth would sink.

My father, you call all the redskins your children. When we have children, we treat them well. That is the reason I make this long talk to get you to take pity on us and let us remain where we are.

Source: J. Gordon Melton, *American Religions* (Santa Barbara, CA: ABC–CLIO, 2000), p. 23.

My father, I wish after my talk is over you would write to my Great Father, the president, that we have a desire to remain a little longer where we now are. I have explained to you that we have thrown all our badness away and keep the good path. I wish our Great Father could hear that. I will now talk to my Great Father, the president.

My Great Father, I don't know if you are the right chief, because I have heard some things go wrong. I wish you to reflect on our situation and let me know. I want to talk to you mildly and in peace, so that we may understand each other. When I saw the Great Spirit, he told me to throw all our bad acts away. We did so. Some of our chiefs said the land belonged to us, the Kickapoos, but this is not what the Great Spirit told me—the lands belongs to him. The Great Spirit told me that no people owned the land—that all was his, and not to forget to tell the white people that when we went into council. When I saw the Great Spirit, he told me, Mention all this to your Great Father. He will take pity on your situation and let you remain on the lands where you are for some years, when you will be able to get through all the bad places. . ., and where you will get to a clear piece of land where you will all live happy. When I talked to the Great Spirit, he told me to make my warriors throw their tomahawks in the bad place. I did so, and every night and morning I raise my hand to the Great Spirit and pray to him to give me success. I expect, my father, that God has put me in a good way—that our children shall see their sister and brothers and our woman will see their children. They will grow up and travel and see their totems The Great Spirit told me, "Our old men had totems. They were good and had many totems. Now you have scarcely any. If you follow my advice, you will soon have totems again." Say this to my Great Father for me.

My Father, every time we eat we raise our hands to the Great Spirit to give us success.

My father, we are sitting by each other here to tell the truth. If you write anything wrong, the Great Spirit will know it. If I say anything not true, the Great Spirit will hear it.

My father, you know how to write and can take down what is said for your satisfaction. I can not, all I do is through the Great Spirit for the benefit of my women and children.

My father, everything belongs to the Great Spirit. If he chooses to make the earth shake, or turn it over, all the skins, white and red, can not stop it. I have done. I trust to the Great Spirit.

RELIGION AND THE
ABOLITIONIST MOVEMENT

The survival and existence of slavery, the South's "peculiar institution," in "the land of the free" caused tensions that eventually led to the American Civil War. Religious leaders brought the issue to the national consciousness, and in their response to it they came down on both sides of the issue, depending largely on geographical positioning.

As early as 1818 the **"Extracts"** of the Presbyterian Church's annual meeting in Philadelphia called for an end to American slavery. Slaves who led the opposition to their condition often claimed divine inspiration, as did Nat Turner in the *Confession* he dictated to a white scribe after his unsuccessful uprising in 1831. Angelina Grimké, who went on to be an early feminist, made an *Appeal to the Christian Women of the South* to work to end the evil of slavery. On the other hand, Archbishop of South Carolina John England, founder of the first Catholic newspaper in the United States, defended it as a part of God's plan in a **Letter** to the U.S. Secretary of State.

Frederick Douglass, the second nationally known slave and after Nat Turner a man who escaped bondage and later purchased his freedom with the aid of the Quakers, often castigated churches, as he did in his **"The Church and Prejudice,"** for not doing more to free the slaves and for their racism. But he also regularly acknowledged, as in his **Address in London,** what a great part religion played in the abolitionist cause.

The issue caused most of the Protestant denominations to divide North and South. For example, from the **Northern Viewpoint,** it was folly to commission as foreign missionaries southern ministers who owned slaves. From the **Southern Viewpoint,** since slavery was legal, the ministers were guiltless. Southern Baptist William Buck argued in a sermon on *The Slavery Question* that slavery was a part of God's plan, and that only slave owners who abused their slaves were guilty of sinful behavior.

White abolitionists often cited religious principles and motivations for their efforts. Harriet Beecher Stowe, who wrote a **Letter to Frederick Douglass** asking for advice as she wrote her *Uncle Tom's Cabin,* galvanized public opinion against slavery by dramatizing the plight of the slave mother Eliza. William Lloyd Garrison, editor of the abolitionist paper *The Liberator*, used religious language in speeches such as his 1854 **"Address on Abolition"** to keep the issue of slavery before the American public for thirty years. Religion played a large part in bringing on the Civil War.

As late as 1861, when the war between the states was a foregone conclusion, the religious debate over slavery continued, even among the nation's Jewish congregations. In a sermon Rabbi M. J. Raphall delivered to his B'nai Jeshuran Congregation in New York City on January 4, **"The Bible View of Slavery,"** he criticized Reverend Henry Ward Beecher for calling slavery unbiblical. In his **"Reply to Dr. Raphall,"** Rabbi Daniel Einhorn scathingly denounced Jewish religious leaders who would defend the evil institution.

4.20

Presbyterian "Extracts" (1818)

T he General Assembly of the Presbyterian Church, having taken into consideration the subject of Slavery, think proper to make known their sentiments upon it to the churches and people under their care.

We consider the voluntary enslaving of one part of the human race by another, as a gross violation of the most precious and sacred rights of human nature; as utterly inconsistent with the law of God, which requires us to love our neighbour as ourselves; and as totally irreconcilable with the spirit and principles of the Gospel of Christ, which enjoin that, "all things whatsoever ye would that men should do to you, do ye even so to them." Slavery creates a paradox in the moral system—it exhibits rational, accountable, and immortal beings, in such circumstances as scarcely to leave them the power of moral action. It exhibits them as dependent on the will of others, whether they shall receive religious instruction; whether they shall know and worship the true God; whether they shall enjoy the ordinances of the Gospel; whether they shall perform the duties and cherish the endearments of husbands and wives, parents and children, neighbours and friends; whether they shall preserve their chastity and purity, or regard the dictates of justice and humanity. Such are some of the consequences of Slavery—consequences not imaginary—but which connect themselves with its very existence. The evils to which the slave is *always* exposed, often take place in fact, and in their very worst degree and form: and where all of them do not take place, as we rejoice to say that in many instances, through the influence of the principles of humanity and religion on the minds of masters, they do not—still the slave is deprived of his natural right, degraded as a human being, and exposed to the danger of passing into the hands of a master who may inflict upon him all the hardships and injuries which inhumanity and avarice may suggest.

Note: Footnotes have been deleted from this reading—ED.
Source: "Extracts," Philadelphia, 1818, pp. 28–33.

From this view of the consequences resulting from the practice into which christian people have most inconsistently fallen, of enslaving a portion of their *brethren* of mankind—for "God hath made of one blood all nations of men to dwell on the face of the earth"—it is manifestly the duty of all Christians who enjoy the light of the present day, when the inconsistency of slavery, both with the dictates of humanity and religion, has been demonstrated, and is generally seen and acknowledged, to use their honest, earnest, and unwearied endeavours, to correct the errors of former times, and as speedily as possible to efface this blot on our holy religion, and to obtain the complete abolition of slavery throughout christendom, and if possible throughout the world.

We rejoice that the church to which we belong commenced, as early as any other in this country, the good work of endeavouring to put an end to slavery, and that in the same work, many of its members have ever since been, and now are, among the most active, vigorous, and efficient labourers. We do, indeed, tenderly sympathize with those portions of our church and our country, where the evil of slavery has been entailed upon them; where a *great*, and *the most virtuous part* of the *community* abhor slavery, and wish its extermination, as sincerely as any others—but where the number of slaves, their ignorance, and their vicious habits generally, render an immediate and universal emancipation inconsistent, alike, with the safety and happiness of the master and the slave. With those who are thus circumstanced, we repeat that we tenderly sympathize.—At the same time, we earnestly exhort them to continue, and, if possible, to increase their exertions to effect a total abolition of slavery.—We exhort them to suffer no greater delay to take place in this most interesting concern, than a regard to the public welfare *truly* and *indispensably* demands.

4.21

Confession (1831)

NAT TURNER

"Seek ye the kingdom of Heaven and all things shall be added unto you." I reflected much on this passage, and prayed daily for light on this subject—As I was praying one day at my plough, the spirit spoke to me, saying "Seek ye the kingdom of heaven and all things shall be added unto you."

Source: *The Confessions of Nat Turner* [recorded by Thomas R. Gray] (Baltimore, MD: Lucas & Deaver, 1831).

Question: What do you mean by the Spirit.

Answer: The Spirit that spoke to the prophets in former days—and I was greatly astonished, and for two years prayed continually, whenever my duty would permit—and then again I had the same revelation, which fully confirmed me in the impression that I was ordained for some great purpose in the hands of the Almighty.

Several years rolled round, in which many events occurred to strengthen me in this my belief. At this time I reverted in my mind to the remarks made of me in my childhood, and the things that had been shown me—and as it had been said of me in my childhood by those by whom I had been taught to pray, both white and black, and in whom I had the greatest confidence, that I had too much sense to be raised, and it I was, I would never be of any use to any one as a slave. Now finding I had arrived to man's estate, and was a slave, and these revelations being made known to me, I began to direct my attention to this great object, to fulfil the purpose for which, by this time, I felt assured I was intended. Knowing the influence I had obtained over the minds of my fellow servants, (not by the means of conjuring and such like tricks—for to them I always spoke of such things with contempt) but by the communions of the Spirit whose revelations I often communicated to them, and they believed and said my wisdom came from God. I now began to prepare them for my purpose, by telling them something was about to happen that would terminate in fulfilling the great promise that had been made to me—About this time I was placed under an overseer, from whom I ran away—and after remaining in the woods thirty days, I returned, to the astonishment of the Negroes on the plantation, who thought I had made my escape to some other part of the country, as my father had done before. But the reason of my return was, that the Spirit appeared to me and said I had my wishes directed to the things of this world, and not to the kingdom of Heaven, and that I should return to the service of my earthly master—"For he who knoweth his Master's will, and doeth it not, shall be beaten with many stripes, and thus have I chastened you." And the negroes found fault, and murmured against me saying that if they had my sense they would not serve any master in the world. And about this time I had a vision—and I saw white spirits and black spirits engaged in battle, and the sun was darkened—the thunder rolled in the Heavens, and blood flowed in streams—and I heard a voice saying, "Such is your luck, such you are called to see, and let it come rough or smooth, you must surely bare it." I now withdrew myself as much as my situation would permit, from the intercourse of my fellow servants, for the avowed purpose of serving the Spirit more fully—and it appeared to me, and reminded me of the things it had already shown me, and that it would then reveal to me the knowledge of the elements, the revolution of the planets, the operation of tides, and changes of the seasons. After this revelation in the year 1825, and the knowledge of the elements being made known to me, I sought more than ever to obtain true holiness before the great day of judgment should appear, and then I began to receive the true knowledge of faith. And from the first steps of righteousness until the last, was I made perfect; and the Holy Ghost was with me, and said, "Behold me as I stand in the Heavens"—and I looked and saw the forms of men in different attitudes—and there were lights in the sky to which the children of darkness gave other names than what they really were—for they were the lights of the Saviour's hands, stretched forth from east to west, even as they were extended on the cross on Calvary for the redemption of sinners. And I wondered greatly at these miracles, and prayed to be informed of a certainty of the meaning thereof—and shortly afterwards, while laboring in the field, I discovered drops of blood on the corn as though it were dew from heaven—and I communicated it to many, both white and black, in the neighborhood—and I then found on the leaves in the woods hieroglyphic characters, and numbers, with the forms of men in different attitudes, portrayed in blood, and representing the figures I had seen before in the heavens. And now the Holy Ghost had revealed itself to me, and made plain the miracles it had shown me—For as the blood of Christ had been shed on this earth, and had ascended to heaven for the salvation of sinners, and was now returning to earth again in the form of dew—and as the leaves on the trees bore the impression of the figures I had seen in the heavens, it was plain to me that the Saviour was about to lay down the yoke he had borne for the sins of men, and the great day of judgment was at hand. About this time I told these things to a white man, (Etheldred T. Brantley) on whom it had a wonderful effect—and he ceased from his wickedness, and was attacked immediately with a cutaneous eruption, and blood oozed from the pores of his skin, and after praying and fasting nine days, he was healed, and the Spirit appeared to me again, and said, as the Saviour had been baptised so should we be also—and when the white people would not let us be baptised by the church, we went down into the water together, in the sight of many who reviled us, and were baptised by the Spirit—After this I rejoiced greatly, and gave thanks to God. And on the 12th of May, 1828, I heard a loud noise in the heavens, and the Spirit instantly appeared to me and said the Serpent was loosened, and Christ had laid down the yoke he had borne for the sins of men, and that I should take it on and fight against the Serpent, for the time was fast approaching when the first should be last and the last should be first.

> **Question:** Do you not find yourself mistaken now?
> **Answer:** Was not Christ crucified?

And by signs in the heavens that it would make known to me when I should commence the great work—and until the first sign appeared, I should conceal it from the knowledge of men—And on the appearance of the sign, (the eclipse of the sun last February) I should arise and prepare myself, and slay my enemies with their own weapons. And immediately on the sign appearing in the heavens, the seal was removed from my lips, and I communicated the great work laid out for me to do, to four in whom I had the greatest confidence (Henry, Hark, Nelson, and Sam)—it was intended by us to have begun the work of death on the 4th July last—Many were the plans formed and rejected by us, and it affected my mind to such a degree, that I fell sick, and the time passed without our coming to any determination how to commence—Still forming new schemes and rejecting them, when the sign appeared again, which determined me not to wait longer.

4.22

Appeal to the Christian Women of the South (1836)

ANGELINA GRIMKÉ

Respected Friends,

It is because I feel a deep and tender interest in your present and eternal welfare that I am willing thus publicly to address you. Some of you have loved me as a relative, and some have felt bound to me in Christian sympathy, and Gospel fellowship; and even when compelled by a strong sense of duty, to break those outward bonds of union which bound us together as members of the same community, and members of the same religious denomination, you were generous enough to give me credit, for sincerity as a Christian, though you believed I had been most strangely deceived. I thanked you then for your kindness, and I ask you *now,* for the sake of former confidence, and former friendship, to read the following pages in the spirit of calm investigation and fervent prayer. . . . Solomon says, "Faithful are the *wounds* of a friend." I do not believe the time has yet come when *Christian women* "will not endure sound doctrine," even on the subject of Slavery, if it is spoken to them in tenderness and love, therefore I now address *you.*

To all of you then, known or unknown, relatives or strangers (for you are all *one* in Christ), I would speak. I have felt for you at this time, when unwelcome light is pouring in upon the world on the subject of slavery; light which even Christians would exclude, if they could, from our country, or at any rate from the southern portion of it, saying, as its rays strike the rock bound coasts of New England and scatter their warmth and radiance over her hills and valleys, and from thence travel onward over the Palisades of the Hudson, and down the soft flowing waters of the Delaware and gild the waves of the Potomac, "hitherto shalt thou come and no further," I know that even professors of His name who

Source: Angelina E. Grimké, *Appeal to the Christian Women of the South* (New York: Arno Press, 1969 [from 1836 pub]) pp. 1–3.

has been emphatically called the "Light of the world" would, if they could, build a wall of adamant around the Southern States whose top might reach unto heaven, in order to shut out the light which is bounding from mountain to mountain and from the hills to the plains and valleys beneath, through the vast extent of our Northern States. But believe me, when I tell you, their attempts will be as utterly fruitless as were the efforts of the builders of Babel; and why? Because moral, like natural light, is so extremely subtle in its nature as to overleap all human barriers, and laugh at the puny efforts of man to control it. All the excuses and palliations of this system must inevitably be swept away, just as other "refuges of lies" have been, by the irresistible torrent of a rectified public opinion. "The *supporters* of the slave system," says Jonathan Dymond in his admirable work on the Principles of Morality, "will *hereafter* be regarded with the *same* public feeling, as he who was an advocate for the slave trade *now is*." It will be, and that very soon, clearly perceived and fully acknowledged by all the virtuous and the candid, that in *principle* it is as sinful to hold a human being in bondage who has been born in Carolina, as one who has been born in Africa. All that sophistry of argument which has been employed to prove, that although it is sinful to send to Africa to procure men and women as slaves, who have never been in slavery, that still, it is not sinful to keep those in bondage who have come down by inheritance, will be utterly overthrown. We must come back to the good old doctrine of our forefathers who declared to the world, "This self evident truth that all men are created equal, and that they have certain *inalienable* rights among which are life, *liberty*, and the pursuit of happiness." It is even a greater absurdity to suppose a man can be legally born a slave under *our free Republican* Government, than under the petty despotisms of barbarian Africa. If then, we have no right to enslave an African, surely we can have none to enslave an American; if it is a self evident truth that *all* men, every where and of every color are born equal, and have an *inalienable right to liberty*, then it is equally true that *no* man can be born a slave, and no man can ever *rightfully* be reduced to *involuntary* bondage and held as a slave, however fair may be the claim of his master or mistress through wills and title-deeds.

4.23

Letter to the U.S. Secretary
of State (1840)

ARCHBISHOP JOHN ENGLAND

Respecting domestic slavery, we distinguish it from the compulsory slavery of an invaded people in its several degrees. I shall touch upon the varieties separately. The first is "voluntary"; that which exists amongst us is not of that description, though I know very many instances where I have found it to be so; but I regard not the cases of individuals, I look to the class. In examining the lawfulness of voluntary slavery, we shall test a principle against which abolitionists contend. They assert, generally, that slavery is contrary to the natural law. The soundness of their position will be tried by inquiring into the lawfulness of holding in slavery a person, who has voluntarily sold himself. Our theological authors lay down a principle, that man in his natural state is master of his own liberty, and may dispose of it as he sees proper; as in the case of a Hebrew (*Exodus* xxi. 5), who preferred remaining with his wife and children as a slave, to going into that freedom to which he had a right; and as in the case of the Hebrew (*Levit* xxv. 47), who, by reason of his poverty, would sell himself to a sojourner or to a stranger. Life and its preservation are more valuable than liberty, and hence when Esther addresses Assuerus (vii. 4), she lays down the principle very plainly and naturally. "For we are sold, I and my people, to be destroyed and slain, and to perish. But if we had been sold for bondsmen and bondswomen, I had held my tongue." The natural law then does not prohibit a man from bartering his liberty and his services to save his life, to provide for his sustenance, to secure other enjoyments which he prefers to that freedom and to that right to his own labour, which he gives in exchange for life and protection. Nor does the natural law prohibit another man from procuring and bestowing upon him those advantages, in return for which he has agreed to bind himself to that other man's service, provided he takes no unjust advantage in the bargain. Thus a state of voluntary slavery is not prohibited by the law of nature; that is, a state in which one man has the dominion over the labour and the ingenuity of another to the end of his life, and consequently in which that labour and ingenuity are the property of him who has the dominion, and are justly applicable to the benefit of the master

Source: *The Works of the Right Reverend John England* (Cleveland, OH: Arthur Clark Co., 1908), V, 195.

and not of the slave. All our theologians have from the earliest epoch sustained, that though in a state of pure nature all men are equal, yet the natural law does not prohibit one man from having dominion over the useful action of another as his slave; provided this dominion be obtained by a just title. That one man may voluntarily give this title to another, is plain from the principle exhibited, and from the divine sanction to which I have alluded.

In one point of view, indeed, we may say that the natural law does not establish slavery, but it does not forbid it—and I doubt how far any of the advocates of abolition would consent to take up for refutation, the following passage of St. Thomas of Aquin,—

"The common possession of all things is said to be of the natural law, because the distinction of possessions and slavery were not introduced by nature, but by the reason of man, for the benefit of human life: and thus the law of nature is not changed by their introduction, but an addition is made thereto."

As well may the wealthy merchant then assert, that it is against the law of nature that one man should possess a larger share of the common fund belonging to the human family for his exclusive benefit, as that it is against the law of nature for one man to be the slave of another. The existence of slavery is considered by our theologians to be as little incompatible with the natural law as is the existence of property. The sole question will be in each case, whether the title on which the dominion is claimed be valid.

I know many slaves who would not accept their freedom; I know some who have refused it; and though our domestic slavery must upon the whole be regarded as involuntary, still the exceptions are not so few as are imagined by strangers.

It may be asked why any one should prefer slavery to freedom. I know many instances where the advantages to the individual are very great; and so, sir, I am confident do you, yet I am not in love with the existence of slavery. I would never aid in establishing it where it did not exist. . . .

The situation of a slave, under a human master, insures to him food, raiment, and dwelling, together with a variety of little comforts; it relieves him from the apprehensions of neglect in sickness, from all solicitude for the support of his family, and in return, all that is required is fidelity and moderate labour. I do not deny that slavery has its evils, but the above are no despicable benefits. Hence I have known many freedmen who regretted their manumission.

4.24

The Church
and Prejudice (1841)

FREDERICK DOUGLASS

A t the South I was a member of the Methodist Church. When I came north, I thought one Sunday I would attend communion, at one of the churches of my denomination, in the town I was staying. The white people gathered round the altar, the blacks clustered by the door. After the good minister had served out the bread and wine to one portion of those near him, he said, "These may withdraw, and others come forward"; thus he proceeded till all the white members had been served. Then he took a long breath, and looking out towards the door, exclaimed, "Come up, colored friends, come up! for you know God is no respecter of persons!" I haven't been there to see the sacraments taken since.

At New Bedford, where I live, there was a great revival of religion not long ago—many were converted and "received" as they said, "into the kingdom of heaven." But it seems, the kingdom of heaven is like a net; at least so it was according to the practice of these pious Christians; and when the net was drawn ashore, they had to set down and cull out the fish. Well, it happened now that some of the fish had rather black scales; so these were sorted out and packed by themselves. But among those who experienced religion at this time was a colored girl; she was baptized in the same water as the rest; so she thought she might sit at the Lord's table and partake of the same sacramental elements with the others. The deacon handed round the cup, and when he came to the black girl, he could not pass her, for there was the minister looking right at him, and as he was a kind of abolitionist, the deacon was rather afraid of giving him offense; so he handed the girl the cup, and she tasted. Now it so happened that next to her sat a young lady who had been converted at the same time, baptized in the same water, and put her trust in the same blessed Saviour; yet when the cup containing the precious blood which had been shed for all, came to her, she rose in disdain, and walked out of the church. Such was the religion she had experienced!

Another young lady fell into a trance. When she awoke, she declared she had been to heaven. Her friends were all anxious to know what and whom she had seen there; so she told the whole story. But there was one good old lady

Source: Philip Foner (ed.), *Life & Writings of Frederick Douglass* (New York: International Publishers, 1950), I: 102–105.

whose curiosity went beyond that of all the others—and she inquired of the girl that had the vision, if she saw any black folks in heaven? After some hesitation, the reply was, *"Oh! I didn't go into the kitchen!"*

Thus you see, my hearers, this prejudice goes even into the church of God. And there are those who carry it so far that it is disagreeable to them even to think of going to heaven, if colored people are going there too. And whence comes it? The grand cause is slavery; but there are others less prominent; one of them is the way in which children in this part of the country are instructed to regard the blacks.

"Yes!" exclaimed an old gentleman, interrupting him— "when they behave wrong, they are told, 'black man come catch you.'"

Yet people in general will say they like colored men as well as any other, but in their proper place! They assign us that place; they don't let us do it for ourselves, nor will they allow us a voice in the decision. They will not allow that we have a head to think, and a heart to feel, and a soul to aspire. They treat us not as men, but as dogs—they cry "Stu-boy!" and expect us to run and do their bidding. That's the way we are liked. You degrade us, and then ask why we are degraded—you shut our mouths, and then ask why we don't speak—you close our colleges and seminaries against us, and then ask why we don't know more.

But all this prejudice sinks into insignificance in my mind, when compared with the enormous iniquity of the system which is its cause—the system that sold my four sisters and my brothers into bondage—and which calls in its priests to defend it even from the Bible! The slaveholding ministers preach up the divine right of the slaveholders to property in their fellow-men. The southern preachers say to the poor slave, "Oh! if you wish to be happy in time, happy in eternity, you must be obedient to your masters; their interest is yours. God made one portion of men to do the working, and another to do the thinking; how good God is! Now, you have no trouble or anxiety; but ah! you can't imagine how perplexing it is to your masters and mistresses to have so much thinking to do in your behalf! You cannot appreciate your blessings; you know not how happy a thing it is for you, that you were born of that portion of the human family which has the working, instead of the thinking to do! Oh! how grateful and obedient you ought to be to your masters! How beautiful are the arrangements of Providence! Look at your hard, horny hands—see how nicely they are adapted to the labor you have to perform! Look at our delicate fingers, so exactly fitted for our station, and see how manifest it is that God designed us to be His thinkers, and you the workers—Oh! the wisdom of God!"—I used to attend a Methodist church, in which my master was a class leader; he would talk most sanctimoniously about the dear Redeemer, who was sent "to preach deliverance to the captives, and set at liberty them that are bruised"—he could pray at morning, pray at noon, and pray at night; yet he could lash up my poor cousin by his two thumbs, and inflict stripes and blows upon his bare back, till the blood streamed to the ground! all the time quoting scripture, for his authority, and appealing to that passage of the Holy Bible which says, "He that knoweth his master's will, and doeth it not, shall be beaten with many stripes!" Such was the amount of this good Methodist's piety.

4.25

Address in London (1846)

FREDERICK DOUGLASS

There are many of these crimes which if the white man did not commit, he would be regarded as a scoundrel and a coward. In South Maryland, there is a law to this effect:—that if a slave shall strike his master, he may be hanged, his head severed from his body, his body quartered, and his head and quarters set up in the most prominent place in the neighbourhood. (Sensation.) If a coloured woman, in the defence of her own virtue, in defence of her own person, should shield herself from the brutal attacks of her tyrannical master, or make the slightest resistance, she may be killed on the spot. (Loud cries of "Shame!") No law whatever will bring the guilty man to justice for the crime.

But you will ask me, can these things be possible in a land professing Christianity? Yes, they are so; and this is not the worst. No, a darker feature is yet to be presented than the mere existence of these facts. I have to inform you that the religion of the southern states, at this time, is the great supporter, the greater sanctioner of the bloody atrocities to which I have referred. (Deep sensation). While America is printing tracts and Bibles; sending missionaries abroad to convert the heathen; expending her money in various ways for the promotion of the Gospel in foreign lands, the slave not only lies forgotten—uncared for, but is trampled under foot by the very churches of the land. What have we in America? Why we have slavery made part of the religion of the land. Yes, the pulpit there stands up as the great defender of this cursed *institution,* as it is called. Ministers of religion come forward, and torture the hallowed pages of inspired wisdom to sanction the bloody deed. (Loud cries of "Shame!") They stand forth as the foremost, the strongest defenders of this "institution." As a proof of this, I need not do more than state the general fact that slavery has existed under the droppings of the sanctuary of the south, for the last 200 years, and there has not been any war between the *religion* and the *slavery* of the south.

Whips, chains, gags, and thumb-screws have all lain under the droppings of the sanctuary, and instead of rusting from off the limbs of the bondman, these droppings have served to preserve them in all their strength. Instead of preaching the Gospel against this tyranny, rebuke, and wrong, ministers of religion have sought, by all and every means, to throw in the background whatever in the Bible could be construed into opposition to slavery, and to bring forward that which they could torture into its support. (Cries of "Shame!") This

Source: London: *The Frederick Douglass Papers* (New Haven, CT: Yale University Press, 1979) pp. 281–283.

I conceive to be the darkest feature of slavery, and the most difficult to attack, because it is identified with religion, and exposes those who denounce it to the charge of infidelity. Yes, those with whom I have been labouring, namely, the old organization Anti-Slavery Society of America, have been again and again stigmatized as infidels, and for what reason? Why, solely in consequence of the faithfulness of their attacks upon the slaveholding religion of the southern states, and the northern religion that sympathizes with it. (Hear, hear.)

I have found it difficult to speak on this matter without persons coming forward and saying, "Douglass, are you not afraid of injuring the cause of Christ? You do not desire to do so, we know; but are you not undermining religion?" This has been said to me again and again, even since I came to this country, but I cannot be induced to leave off these exposures. (Loud cheers.)

I love the religion of our blessed Saviour; I love that religion that comes from above, in the "wisdom of God, which is first pure, then peaceable, gentle, and easy to be entreated, full of mercy and good fruits, without partiality and without hypocrisy." I love that religion that sends its votaries to bind up the wounds of him that has fallen among thieves. I love that religion that makes it the duty of its disciples to visit the fatherless and widow in their affliction. I love that religion that is based upon the glorious principle, of love to God and love to man (cheers), which makes its followers do unto others as they themselves would be done by. If you demand liberty to yourself, it says, grant it to your neighbours. If you claim a right to think for yourselves, it says, allow your neighbours the same right. If you claim to act for yourselves, it says, allow your neighbours the same right. It is because I love this religion that I hate the slave-holding, the woman-whipping, the mind-darkening, the soul-destroying religion that exists in the southern states of America. (Immense cheering.) It is because I regard the one as good, and pure, and holy, that I cannot but regard the other as bad, corrupt, and wicked. Loving the one I must hate the other, holding to the one I must reject the other, and I, therefore, proclaim myself an infidel to the slaveholding religion of America. (Reiterated cheers.)

Why, as I said in another place, to a smaller audience the other day, in answer to the question, "Mr. Douglass, are there not Methodist churches, Baptist churches, Congregational churches, Episcopal churches, Roman Catholic churches, Presbyterian churches in the United States, and in the southern states of America, and do they not have revivals of religion, accessions to their ranks from day to day, and will you tell me that these men are not followers of the meek and lowly Saviour?" Most unhesitatingly I do. Revivals in religion, and revivals in the slave trade, go hand in hand together. (Cheers.) The church and the slave prison stand next to each other, the groans and cries of the heartbroken slave are often drowned in the pious devotions of his religious master. (Hear, hear.) The church-going bell and the auctioneer's bell chime in with each other; the pulpit and the auctioneer's block stand in the same neighbourhood; while the blood-stained gold goes to support the pulpit, the pulpit covers the infernal business with the garb of Christianity. We have men sold to build churches, women sold to support missionaries, and babies sold to buy Bibles and communion services for the churches.

4.26

Baptists Divide

NORTHERN VIEWPOINT (1845)

The history of the proceedings, which led to the separation of the South from the General Convention, may be given in few words. In November, 1844, "The Baptist State Convention of Alabama" adopted a preamble and certain resolutions, which they forwarded to the Acting Board, at Boston, by one of which resolutions the Board understood the Convention of Alabama as intending to demand of the Board distinctly to avow, whether they would or would not appoint a slaveholder a missionary. To this demand, after expressing regret that it had been made, as unnecessary, and stating that in thirty years in which the Board had existed, no slaveholder, to their knowledge, had applied to be appointed a missionary, and that such an event as a slaveholder's taking slaves with him, could not, for reasons expressed, possibly occur, the Board frankly and plainly answered in the following words: "If, however, any one should offer himself as a missionary, having slaves, and insist on retaining them as his property, we could not appoint him. One thing is certain, we never can be a party to any arrangement which would imply approbation of slavery."

The publication of this answer of the Board was immediately followed by the manifestation of excited feeling on the part of the South. Agitation and discussion were kept up till May, in the present year, when a Southern Baptist Convention was held at Augusta, in Georgia. This Convention resolved to withdraw from the General Convention, and to form a separate organization for supporting missions. . . .

How was it possible for the Board to act otherwise than they did act? They were asked, not by strangers, but by persons directly interested in the question, and to whom the Board stood in the fiduciary relation of agents or trustees, whether they would appoint a slaveholder a missionary. The question was in the most general form, and of course, importing a slaveholder under the common and ordinary circumstances of slaveholding. The Board could not say it was a matter of doubt or uncertainty in their minds how they should act in such case. They had a clear and decided opinion. The only alternative was, to express, or conceal their opinion. If any man thinks that the members of the Board, as upright men and Christians, might have concealed their opinions on this subject, with a view to obtain money from the South, which might not be obtained if their opinions were expressed, we have no argument to offer to

Source: Northern Viewpoint: *Christian Review* (40). 481–482, 496–497; Southern Viewpoint: *Christian Review* 41: 114–115ff.

that man, and must decline all discussion with him. His standard of morals, and of upright and honorable conduct must be such as to preclude the possibility of his appreciating the motives which actuated the Board. The members of the Board, at the time of accepting their appointment, had no reason to believe that, with their known views and feelings on the subject of slavery, the South would expect that they could, according to their sense of duty, appoint slave-holders as missionaries. The opinions of the members of the Board on the subject of slavery being well known, the course of action which would natu-rally follow, under the influence of those opinions, was properly supposed to be understood and acquiesced in by all interested, and it could not be neces-sary to make, uncalled for, any particular declaration as to that course of action. It was enough that the general opinions and feelings of the Board were well understood, if nothing more specific was desired. But when the Board is dis-tinctly asked if they would appoint a slaveholder a missionary, and a distinct avowal of the opinion of the Board on this subject is desired by a party in interest, it seems to us clear, beyond doubt, that the Board could do nothing but the precise thing they in fact did.

SOUTHERN VIEWPOINT (1845)

. . . If a slaveholder cannot be appointed a missionary, lest the appointment should imply, on the part of the Board, approbation of slavery, neither can he be appointed an agent, or to any office, for the same reason. Nor does the con-sequence stop here. If a slaveholder is unfit to be appointed to office, then those persons who own no slaves, but countenance slavery, are connected with slaveholding churches, and derive their authority to preach the gospel from them, are equally unfit; and these two classes embrace all the ministers in the South. We now ask—we put it to the common sense and candor of every man, Is it fair, is it equal—that the South shall participate in all the burdens of the Convention, and be excluded from all its privileges? Our lot has been cast in a land where slavery prevails. We did not originate it. Many of us lament most sincerely its existence. We did not choose the place of our birth. Many of us had slavery entailed on us by laws which we did not enact, and which we could not, even if it were politic to do so, repeal. We must, in many cases, retain possession of our slaves, or disregard the laws of the land, and the princi-ples of humanity and religion. We claim for ourselves the right of acting in regard to this delicate and embarrassing subject, according to the dictates of our own consciences, without foreign control or interference. And we ask again; Is it just that we should be summarily excluded, by the mere action of the Board, from all participation in the work of sending the gospel to the hea-then, save that of contributing money to the treasury? . . .

The separation has taken place. Posterity will judge of the matter, and lay the responsibility where it ought to be laid. At any rate, we must all soon appear at a tribunal where no sophistry can deceive, and no partiality pervert judgment. In view of this solemn reckoning, the best of us have great cause to exclaim, "Lord, enter not into judgment with thy servants." Henceforward, let there be no strife between the North and South. We are brethren. Our interest is one and indivisible. Entertaining similar views of the kingdom of Christ, we should vie with each other in labors and sacrifices to extend and perpetuate it.

4.27

The Slavery Question (1849)

WILLIAM BUCK

Now we maintain that God appoved of, and by solemn covenant and compact with Abraham, ratified and confirmed the relation of master and slave which subsisted between him and those servants, bought with his money and born in his house, forever; and in this position we are amply sustained, not only by the covenant itself, but by the testimony of Abraham's chief servant, who testified to Laban and Bethuel, that the "LORD *had given to his master man-servants and maid-servants.*"

It seems to us, therefore, that it would be the height of impiety to challenge the Divine procedure in this transaction, or to institute a doubt that the relation subsisting between Abraham and his servants was not perfectly consistent with the moral perfections of the Deity.

★ ★ ★

Slavery, as thus defined, was incorporated into the Mosaic law, by divine authority, and recognised by our Saviour and his Apostles: and we now proceed to show by a brief examination of the Mosaic law, and the history of the times, that the slavery of the Scriptures was conceived in divine benevolence, and intended, mainly, to secure the happiness of the slave—to preserve life—to afford protection and to furnish the means of moral culture, to those who would otherwise have been destitute of one or all of these great blessings. Slavery was never intended by God to minister to the cupidity and luxury of the master without an adequate, and even more than an adequate return of

Source: William C. Buck, *The Slavery Question* (Louisville, KY: Harney, Hughes, & Hughes, 1849) pp. 9, 10, 22–23.

good to the slave. *Its principle design was, benevolence to the poor and defenceless, and religious instruction to Idoliters, etc.:* and this we hope to moke appear.

★ ★ ★

Slavery in this country, as defined by a certain class of laws, and as carried out in the practice of thousands of slaveholders, is not the slavery of the Bible and cannot be defended by an appeal to its laws or examples, as we have briefly stated in another place. That kind of slavery which makes no provision for the improvement and moral training of the slave, which disregards the marriage relation and the common laws of humanity and justice, *is a perversion of slavery,* and has no more affinity to the slavery of the Scriptures than socialism or concubinage has to the marriage relation as recognised by the law of God. Such a system of slavery may justly be denounced as *sinful and only sinful;* and we doubt not that thousands are heaping to themselves wrath against the day of wrath, by such a system of slaveholding. But we no more condemn slavery in the abstract, because wicked men have thus perverted and abused it than we condemn the marriage relation, because wicked men have contemned and violated its solemn and holy obligations.—As we have elsewhere said, we feel confident that there are multiplied thousands of slaveholders in this country, who hold their slaves in the fear of God, and whose conduct in relation to them is regulated by the law of Christ, remembering that they have a master in Heaven, to whom they must render an account. Thousands make sacrifices and sustain discomforts for the good of their slaves as purely disinterested as any act of Christian benevolence can be, and certainly to as great an amount as in any other department of benevolent effort. Hence the injustice and the impiety of the sweeping condemnation of Southern slaveholders by the Abolitionists of the North.

While therefore we are constrained, from the testimony of the Bible, to believe that slavery as therein warranted and provided for was benevolently provided for the benefit of the poor, still in consequence of the extensive perversion, of it in this country, and its consequent evil influences upon the moral and social interests of the white population, we can but regard it as, at this time, a social and political evil which calls for appropriate remedies and correctives, of which we shall speak hereafter.

We now pass on to enquire into its effects upon the African race, and in order to do this we must contrast the condition of the native Africans, both at the time that slavery was introduced into this country and at the present time, with the present and prospective condition of the African race in this country. Of their condition in Africa, socially, civilly and morally, we have heretofore spoken, and as we aim to be as concise as possible, we beg the reader to refer to what we there said and to contrast their condition, as there described, with what, from his own observation, he would esteem the condition of the blacks, as a whole, in this country, to be at the present time; and notwithstanding the cruelty and injustice which has been practised towards them, in too many instances, both in the slave and free States, still every honest and candid man must, unhesitatingly, admit, to say nothing of the future, that their condition has been vastly improved by being brought as slaves to this country. They are in a great measure civilized. They have acquired an extensive practical knowledge of agriculture and the mechanical arts; and many of them have made considerable advances in literary and scientific acquirements. Besides all this, and still better, many thousands of them have become joyfully and savingly interested in the redemption that is in Christ Jesus. Compared with the natives of Africa, the Africans in this country are a civilised and christianised people; and are rapidly approaching that state of intellectual improvement and moral refinement which will fit them for *self-government and national independence.*

But we must not limit our estimates of the effects of American slavery to what has been developed in reference to the African race in this country, either in the past or the present. We have sufficient data, we think, upon which to found calculations for the future, and to hope for and expect results, in favor of that race, both to those in this country and in Africa, still more beneficial and universal than have as yet appeared. We hope—*ah, we believe,* that God is preparing, by means of African slavery in this country, *a nation* of civilised and christianized men and women, to be transplanted to Africa, by whom to redeem that land from barbarism, anarchy and blood, and to shed upon it the light and the blessedness of the glorious Gospel of Christ. To us this is a subject of so much interest that we are desirous to present our views upon it in as connected a form as possible, and as this number is already as long as it should be, we shall defer what we have to say further upon this subject to our next.

4.28

Letter to Frederick Douglass (1851)

HARRIET BEECHER STOWE

Brunswick, July 9, 1851.

Frederick Douglass, Esq.:

Sir,—You may perhaps have noticed in your editorial readings a series of articles that I am furnishing for the "Era" under the title of "Uncle Tom's Cabin, or Life among the Lowly."

In the course of my story the scene will fall upon a cotton plantation. I am very desirous, therefore, to gain information from one who has been an actual laborer on one, and it occurred to me that in the circle of your acquaintance there might be one who would be able to communicate to me some such information as I desire. I have before me an able paper written by a Southern planter, in which the details and *modus operandi* are given from his point of sight. I am anxious to have something more from another standpoint. I wish to be able to make a picture that shall be graphic and true to nature in its details. Such a person as Henry Bibb, if in the country, might give me just the kind of information I desire. You may possibly know of some other person. I will subjoin to this letter a list of questions, which in that case you will do me a favor by inclosing to the individual, with the request that he will at earliest convenience answer them.

For some few weeks past I have received your paper through the mail, and have read it with great interest, and desire to return my acknowledgments for it. It will be a pleasure to me at some time when less occupied to contribute something to its columns. I have noticed with regret your sentiments on two subjects,—the church and African colonization, . . . with the more regret because I think you have a considerable share of reason for your feelings on both these subjects; but I would willingly, if I could, modify your views on both points.

In the first place you say the church is "pro-slavery." There is a sense in which this may be true. The American church of all denominations, taken as a body, comprises the best and most conscientious people in the country. I do not say it comprises none but these, or that none such are found out of it, but

Source: *Life & Letters of Harriet Beecher Stowe* (ed. Annie Fields), (Boston: Houghton-Mifflin, 1898).

only if a census were taken of the purest and most high-principled men and women of the country, the majority of them would be found to be professors of religion in some of the various Christian denominations. This fact has given to the church great weight in this country,—the general and predominant spirit of intelligence and probity and piety of its majority has given it that degree of weight that it has the power to decide the great moral questions of the day. Whatever it unitedly and decidedly sets itself against as moral evil it can put down. In this sense the church is responsible for the sin of slavery. Dr. Barnes has beautifully and briefly expressed this on the last page of his work on slavery, when he says: "Not all the force out of the church could sustain slavery an hour if it were not sustained in it." It then appears that the church has the power to put an end to this evil and does not do it. In this sense she may be said to be pro-slavery. But the church has the same power over intemperance, and Sabbath-breaking, and sin of all kinds. There is not a doubt that if the moral power of the church were brought up to the New Testament standpoint it is sufficient to put an end to all these as well as to slavery. But I would ask you, Would you consider it a fair representation of the Christian church in this country to say that it is pro-intemperance, pro-Sabbath-breaking, and pro everything that it might put down if it were in a higher state of moral feeling? If you should make a list of all the abolitionists of the country, I think that you would find a majority of them in the church,—certainly some of the most influential and efficient ones are ministers.

I am a minister's daughter, and a minister's wife, and I have had six brothers in the ministry (one is in heaven); I certainly ought to know something of the feelings of ministers on this subject. I was a child in 1820 when the Missouri question was agitated, and one of the strongest and deepest impressions on my mind was that made by my father's sermons and prayers, and the anguish of his soul for the poor slave at that time. I remember his preaching drawing tears down the hardest faces of the old farmers in his congregation.

I will remember his prayers morning and evening in the family for "poor, oppressed, bleeding Africa," that the time of her deliverance might come; prayers offered with strong crying and tears, and which indelibly impressed my heart and made me what I am from my very soul, the enemy of all slavery. Every brother I have has been in his sphere a leading anti-slavery man. One of them was to the last the bosom friend and counselor of Lovejoy. As for myself and husband, we have for the last seventeen years lived on the border of a slave State, and we have never shrunk from the fugitives, and we have helped them with all we had to give. I have received the children of liberated slaves into a family school, and taught them with my own children, and it has been the influence that we found in the church and by the altar that has made us do all this. Gather up all the sermons that have been published on this offensive and unchristian Fugitive Slave Law, and you will find that those against it are numerically more than those in its favor, and yet some of the strongest opponents have not published their sermons. Out of thirteen ministers who meet with my husband weekly for discussion of moral subjects, only three are found who will acknowledge or obey this law in any shape.

After all, my brother, the strength and hope of your oppressed race does lie in the church,—in hearts united to Him of whom it is said, "He shall spare the souls of the needy, and precious shall their blood be in his sight." Everything is against you, but Jesus Christ is for you, and He has not forgotten his church, misguided and erring though it be. I have looked all the field over with despairing eyes; I see no hope but in Him. This movement must and will become a purely religious one. The light will spread in churches, the tone of feeling will rise, Christians North and South will give up all connection with, and take up their testimony against, slavery, and thus the work will be done.

4.29

Uncle Tom's Cabin (1853)

HARRIET BEECHER STOWE

An hour before sunset, she entered the village of T—, by the Ohio river, weary and foot-sore, but still strong in heart. Her first glance was at the river, which lay, like Jordan, between her and the Canaan of liberty on the other side.

It was now early spring, and the river was swollen and turbulent; great cakes of floating ice were swinging heavily to and fro in the turbid waters. Owing to the peculiar form of the shore on the Kentucky side, the land bending far out into the water, the ice had been lodged and detained in great quantities, and the narrow channel which swept round the bend was full of ice, piled one cake over another, thus forming a temporary barrier to the descending ice, which lodged, and formed a great undulating raft, filling up the whole river, and extending almost to the Kentucky shore.

Eliza stood, for a moment contemplating this unfavorable aspect of things, which she saw at once must prevent the usual ferry-boat from running, and then turned into a small public house on the bank, to make a few inquiries.

The hostess, who was busy in various fizzing and stewing operations over the fire, preparatory to the evening meal, stopped, with a fork in her hand, as Eliza's sweet and plaintive voice arrested her.

"What is it?" she said.

"Isn't there any ferry or boat, that takes people over to B—, now?" she said.

Source: Harriet Beecher Stowe, *Uncle Tom's Cabin* (London: Ingram, Cooke, 1853).

Harriet Beecher Stowe, author of *Uncle Tom's Cabin*.

"No, indeed!" said the woman, "the boats has stopped running."

Eliza's look of dismay and disappointment struck the woman, and she said, inquiringly,

"May be you're wanting to get over?—anybody sick? Ye seem mighty anxious?"

"I've got a child that's very dangerous," said Eliza. "I never heard of it till last night, and I've walked quite a piece to-day, in hopes to get to the ferry."

"Well, now, that's onlucky," said the woman, whose motherly sympathies were much aroused; "I'm re'lly consarned for ye. Solomon!" she called, from the window, towards a small back building. A man, in leather apron and very dirty hands, appeared at the door.

"I say, Sol," said the woman, "is that ar man going to tote them bar'ls over to-night?"

"He said he should try, if 't was any way prudent," said the man.

"There's a man a piece down here, that's going over with some truck this evening, if he durs' to; he'll be in here to supper to-night, so you'd better set down and wait. That's a sweet little fellow," added the woman, offering him a cake.

But the child, wholly exhausted, cried with weariness.

"Poor fellow! he isn't used to walking, and I've hurried him on so," said Eliza.

"Well, take him into this room," said the woman, opening into a small bed-room, where stood a comfortable bed. Eliza laid the weary boy upon it, and held his hands in hers till he was fast asleep. For her there was no rest. As a fire in her bones, the thought of the pursuer urged her on; and she gazed with longing eyes on the sullen, surging waters that lay between her and liberty.

★ ★ ★

It was about three-quarters of an hour after Eliza had laid her child to sleep in the village tavern that the party came riding into the same place. Eliza was standing by the window, looking out in another direction, when Sam's quick eye caught a glimpse of her. Haley and Andy were two yards behind. At this crisis, Sam contrived to have his hat blown off, and uttered a loud and charac-teristic ejaculation, which startled her at once; she drew suddenly back; the whole train swept by the window, round to the front door.

A thousand lives seemed to be concentrated in that one moment to Eliza. Her room opened by a side door to the river. She caught her child, and sprang down the steps towards it. The trader caught a full glimpse of her, just as she was disappearing down the bank; and throwing himself from his horse, and calling loudly on Sam and Andy, he was after her like a hound after a deer. In that dizzy moment her feet to her scarce seemed to touch the ground, and a moment brought her to the water's edge. Right on behind they came; and, nerved with strength such as God gives only to the desperate, with one wild cry and flying leap, she vaulted sheer over the turbid current by the shore, and on to the raft of ice beyond. It was a desperate leap—impossible to anything but madness and despair; and Haley, Sam, and Andy, instinctively cried out, and lifted up their hands, as she did it.

The huge green fragment of ice on which she alighted pitched and creaked as her weight came on it, but she staid there not a moment. With wild cries and desperate energy she leaped to another and still another cake;—stumbling—leaping—slipping—springing upwards again! Her shoes are gone—her stockings cut from her feet—while blood marked every step; but she saw nothing, felt nothing, till dimly, as in a dream, she saw the Ohio side, and a man helping her up the bank.

"Yer a brave gal, now, whoever ye ar!" said the man, with an oath.

Eliza recognized the voice and face of a man who owned a farm not far from her old home.

"O, Mr. Symmes!—save me—do save me—do hide me!" said Eliza.

"Why, what's this?" said the man. "Why, if 'tan't Shelby's gal!"

"My child!—this boy!—he'd sold him! There is his Mas'r," said she, point-ing to the Kentucky shore. "O, Mr. Symmes, you've got a little boy!"

"So I have," said the man, as he roughly, but kindly, drew her up the steep bank. "Besides, you're a right brave gal. I like grit, wherever I see it."

When they had gained the top of the bank, the man paused.

"I'd be glad to do something for ye," said he; "but then there's nowhar I could take ye. The best I can do is tell ye to go *thar*," said he, pointing to a large white house which stood by itself, off the main street of the village. "Go thar; they're kind folks. Thar's no kind o' danger but they'll help you,—they're up to all that sort o' thing."

"The Lord bless you!" said Eliza, earnestly.

"No 'casion, no 'casion in the world," said the man. "What I've done's of no 'count."

"And, oh, surely, sir, you won't tell any one!"

"Go to thunder, gal! What do you take a feller for? In course not," said the man. "Come, now, go along like a likely, sensible gal, as you are. You've arnt your liberty, and you shall have it, for all me."

The woman folded her child to her bosom, and walked firmly and swiftly away. The man stood and looked after her.

"Shelby, now, mebee won't think this yer the most neighborly thing in the world; but what's a feller to do? If he catches one of my gals in the same fix, he's welcome to pay back. Somehow I never could see no kind o' critter a strivin' and pantin', and trying to clar theirselves, with the dogs arter 'em, and go agin 'em. Besides, I don't see no kind of 'casion for me to be hunter and catcher for other folks, neither."

So spoke this poor, heathenish Kentuckian, who had not been instructed in his constitutional relations, and consequently was betrayed into acting in a sort of Christianized manner, which, if he had been better situated and more enlightened, he would not have been left to do.

Haley had stood a perfectly amazed spectator of the scene, till Eliza had disappeared up the bank, when he turned a blank, inquiring look on Sam and Andy.

"That ar was a tolerable fair stroke of business," said Sam.

"The gal's got seven devils in her, I believe!" said Haley. "How like a wild-cat she jumped!"

"Wal, now," said Sam, scratching his head, "I hope Mas'r'll 'scuse us tryin' dat ar road. Don't think I feel spry enough for dat ar, no way!" and Sam gave a hoarse chuckle.

"*You* laugh!" said the trader, with a growl.

"Lord bless you, Mas'r, I couldn't help it, now," said Sam, giving way to the long pent-up delight of his soul. "She looked so curi's, a leapin' and springin'—ice a crackin'—and only to hear her,—plump! ker chunk! ker splash! Spring! Lord! How she goes it!" and Sam and Andy laughed till the tears rolled down their cheeks.

"I'll make ye laugh t'other side yer mouths!" said the trader, laying about their heads with his riding-whip.

Both ducked, and ran shouting up the bank, and were on their horses before he was up.

"Good-evening, Mas'r!" said Sam, with much gravity. "I berry much 'spect Missis be anxious 'bout Jerry. Mas'r Haley won't want us no longer. Missis wouldn't hear of our ridin' the critters over Lizy's bridge to-night;" and, with a facetious poke into Andy's ribs, he started off, followed by the latter, at full speed,—their shouts of laughter coming faintly on the wind.

4.30

Address on Abolition (1854)

WILLIAM LLOYD GARRISON

Let me define my positions, and at the same time challenge anyone to show wherein they are untenable.

I am a believer in that portion of the Declaration of American Independence in which it is set forth, as among self-evident truths, "that all men are created equal; that they are endowed by their Creator with certain inalienable rights; that among these are life, liberty, and the pursuit of happiness." Hence, I am an abolitionist. Hence, I cannot but regard oppression in every form—and most of all, that which turns a man into a thing—with indignation and abhorrence. Not to cherish these feelings would be recreancy to principle. They who desire me to be dumb on the subject of slavery, unless I will open my mouth in its defense, ask me to give the lie to my professions, to degrade my manhood, and to stain my soul. I will not be a liar, a poltroon, or a hypocrite, to accommodate any party, to gratify any sect, to escape any odium or peril, to save any interest, to preserve any institution, or to promote any object. Convince me that one man may rightfully make another man his slave, and I will no longer subscribe to the Declaration of Independence. Convince me that liberty is not the inalienable birthright of every human being, of whatever complexion or clime, and I will give that instrument to the consuming fire. I do not know how to espouse freedom and slavery together. I do not know how to worship God and Mammon at the same time. If other men choose to go upon all fours, I choose to stand erect, as God designed every man to stand. If, practically falsifying its heaven-attested principles, this nation denounces me for refusing to imitate its example, then, adhering all the more tenaciously to those principles, I will not cease to rebuke it for its guilty inconsistency. Numerically, the contest may be an unequal one, for the time being; but the author of liberty and the source of justice, the adorable God, is more than multitudinous, and he will defend the right. My crime is that I will not go with the multitude to do evil. My singularity is that when I say that freedom is of God and slavery is of the devil, I mean just what I say. My fanaticism is that I insist on the American people abolishing slavery or ceasing to prate of the rights of man . . .

The abolitionism which I advocate is as absolute as the law of God, and as unyielding as his throne. It admits of no compromise. Every slave is a stolen man; every slaveholder is a man stealer. By no precedent, no example, no law,

Source: William Lloyd Garrison, *The Liberator*, found at http://users.aol.com

no compact, no purchase, no bequest, no inheritance, no combination of circumstances, is slaveholding right or justifiable. While a slave remains in his fetters, the land must have no rest. Whatever sanctions his doom must be
pronounced accursed. The law that makes him a chattel is to be trampled
underfoot; the compact that is formed at his expense, and cemented with his
blood, is null and void; the church that consents to his enslavement is horribly
atheistical; the religion that receives to its communion the enslaver is the
embodiment of all criminality. Such, at least, is the verdict of my own soul, on
the supposition that I am to be the slave; that my wife is to be sold from me for
the vilest purposes; that my children are to be torn from my arms, and disposed
of to the highest bidder, like sheep in the market. And who am I but a man?
What right have I to be free, that another man cannot prove himself to possess
by nature? Who or what are my wife and children, that they should not be
herded with four-footed beasts, as well as others thus sacredly related? . . .

If the slaves are not men; if they do not possess human instincts, passions,
faculties, and powers; if they are below accountability, and devoid of reason; if
for them there is no hope of immortality, no God, no heaven, no hell; if, in
short, they are what the slave code declares them to be, rightly "deemed, sold,
taken, reputed and adjudged in law to be chattels personal in the hands of their
owners and possessors, and their executors, administrators and assigns, to all
intents, constructions, and purposes whatsoever"; then, undeniably, I am mad,
and can no longer discriminate between a man and a beast. But, in that case,
away with the horrible incongruity of giving them oral instruction, of teaching them the catechism, of recognizing them as suitably qualified to be members of Christian churches, of extending to them the ordinance of baptism, and
admitting them to the communion table, and enumerating many of them as
belonging to the household of faith! Let them be no more included in our
religious sympathies or denominational statistics than are the dogs in our
streets, the swine in our pens, or the utensils in our dwellings. It is right to
own, to buy, to sell, to inherit, to breed, and to control them, in the most
absolute sense. All constitutions and laws which forbid their possession ought
to be so far modified or repealed as to concede the right.

But, if they are men; if they are to run the same career of immortality with
ourselves; if the same law of God is over them as over all others; if they have
souls to be saved or lost; if Jesus included them among those for whom he laid
down his life; if Christ is within many of them "the hope of glory"; then, when
I claim for them all that we claim for ourselves, because we are created in the
image of God, I am guilty of no extravagance, but am bound, by every principle of honor, by all the claims of human nature, by obedience to Almighty
God, to "remember them that are in bonds as bound with them," and to
demand their immediate and unconditional emancipation . . .

These are solemn times. It is not a struggle for national salvation; for the
nation, as such, seems doomed beyond recovery. The reason why the South
rules, and the North falls prostrate in servile terror, is simply this: with the
South, the preservation of slavery is paramount to all other considerations—
above party success, denominational unity, pecuniary interest, legal integrity,

and constitutional obligation. With the North, the preservation of the Union is placed above all other things—above honor, justice, freedom, integrity of soul, the Decalogue and the Golden Rule—the infinite God himself. All these she is ready to discard for the Union. Her devotion to it is the latest and the most terrible form of idolatry. She has given to the slave power a carte blanche, to be filled as it may dictate—and if, at any time, she grows restive under the yoke, and shrinks back aghast at the new atrocity contemplated, it is only necessary for that power to crack the whip of disunion over her head, as it has done again and again, and she will cower and obey like a plantation slave—for has she not sworn that she will sacrifice everything in heaven and on earth, rather than the Union?

What then is to be done? Friends of the slave, the question is not whether by our efforts we can abolish slavery, speedily or remotely—for duty is ours, the result is with God; but whether we will go with the multitude to do evil, sell our birthright for a mess of pottage, cease to cry aloud and spare not, and remain in Babylon when the command of God is "Come out of her, my people, that ye be not partakers of her sins, and that ye receive not of her plagues." Let us stand in our lot, "and having done all, to stand." At least, a remnant shall be saved. Living or dying, defeated or victorious, be it ours to exclaim, "No compromise with slavery! Liberty for each, for all, forever! Man above all institutions! The supremacy of God over the whole earth!"

4.31

The Bible View
of Slavery (1861)

RABBI M.J. RAPHALL

Having thus, on the authority of the sacred Scripture, traced slavery back to the remotest period, I next request your attention to the question, "Is slaveholding condemned as a sin in sacred Scripture?" How this question can at all arise in the mind of any man that has received a religious education, and is acquainted with the history of the Bible, is a phenomenon I cannot

Source: http://www.jewish-history.com

explain to myself, and which fifty years ago no man dreamed of. But we live in times when we must not be surprised at anything. Last Sunday an eminent preacher is reported to have declared from the pulpit, "The Old Testament requirements served their purpose during the physical and social development of mankind, and were rendered no longer necessary now when we were to be guided by the superior doctrines of the New in the moral instruction of the race." I had always thought that in the "moral instruction of the race," the requirements of Jewish Scriptures and Christian Scriptures were identically the same; that to abstain from murder, theft, adultery, that "to do justice, to love mercy, and to walk humbly with G[o]d," were "requirements" equally imperative in the one course of instruction as in the other. But it appears I was mistaken. "We have altered all that now," says this eminent divine, in happy imitation of Molière's physician, whose new theory removed the heart from the left side of the human body to the right. But when I remember that the "now" refers to a period of which you all, though no very aged men, witnessed the rise; when, moreover, I remember that the "WE" the reverend preacher speaks of, is limited to a few impulsive declaimers, gifted with great zeal, but little knowledge; more eloquent than learned; better able to excite our passions than to satisfy our reason; and when, lastly, I remember the scorn with which sacred Scripture (Deut. xxxii. 18) speaks of "newfangled notions, lately sprung up, which your fathers esteemed not;" when I consider all this, I think you and I had rather continue to take our "requirements for moral instruction" from Moses and the Prophets than from the eloquent preacher of Brooklyn [Henry Ward Beecher]. But as that reverend gentleman takes a lead among those who most loudly and most vehemently denounce slaveholding as a sin, I wished to convince myself whether he had any Scripture warranty for so doing; and whether such denunciation was one of those "requirements for moral instruction" advanced by the New Testament. I have accordingly examined the various books of Christian Scripture, and find that they afford the reverend gentleman and his compeers no authority whatever for his and their declamations. The New Testament nowhere, directly or indirectly, condemns slaveholding, which, indeed, is proved by the universal practice of all Christian nations during many centuries. Receiving slavery as one of the conditions of society, the New Testament nowhere interferes with or contradicts the slave code of Moses; it even preserves a letter written by one of the most eminent Christian teachers to a slaveowner on sending back to him his runaway slave. And when we next refer to the history and "requirements" of our own sacred Scriptures, we find that on the most solemn occasion therein recorded, when G[o]d gave the Ten Commandments on Mount Sinai—

> There where His finger scorched, the tablet shone;
> There where His shadow on his people shone His glory, shrouded in its garb of fire,
> Himself no eye might see and not expire.

Even on that most solemn and most holy occasion, slaveholding is not only recognized and sanctioned as an integral part of the social structure, when it is commanded that the Sabbath of the L[o]rd is to bring rest to *Avdecha ve'Amasecha,* "Thy male slave and thy female slave" (Exod. xx. 10; Deut. v. 14). But the property in slaves is placed under the same protection as any other species of lawful property, when it is said, "Thou shalt not covet thy neighbor's house, or his field, or his male slave, or his female slave, or his ox, or his ass, or aught that belongeth to thy neighbor" (Ibid. xx. 17; v.21). That the male slave and the female slave here spoken of do not designate the Hebrew bondman, but the heathen slave, I shall presently show you. That the Ten Commandments are the word of G[o]d, and as such, of the very highest authority, is acknowledged by Christians as well as by Jews. I would therefore ask the reverend gentleman of Brooklyn and his compeers—How dare you, in the face of the sanction and protection afforded to slave property in the Ten Commandments—how dare you denounce slaveholding as a sin? When you remember that Abraham, Isaac, Jacob, Job—the men with whom the Almighty conversed, with whose names he emphatically connects his own most holy name, and to whom He vouchsafed to give the character of "perfect, upright, fearing G[o]d and eschewing evil" (Job i. 8)—that all these men were slave-holders, does it not strike you that you are guilty of something very little short of blasphemy? And if you answer me, "Oh, in their time slaveholding was lawful, but now it has become a sin," I in my turn ask you, "When and by what authority you draw the line? Tell us the precise time when slaveholding ceased to be permitted, and became sinful?" When we remember the mischief which this inventing a new sin, not known in the Bible, is causing; how it has exasperated the feelings of the South, and alarmed the conscience of the North, to a degree that men who should be brothers are on the point of embruing their hands in each other's blood, are we not entitled to ask the reverend preacher of Brooklyn, "What right have you to insult and exasperate thousands of G[o]d-fearing, law-abiding citizens, whose moral worth and patriotism, whose purity of conscience and of life, are fully equal to your own? What right have you to place yonder grey-headed philanthropist on a level with a murderer, or yonder mother of a family on a line with an adulteress, or yonder honorable and honest man in one rank with a thief, and all this solely because they exercise a right which your own fathers and progenitors, during many generations, held and exercised without reproach or compunction. You profess to frame your "moral instruction of the race" according to the "requirements" of the New Testament—but tell us where and by whom it was said, "Whosoever shall say to his neighbor, *rakah* (worthless sinner), shall be in danger of the council; but whosoever shall say, thou fool, shall be in danger of the judgement." My friends, I find, and I am sorry to find, that I am delivering a pro-slavery discourse. I am no friend to slavery in the abstract, and still less friendly to the practical working of slavery. But I stand here as a teacher in Israel; not to place before you my own feelings and opinions, but to propound to you the word of G[o]d, the Bible view of slavery. With a due sense of my responsibility, I must state to you the truth and nothing but the truth, however unpalatable or unpopular that truth may be.

4.32

Reply to Dr. Raphall (1861)

DAVID EINHORN

At the moment that I am writing this down, January 9th, the thunder-cloud still hangs heavily over our head, and hides the future of our beloved land in dense mist. Perhaps some of you in our midst may consider it unjustifiable that at such a time I have thus unequivocally expressed my conviction in the foregoing regarding the law of Moses about slavery. The Jew has special cause to be conservative, and he is doubly and triply so in a country which grants him all the spiritual and material privileges he can wish for, he wants peace at every price and trembles for the preservation of the Union like a true son for the life of a dangerously sick mother. From the depth of my soul, I share your patriotic sentiments, and cherish no more fervent wish than that God may soon grant us the deeply yearned-for peace. Still no matter which political party we may belong to the sanctity of our Law must never be drawn into political controversy, nor disgraced in the interest of this or that political opinion, as it is in this instance, and with such publicity besides, and in the holy place! The spotless morality of the Mosaic principles is our pride and our fame, and our weapon since thousands of years. This weapon we cannot forfeit without pressing a mighty sword into the hands of our foes. This pride and renown, the only one which we possess, we will not and dare not allow ourselves to be robbed of. This would be unscrupulous, prove the greatest triumph of our adversaries and our own *destruction*, and would be paying too dearly for the fleeting, wavering favor of the moment. Would it not then be justly said, as in fact it has already been done, in consequence of the incident referred to: *Such* are the Jews! Where they are oppressed, they boast of the humanity of their religion; but where they are free, their Rabbis declare slavery to have been sanctioned by God, even mentioning the holy act of the Revelation on Sinai in defense of it. Whereas Christian clergymen even in the Southern States, and in presence of the nation's Representatives in part, though admonishing to toleration openly disapprove of it and in part *apologize* for it, owing to existing conditions!

I am no politician and do not meddle in politics. But to proclaim slavery in the name of Judaism to be a God-sanctioned institution the Jewish-religious

Source: http://www.jewish-history.com

press must raise objections to this, if it does not want itself and Judaism branded forever. Had a Christian clergyman in Europe delivered the Raphall address the Jewish-orthodox as well as Jewish-reform press would have been set going to call the wrath of heaven and earth upon such falsehoods, to denounce such disgrace, and . . . And are we in America to ignore this mischief done by a *Jewish* preacher? Only such Jews, who prize the dollar more highly than their God and their religion, can demand or even approve of this!

EINHORN

CHAPTER 5

✳

Crisis and Rebirth

Religion and The American Civil War

Observers of American religious life have noticed that alongside the various denominations to which Americans give their loyalties stands what some call a "civil religion" and others call a "political religion." Patterned after the Jewish and Christian traditions, this other American religion gives meaning to the American historical experience and bridges the social gaps created by competing denominations. Catholics, Protestants, and Jews are included in this other American congregation, and they can worship there without feeling they are compromising their particular faiths.

In the American political religion, the late eighteenth century struggle for independence was the American Exodus, the escape from Egyptian (colonial) Bondage and entry into the Promised Land of nationhood. George Washington was the American Moses. According to this theory, the American Civil War was the great national Golgotha, the crisis that almost destroyed the republic; and its resolution, the national Resurrection from the Dead, was its transition from the Old to the New Testament. In this schema, Abraham Lincoln was the American Christ.

It is no wonder that religious groups and their spokespeople played such a large part in this great national upheaval. It is no wonder that the war broke religious groups apart. It is no wonder that Americans saw the conflict in a religious light and used religious language to explain it. It is no wonder that

215

both African American and white Americans saw it as the scene of national redemption or that President Lincoln was portrayed as the Redeemer who gave his life, appropriately on Easter weekend, for the sins of the nation.

RELIGIOUS REACTIONS TO AND JUSTIFICATION FOR THE WAR

Just as religious groups and their spokespeople manned the debate over slavery, which led to the Civil War, so did they man the choirs that cheered on the troops of both sides. Catholic, Protestant, and Jewish leaders strongly supported both the Union and the Confederate causes, depending largely on where they lived.

Thanksgiving sermons by Southern Presbyterian Benjamin Morgan Palmer in New Orleans, **"The South: Her Peril and Duty,"** and by Northern Congregationalist Henry Ward Beecher in Brooklyn, **"Modes and Duties of Emancipation,"** demonstrate the strong religious emotions the war evoked. So does the exchange between Rabbi Samuel Isaacs in his **Editorials** for the *Jewish Messenger* and the **Response** of his anonymous but verbose Jewish critic from Louisiana.

Not only clergymen but also poets and musicians used religious language to support both sides of the war, as we see in Julia Ward Howe's **"Battle Hymn of the Republic,"** George Miles's **"God Save the South,"** and E. K. Blunt's **"The Southern Cross."**

5.1

The South: Her Peril and Duty (1860)

BENJAMIN MORGAN PALMER

Need I pause to show how this system of servitude underlies and supports our material interests; that our wealth consists in our lands and in the serfs who till them; that from the nature of our products they can only be cultivated by labor which must be controlled in order to be certain; that any other than a tropical race must faint and wither beneath a tropical sun? Need I pause to show how this system is interwoven with our entire social fabric; that these slaves form parts of our households, even as our children; and that, too, through a relationship recognized and sanctioned in the Scriptures of God even as the other? Must I pause to show how it has fashioned our modes of life, and determined all our habits of thought and feeling, and moulded the very type of our civilization? How then can the hand of violence be laid upon it without involving our existence? The so-called free States of this country are working out the social problem under conditions peculiar to themselves. These conditions are sufficiently hard, and their success is too uncertain to excite in us the least jealousy of their lot. With a teeming population, which the soil cannot support; with their wealth depending upon arts, created by artificial wants; with an external friction between the grades of their society; with their labor and their capital grinding against each other like the upper and nether millstones; with labor cheapened and displaced by new mechanical inventions, bursting more asunder the bonds of brotherhood— amid these intricate perils we have ever given them our sympathy and our prayers, and have never sought to weaken the foundations of their social order. God grant them complete success in the solution of all their perplexities! . . .

This duty is bound upon us again as the constituted guardians of the slaves themselves. Our lot is not more implicated in theirs, than their lot in ours; in our mutual relations we survive or perish together. . . . My servant, whether born in my house or bought with my money, stands to me in the relation of a child. Though providentially owing me service, which, providentially, I am bound to exact, he is, nevertheless, my brother and my friend, and I am to him a guardian and a father. He leans upon me for protection, for counsel, and for blessing; and so long as the relation continues, no power but the power of

Source: *The Life & Letters of Benjamin Morgan Palmer* (Richmond, 1906), found at
http://www.brandywinesources.com

Almighty God shall come between him and me. Were there no argument but this, it binds upon us the providential duty of preserving the relation that we may save him from a doom worse than death.

It is a duty which we owe, further, to the civilized world. It is a remarkable fact that during these thirty years of unceasing warfare against slavery, and while a lying spirit has inflamed the world against us, that world has grown more and more dependent upon it for sustenance and wealth. Every tyro knows that all branches of industry fall back upon this soil. We must come, every one of us, to the bosom of this great mother for nourishment. In the happy partnership which has grown up in providence between the tribes of this confederacy, our industry has been concentrated upon agriculture. To the North we have cheerfully resigned all the profits arising from manufacture and commerce. Those profits they have, for the most part, fairly earned, and we have never begrudged them. . . .

[I]n this great struggle, we defend the cause of God and religion. The abolition spirit is undeniably atheistic. . . . Among a people so generally religious as the American, a disguise must be worn; but it is the same old threadbare disguise of the advocacy of human rights. . . . [T]he decree has gone forth which strikes at God by striking at all subordination and law. Availing itself of the morbid and misdirected sympathies of men, it has entrapped weak consciences in the meshes of its treachery; and now, at last, has seated its high priest upon the throne, clad in the black garments of discord and schism, so symbolic of its ends. Under this suspicious cry of reform, it demands that every evil shall be corrected, or society become a wreck—the sun must be stricken from the heavens, if a spot is found upon his disk. The Most High, knowing his own power, which is infinite, and his own wisdom, which is unfathomable, can afford to be patient. But these self-constituted reformers must quicken the activity of Jehovah or compel his abdication. In their furious haste, they trample upon obligations sacred as any which can bind the conscience. It is time to reproduce the obsolete idea that Providence must govern man, and not that man shall control Providence. In the imperfect state of human society, it pleases God to allow evils which check others that are greater. As in the physical world, objects are moved forward, not by a single force, but by the composition of forces; so in his moral administration, there are checks and balances whose intimate relations are comprehended only by himself. But what reck they of this—these fierce zealots who undertake to drive the chariot of the sun? Working out the single and false idea which rides them like a nightmare, they dash athwart the spheres, utterly disregarding the delicate mechanism of Providence, which moves on, wheels within wheels, with pivots and balances and springs, which the great Designer alone can control. This spirit of atheism, which knows no God who tolerates evil, no Bible which sanctions law, and no conscience that can be bound by oaths and covenants, has selected us for its victims, and slavery for its issue. Its banner-cry rings out already upon the air— "liberty, equality, fraternity," which simply interpreted mean bondage, confiscation and massacre.

5.2

Modes and Duties
of Emancipation (1861)

HENRY WARD BEECHER

S ince we must accept this war, with all its undeniable evils, it is a matter for thanksgiving that the citizens and their lawful government of these United States can appeal to the Judge of the universe and to all right-minded men, to bear witness that it is not a war waged in the interest of any base passion, but, truly and religiously, in the defense of the highest interests ever committed to national keeping. It is not, on our side, a war of passion; nor of avarice; nor of anger; nor of revenge; nor of fear and jealousy.

★ ★ ★

We are contending, not for that part of the Constitution which came in any way from Roman law, and expressed justice as it had been developed in the iron-hearted realm; but for that part which Christianity gave us, and which has been working forth into laws and customs for eighteen hundred years. The principle now in conflict is that very one which gives unity to history: it is that golden thread that leads us through the dark maze of nearly two-thousand years, and connects us with the immortal Head of the Church,—the principle of man's rights based upon the divinity of his origin. Man from God, God a Father, and the race brothers, all alike standing on one great platform of justice and love,—the principle herein expressed has been the foundation of the struggle of eighteen hundred years; and it has been embodied (thanks to Puritan influence) in our Constitution. And this the exponent of Southern views plainly declares to be the point of offense in our government. He says, in unmeasured terms, and with impious boldness, that it is to put down that principle that the South are up in arms to-day.

Is it no cause for thanksgiving, then, that since we must war, God has called us to battle on ground so high, for ends so noble, in a cause so pure, and for results so universal? For this is not a battle for ourselves alone. Every great deed nobly done is done for all mankind. A battle on the Potomac for our Constitution, as a document of liberty, is the world's battle. We are fighting,

Source: Henry Ward Beecher, *Patriotic Addresses 1850–1885* (New York: Fords, Howard, & Halbert, 1889) pp. 323, 327–329.

not merely for our liberty, but for those ideas that are the seeds and strength of liberty throughout the earth. There is not a man that feels the chain, there is not a man whose neck is stiff under the yoke, whether that man be serf, yeoman, or slave, who has not an interest in the conflict that we are set, in the providence of God, to wage against this monstrous doctrine of iniquity. There is honey in that lion!

II. It is matter of thanksgiving that we have not sought this war, but, by a long and magnanimous course, have endured shame, and political loss, and disturbance the most serious, rather than peril the Union. Indeed, I am bound to say that, so strong was the national feeling with us, and so weak with Southern men, that we made an idol of that which they trod under foot with contempt; and like idolaters we threw ourselves down at the expense of our very self-respect before our idol of the Union. I do not mean that it would have been wrong to have taken the initiative in a cause so sacred as that which impels this conflict; but if, where the end is right and the cause is sacred, it can also be shown that there has been patience, honest and long-continued effort to preserve the right by peaceful methods,—by reasoning and by moral appeal,—and that that most desperate of all remedies, war, has been forced upon us (not sought, nor wished, but accepted reluctantly) by the overt act of the rebellious States, then this patience and forbearance will give an added luster to our cause.

I make these remarks out of respect to the Christian Public Sentiment of Nations. Contiguity is raising up a new element of power on the globe; and we do not hesitate to pay a just respect to the opinions and expectations which Christian men and philanthropists of other lands have entertained. We stand up boldly before the earnest peace men, the kind advisers, the yearning mediators, yea, and before the body of Christ,—his Church on earth,—and declare that this war, which we could not avert without giving up all that Christian civilization has set us to guard and transmit, cannot be abandoned without betraying every principle of justice, rectitude, and liberty. We do not fear search and trial before the tribunal of the Christian world! In the end, those who should have given sympathy, but have given, instead, chilling advice and ignorant rebuke, shall confess their mistake, and own our fealty to God, to government, and to mankind. When it would have swelled our sails, there was no breath of applause or sympathy. When the gale is no longer needed, and our victorious voyage is ended, we shall have incense and admiration enough! But, meanwhile, God has called us to war upon a plane higher than feet ever trod before. Though we did not seek it, but prayed against it, and with long endurance sought to avoid and avert it, and reluctantly accepted it; now that it has come; it is infinite satisfaction to know that we can stand acquitted before the Christianity of the globe in such a conflict as this. There is honey in that lion!

5.3

Jewish Editorials (1860–1861)

RABBI SAMUEL MAYER ISAACS

EDITORIAL (1860)

The Union . . . has been the source of happiness for our ancestors and ourselves. Under the protection of the freedom guaranteed us by the Constitution, we have lived in the enjoyment of full and perfect equality with our fellow citizens. We are enabled to worship the Supreme Being according to the dictates of conscience, we can maintain the position to which our abilities entitle us, without our religious opinions being an impediment to advancement. This Republic was the first to recognize our claims to absolute equality, with men of whatever religious denomination. Here we can sit "each under his vine and fig tree, with none to make him afraid."

"STAND BY THE FLAG!" (1861)

It is almost a work of supererogation for us to call upon our readers to be loyal to the Union, which protects them. It is needless for us to say anything to induce them to proclaim their devotion to the land in which they live. But we desire our voice, too, to be heard at this time, joining in the hearty and spontaneous shout ascending from the whole American people, to stand by the stars and stripes!

Already we hear of many of our young friends taking up arms in defense of their country, pledging themselves to assist in maintaining inviolate its integrity, and ready to respond, if need be, with their lives, to the call of the constituted authorities, in the cause of law and order.

The time is past for forbearance and temporizing. We are now to act, and sure we are, that those whom these words may reach, will not be backward in realizing the duty that is incumbent upon them—to rally as one man for the Union and the Constitution. The Union—which binds together, by so many sacred ties, millions of free men—which extends its hearty invitation to the oppressed of all nations, to come and be sheltered beneath its protecting wings—shall it be severed, destroyed, or even impaired? Shall those, whom we once called our brethren, be permitted to overthrow the fabric reared by

Source: 1860: *Jewish Messenger,* December 28, 1860; 1861: Jewish Messenger, April 26, 1861.

the noble patriots of the revolution, and cemented with their blood? And the Constitution—guaranteeing to all, the free exercise of their religious opinions—extending to all, liberty, justice, and equality—the pride of Americans, the admiration of the world—shall that Constitution be subverted, and anarchy usurp the place of a sound, safe and stable government, deriving its authority from the consent of the American People?

The voice of millions yet unborn, cried out, "Forbid it, Heaven!" The voice of the American people declares in tones not to be misunderstood: "It shall not be!"

Then stand by the Flag! What death can be as glorious as that of the patriot, surrendering his life in defense of his country—pouring forth his blood on the battlefield—to live forever in the hearts of a grateful people. Whether native or foreign born, Gentile or Israelite, stand by it, and you are doing your duty, and acting well your part on the side of liberty and justice! We know full well that our young men, who have left their homes to respond to the call of their country, will, on their return, render a good account of themselves. We have no fears for their bravery and patriotism. Our prayers are with them. God speed them on the work which they have volunteered to perform!

And if they fall—if, fighting in defense of that flag, they meet a glorious and honorable death, their last moments will be cheered by the consciousness that they have done their duty, and grateful America will not forget her sons, who have yielded up their spirit in her behalf.

And as for us, who do not accompany them on their noble journey, our duty too, is plain. We are to pray to Heaven that He may restore them soon again to our midst, after having assisted in vindicating the honor and integrity of the flag they have sworn to defend; and we are to pledge ourselves to assume for them, should they fall in their country's cause, the obligation of supporting those whom their departure leaves unprotected. Such is our duty. Let them, and all of us, renew our solemn oath that, whatever may betide, we will be true to the Union and the Constitution, and

STAND BY THE FLAG!

5.4

Southern Jewish Response (1861)

Whereas, we received the *Jewish Messenger* of the 26th of April, a paper published in New York, in which an appeal has been made to all, whether native or foreign born, Christian or Israelite. An article headed "Stand by the Flag!" in which the editor makes an appeal to support the Stars and Stripes, and to rally as one man for the Union and the Constitution. Therefore be it.

Resolved, That we, the Hebrew congregation of Shreveport, scorn and repel your advice, although we might be called Southern rebels; still, as law-abiding citizens, we solemnly pledge ourselves to stand by, protect, and honor the flag, with its stars and stripes, the Union and Constitution of the Southern Confederacy with our lives, liberty, and all that is dear to us.

Resolved, That we, the members of said congregation, bind ourselves to discontinue the subscription of the *Jewish Messenger,* and all Northern papers opposed to our holy cause, and also to use all honorable means in having said paper banished from our beloved country.

Resolved, That while we mistook your paper for a religious one, which ought to be strictly neutral in politics, we shall from this out treat it with scorn, as a black republican paper, and not worthy of Southern patronage, and that, according to our understanding, church and politics ought never to be mingled, as it has been the ruination of any country captivated by the enticing words of preachers.

Resolved, That we, the members of said congregation, have lost all confidence and regard to the Rev. Samuel Mayer Isaacs, editor and proprietor of the *Jewish Messenger,* and see in him an enemy to our interest and welfare, and believe it to be more unjust for one who preaches the Word of G[o]d, and to advise us to act as traitors and renegades to our adopted country, and raise hatred and dissatisfaction in our midst, and assisting to start a bloody civil war amongst us.

Resolved, That we believe, like the *Cohanim* of old the duties of those who preach the Holy Word to be first in the line of battle, and to cheer up those fighting against their oppressors, in place of those who are proclaiming now, from their pulpits, words to encourage an excited people, and praying for bloody vengeance against us.

Resolved, That a copy of these resolutions be sent to the editor of the *Jewish Messenger.*

Resolved, That papers friendly to the Southern cause are politely requested to publish the foregoing resolutions.

M. Baer, President
Ed. Eberstadt, Secretary, pro tem.

Source: *Jewish Messenger,* June 7, 1861.

5.5

Battle Hymn of the Republic (1861)

JULIA WARD HOWE

It would be impossible for me to say how many times I have been called upon to rehearse the circumstances under which I wrote the "Battle Hymn of the Republic." I have also had occasion more than once to state the simple story in writing. As this oft-told tale has no unimportant part in the story of my life, I will briefly add it to these records. I distinctly remember that a feeling of discouragement came over me as I drew near the city of Washington at the time already mentioned. I thought of the women of my acquaintance whose sons or husbands were fighting our great battle; the women themselves serving in the hospitals, or busying themselves with the work of the Sanitary Commission. My husband, as already said, was beyond the age of military service, my eldest son but a stripling; my youngest was a child of not more than two years. I could not leave my nursery to follow the march of our armies, neither had I the practical deftness which the preparing and packing of sanitary stores demanded. Something seemed to say to me, "You would be glad to serve, but you cannot help any one; you have nothing to give, and there is nothing for you to do." Yet, because of my sincere desire, a word was given me to say, which did strengthen the hearts of those who fought in the field and of those who languished in the prison.

We were invited, one day, to attend a review of troops at some distance from the town. While we were engaged in watching the manoeuvres, a sudden movement of the enemy necessitated immediate action. The review was discontinued, and we saw a detachment of soldiers gallop to the assistance of a small body of our men who were in imminent danger of being surrounded and cut off from retreat. The regiments remaining on the field were ordered to march to their cantonments. We returned to the city very slowly, of necessity, for the troops nearly filled the road. My dear minister was in the carriage with me, as were several other friends. To beguile the rather tedious drive, we sang from time to time snatches of the army songs so popular at that time, concluding, I think with.

"John Brown's body lies a-mouldering in the ground;
His soul is marching on."

Source: Julia Ward Howe, *Reminiscences* (Boston: Houghton-Mifflin, 1899).

The soldiers seemed to like this, and answered back, "Good for you!" Mr. Clarke said, "Mrs. Howe, why do you not write some good words for that stirring tune?" I replied that I had often wished to do this, but had not as yet found in my mind any leading toward it.

I went to bed that night as usual, and slept, according to my wont, quite soundly. I awoke in the gray of the morning twilight; and as I lay waiting for the dawn, the long lines of the desired poem began to twine themselves in my mind. Having thought out all the stanzas, I said to myself, "I must get up and write these verses down, lest I fall asleep again and forget them." So, with a sudden effort, I sprang out of bed, and found in the dimness an old stump of a pen which I remembered to have used the day before. I scrawled the verses almost without looking at the paper. I had learned to do this when, on previous occasions, attacks of versification had visited me in the night, and I feared to have recourse to a light lest I should wake the baby, who slept near me. I was always obliged to decipher my scrawl before another night should intervene, as it was only legible while the matter was fresh in my mind. At this time, having completed my writing, I returned to bed and fell asleep, saying to myself, "I like this better than most things that I have written."

The poem, which was soon after published in the *Atlantic Monthly,* was somewhat praised on its appearance, but the vicissitudes of the war so engrossed public attention that small heed was taken of literary matters. I knew, and was content to know, that the poem soon found its way to the camps, as I heard from time to time of its being sung in chorus by the soldiers.

As the war went on, it came to pass that Chaplain McCabe, newly released from Libby Prison, gave a public lecture in Washington, and recounted some of his recent experiences. Among them was the following: He and the other Union prisoners occupied one large, comfortless room, in which the floor was their only bed. An official in charge of them told them, one evening, that the Union arms had just sustained a terrible defeat. While they sat together in great sorrow, the negro who waited upon them whispered to one man that the officer had given them false information, and that the Union soldiers had, on the contrary, achieved an important victory. At this good news they all rejoiced, and presently made the walls ring with my Battle Hymn, which they sang in chorus, Chaplain McCabe leading. The lecturer recited the poem with such effect that those present began to inquire, "Who wrote this Battle Hymn?" It now became one of the leading lyrics of the war. In view of its success, one of my good friends said, "Mrs. Howe ought to die now, for she has done the best that she will ever do." I was not of this opinion, feeling myself still "full of days' works," although I did not guess at the new experiences which then lay before me.

★ ★ ★

Mine eyes have seen the glory of the coming of the Lord
He is trampling out the vintage where the grapes of wrath are stored,
He has loosed the fateful lightening of His terrible swift sword
His truth is marching on.

Glory! Glory! Hallelujah!
Glory! Glory! Hallelujah!
Glory! Glory! Hallelujah!
His truth is marching on.

I have seen Him in the watch-fires of a hundred circling camps
They have builded Him an altar in the evening dews and damps
I can read His righteous sentence by the dim and flaring lamps
His day is marching on.

Glory! Glory! Hallelujah!
Glory! Glory! Hallelujah!
Glory! Glory! Hallelujah!
His truth is marching on.

I have read a fiery gospel writ in burnish'd rows of steel,
"As ye deal with my contemners, So with you my grace shall deal";
Let the Hero, born of woman, crush the serpent with his heel
Since God is marching on.

Glory! Glory! Hallelujah!
Glory! Glory! Hallelujah!
Glory! Glory! Hallelujah!
His truth is marching on.

He has sounded forth the trumpet that shall never call retreat
He is sifting out the hearts of men before His judgment-seat
Oh, be swift, my soul, to answer Him! be jubilant, my feet!
Our God is marching on.

Glory! Glory! Hallelujah!
Glory! Glory! Hallelujah!
Glory! Glory! Hallelujah!
His truth is marching on.

In the beauty of the lilies Christ was born across the sea,
With a glory in His bosom that transfigures you and me:
As He died to make men holy, let us die to make men free,
While God is marching on.

Glory! Glory! Hallelujah!
Glory! Glory! Hallelujah!
Glory! Glory! Hallelujah!
His truth is marching on.

5.6

God Save the South (1861)

GEORGE MILES

GOD save the South!
   God save the South!
Her altars and firesides—
   God save the South!
Now that the war is nigh—
Now that we arm to die—
Chanting our battle-cry,
Freedom or death!

God be our shield!
At home or a-field,
Stretch Thine arm over us,
   Strengthen and save!
What though they're five to one,
Forward each sire and son,
Strike till the war is done,
   Strike to the grave.

God make the right
Stronger than might!
Millions would trample us
   Down in their pride.
   Lay, Thou, their legions low;
Roll back the ruthless foe;
Let the proud spoiler know
   God's on our side!

Hark! honor's call,
Summoning all—
Summoning all of us
   Up to the strife.
Sons of the South, awake!
Strike till the brand shall break!
Strike for dear honor's sake,
   Freedom and Life!

Source: H.M. Wharton (ed.), *War Songs & Poems of the Southern Confederacy* (Chicago: Winston Co. 1904) pp. 281–283.

Rebels before
Were our fathers of yore;
Rebel, the glorious name
    Washington bore.
Why, then, be ours the same
Title be snatched from shame;
Making it first in fame,
    Odious no more.

War to the hilt!
Their's be the guilt,
Who fetter the freeman
    To ransom the slave.
Up, then, and undismayed,
Sheathe not the battle-blade,
Till the last foe is laid
    Low in the grave.

5.7

The Southern Cross (1863)

E.K. BLUNT

IN the name of God! Amen!
    Stand for our Southern rights;
On our side, Southern men,
    The God of battles fights:
Fling the invaders far—
    Hurl back their work of woe—
Thy voice is the voice of a brother,
    But the hands are the hands of a foe.
They come with a trampling army,
    Invading our native sod—
Stand, Southrons! fight and conquer
    In the name of the mighty God

Source: H.M. Wharton (ed.), *War Songs & Poems of the Southern Confederacy* (Chicago: Winston Co. 1904) pp. 283–284.

They are singing our song of triumph,
    Which proclaimed us proud and free—
While breaking away the heartstrings
    Of our nation's harmony.
Sadly it floateth from us,
    Sighing o'er land and wave;
Till, mute on the lips of the poet,
    It sleeps in its Southern grave.
Spirit and song departed!
    Minstrel and minstrelsy!
We mourn ye, heavy hearted,—
    But we will—we will be free!

    They are waving our flag above us,
        With the despot's tyrant will;
    With our blood they have stained its colors,
        And they call it holy still.
    With tearful eyes, but steady hand,
        We'll tear its stripes apart,
    And fling them, like broken fetters,
        That may not bind the heart.
    But we'll save our stars of glory,
        In the might of the sacred sign
    Of Him who has fixed forever
        One "Southern Cross" to shine.

Stand, Southrons! fight and conquer!
    Solemn, and strong, and sure!
The fight shall not be longer
    Than God shall bid endure.
By the life that but yesterday
    Waked with the infant's breath!
By the feet which, ere morning, may
    Tread to the soldier's death!
By the blood which cries to heaven—
    Crimson upon our sod!
Stand, Southrons! fight and conquer,
    In the name of the mighty God!

———————————————

BLACK EMANCIPATION AND NATIONAL LIBERATION

On January 1, 1863, President Lincoln issued the Emancipation Proclamation, which had taken several months to compose. Abolitionists thought it was past due, while defenders of states' rights thought it both precipitous and unconstitutional. No one believed that it alone ended slavery in the United States. Lincoln declared free the slaves in territories in a state of rebellion, while leaving in bondage slaves in territories loyal to the United States. As Lincoln himself had always said, a Constitutional Amendment (the Thirteenth) was needed to bring an end to the institution.

Yet the Proclamation had a dramatic effect both in the North and in the South, both on whites and on African Americans. After he saw its first draft, Senator Charles Sumner of Massachusetts, in an **"Address at Faneuil Hall,"** publicly thanked God for it. In his own **"Statement on Emancipation Proclamation,"** President of the Confederacy Jefferson Davis referred to the Creator as he condemned the draft. Daniel Payne called the emancipated slaves **Ransomed** and welcomed them to citizenship. In his autobiography *Up from Slavery,* Booker T. Washington much later recalled the joy, tempered almost immediately by the realization of responsibility, that the Proclamation brought to his slave community.

5.8

Address at Faneuil Hall (1862)

CHARLES SUMNER

Thank God that I live to enjoy this day! Thank God that my eyes have not closed without seeing this great salvation! The skies are brighter and the air is purer now that Slavery is handed over to judgment.

By the proclamation of the President, all persons held as slaves January 1, 1863, within any State or designated part of a State, the people whereof shall

Source: Charles Sumner, *The Works of Charles Sumner*, (Boston: Lee & Shepard, 1870.)

then be in rebellion against the United States, shall be then, thenceforward, and forever free; and the Executive Government of the United States, including the military and naval authority thereof, will recognize and maintain the freedom of such persons, and will do no act or acts to repress such persons, or any of them, in any efforts they may make for their actual freedom. Beyond these most effective words, which do not go into operation before the new year, are other words of immediate operation, constituting a present edict of Emancipation. The President recites the recent Acts of Congress applicable to this question, and calls upon all persons in the military and naval service to observe, obey, and enforce them. But these Acts provide that all slaves of Rebels, taking refuge within the liens of our army, all slaves captured from Rebels or deserted by them, and all slaves found within any place occupied by Rebel forces and afterwards occupied by forces of the United States, shall be forever free of servitude, and not again held as slaves; and these Acts further provide that no person in the military or naval service shall, under any pretence whatever, assume to decide on the validity of any claim to a slave, or surrender any such person to his claimant, on pain of being dismissed from the service: so that by these Acts, now proclaimed by the President, Freedom is practically secured to all who find shelter within our lines, and the glorious flag of the Union, wherever it floats, becomes the flag of Freedom. . . .

And now, thank God, the word is spoken!—greater word was seldom spoken. Emancipation has begun, and our country is already elevated and glorified. The war has not changed in object, but it has changed in character. Its object now, as at the beginning, is simply to put down the Rebellion; but its character is derived from the new force at length enlisted, stamping itself upon all that is done, and absorbing the whole war to itself. Vain will it be again to delude European nations into foolish belief that Slavery has nothing to do with the war, that it is a war for empire on one side and independence on the other, and that all generous ideas are on the side of the Rebellion. And vain, also, will be that other European cry,—whether from an intemperate press or the cautious lips of statesmen,—that separation is inevitable, and that our Government is doomed to witness the dismemberment of the Republic. With this new alliance, such forbodings will be falsified, the wishes of the fathers will be fulfilled, and the rights of human nature, which were the declared object of our Revolution, vindicated. Thus inspired, the sword of Washington—that sword which, according to his last will and testament, was to be drawn only in self-defence, or in defence of country and its rights—will once more marshal our armies to victory, while the national flag, wherever it floats, will give freedom to all beneath its folds, and the proud inscription be at last triumphantly verified: "Liberty and Union, now and forever, one and inseparable."

5.9

Statement on Emancipation Proclamation (1863)

JEFFERSON DAVIS

The public journals of the North have been received, containing a proclamation, dated on the 1st day of the present month, signed by the President of the United States, in which he orders and declares all slaves within ten of the States of the Confederacy to be free, except such as are found within certain districts now occupied in part by the armed forces of the enemy. We may well leave it to the instincts of that common humanity which a beneficent Creator has implanted in the breasts of our fellowmen of all countries to pass judgement on a measure by which several millions of human beings of an inferior race, peaceful and contended laborers in their sphere, are doomed to extermination, while at the same time they are encouraged to a general assassination of their masters by the insidious recommendation "to abstain from violence unless in necessary self-defense." Our own detestation of those who have attempted the most execrable measure recorded in the history of guilty man is tempered by profound contempt for the impotent rage which it discloses. So far as regards the action of this Government on such criminals as may attempt its execution, I confine myself to informing you that I shall, unless in your wisdom you deem some other course more expedient, deliver to the several State authorities all commissioned officers of the United States that may hereafter be captured by our forces in any of the States embraced in the proclamation, that they may be dealt within in accordance with the laws of those States providing for the punishment of criminals engaged in exciting servile insurrection. The enlisted soldiers I shall continue to treat as unwilling instruments in the commission of these crimes, and shall direct their discharge and return to their homes on the proper and usual parole.

Source: http://www.civilwaribluegrass.net

5.10

Welcome to the Ransomed
(1863)

DANIEL PAYNE

We are gathered to celebrate the emancipation, yea, rather, the *Redemption* of the enslaved people of the District of Columbia, the exact number of whom we have no means of ascertaining, because, since the benevolent intention of Congress became manifest, many have been removed by their owners beyond the reach of this beneficent act.

Our pleasing task then, is to welcome to the Churches, the homesteads, and circles of free colored Americans, those who remain to enjoy *the boon of holy Freedom.*

Brethren, sisters, friends, we say welcome to our Churches, welcome to our homesteads, welcome to our social circles.

Enter the great family of Holy Freedom; not to *lounge in sinful indolence,* not to *degrade yourselves by vice,* nor to *corrupt society by licentiousness,* neither to *offend the laws by crime,* but to the *enjoyment of a well regulated liberty,* the off-spring of generous laws; of law as just as generous, as righteous as just—a liberty to be *perpetuated* by equitable law, and sanctioned by the divine; for law is never equitable, righteous, just, until it harmonizes with the will of Him, who is *"King* of kings, and *Lord* of lords," and who commanded Israel to *have but one law for the home-born* and the *stranger.*

We repeat ourselves, welcome then *ye ransomed ones;* welcome *not* to indolence, to vice, licentiousness, and crime, but to a well-regulated liberty, sanctioned by the Divine, maintained by the Human law.

Welcome to habits of industry and thrift—to duties of religion and piety—to obligations of law, order, government—of government divine, of government human: these two, though not one, are inseparable. The man who refuses to obey divine law, will never obey human laws. *The divine first,* the *human next.* The latter is the consequence of the former, and follows it as light does the rising sun.

We invite you to our Churches, because we desire you to be religious; to be more than religious; we urge you *to be godly.* We entreat you to never be content until you are emancipated from sin, from sin without, and from sin within you. But this kind of freedom is attained only through the faith of Jesus,

Source: Daniel Payne, *Sermons and Addresses,* 1853–1891 (New York: Arno, 1972) pp. 6–7.

love for Jesus, obedience to Jesus. As certain as the American Congress has *ransomed* you, so certain, yea, more certainly has Jesus redeemed you from the guilt and power of sin by his own precious blood.

As you are now free in body, so now seek to be free in soul and spirit, from sin and Satan. The *noblest freeman is he whom Christ makes free.*

5.11

Up from Slavery (1928)

BOOKER T. WASHINGTON

The night before the eventful day, word was sent to the slave quarters to the effect that something unusual was going to take place at the "big house" the next morning. There was little, if any, sleep that night. All was excitement and expectancy. Early the next morning word was sent to all the slaves, old and young, to gather at the house. In company with my mother, brother, and sister, and a large number of other slaves, I went to the master's house. All of our master's family were either standing or seated on the veranda of the house, where they could see what was to take place and hear what was said. There was a feeling of deep interest, or perhaps sadness, on their faces, but not bitterness. As I now recall the impression they made upon me, they did not at the moment seem to be sad because of the loss of property, but rather because of parting with those whom they had reared and who were in many ways very close to them. The most distinct thing that I now recall in connection with the scene was that some man who seemed to be a stranger (a United States officer, I presume) made a little speech and then read a rather long paper—the Emancipation Proclamation, I think. After the reading we were told that we were all free, and could go when and where we pleased. My mother, who was standing by my side, leaned over and kissed her children, while tears of joy ran down her cheeks. She explained to us what it all meant, that this was the day for which she had been so long praying, but fearing that she would never live to see.

For some minutes there was great rejoicing, and thanksgiving, and wild scenes of ecstasy. But there was no feeling of bitterness. In fact, there was pity among the slaves for our former owners. The wild rejoicing on the part of the

Source: Booker T. Washington, *Up from Slavery* (Cambridge, MA: Houghton-Mifflin, 1928) pp. 20–22.

emancipated coloured people lasted but for a brief period, for I noticed that by the time they returned to their cabins there was a change in their feelings. The great responsibility of being free, of having charge of themselves, of having to think and plan for themselves and their children, seemed to take possession of them. It was very much like suddenly turning a youth of ten or twelve years out into the world to provide for himself. In a few hours the great questions with which the Anglo-Saxon race had been grappling for centuries had been thrown upon these people to be solved. These were the questions of a home, a living, the rearing of children, education, citizenship, and the establishment and support of churches. Was it any wonder that within a few hours the wild rejoicing ceased and a feeling of deep gloom seemed to pervade the slave quarters? To some it seemed that, now that they were in actual possession of it, freedom was a more serious thing than they had expected to find it. Some of the slaves were seventy or eighty years old; their best days were gone. They had no strength with which to earn a living in a strange place and among strange people, even if they had been sure where to find a new place of abode. To this class the problem seemed especially hard. Besides, deep down in their hearts there was a strange and peculiar attachment to "old Marster" and "old Missus," and to their children, which they found it hard to think of breaking off. With these they had spent in some cases nearly a half-century, and it was no light thing to think of parting. Gradually, one by one, stealthily at first, the older slaves began to wander from the slave quarters back to the "big house" to have a whispered conversation with their former owners as to the future.

ABRAHAM LINCOLN AND NATIONAL REDEMPTION

Until 1858, Abraham Lincoln was an unlikely candidate to lead the country through its greatest crisis. Only after he gained great prestige and respect for his debates with Stephen A. Douglas in the losing race for the U.S. Senate did many people consider him a viable presidential candidate. Even after his election in 1860, few people would have wagered that he would be a successful president who would win the war and become a national hero. No one would have guessed that in his death he would achieve martyrdom and become a religious icon, as some would refer to him the American Redeemer.

While Lincoln never joined a church and as a young man was an avowed agnostic, as he neared the presidency he seemed to grow more religious, at least publicly, using religious language in his speeches and expressing his **Thoughts** on God's will, never claiming to know exactly what it was. He

Courtesy of the Abraham Lincoln Presidential Library & Museum

WASHINGTON AND LINCOLN.
THE FATHER AND THE SAVIOUR OF OUR COUNTRY.

Lincoln with Washington, icons of the American
Political Religion

demonstrated his piety, or at least his wise use of religion, in his 1863
"Proclamation of a National Fast-Day" and in his **"Second Inaugural
Address,"** delivered just one month before his assassination.

Lincoln's death on Easter weekend transformed him into a figure larger
than life, and he quickly rose to be the leading actor in the drama of American
Redemption. Pastor Gilbert Haven called him **"The Uniter and Liberator
of America,"** poet Herman Melville called him **"The Martyr,"** and Vachel
Lindsay portrayed him as still living among his people and grieving over their
follies in the poem **"Abraham Lincoln Walks at Midnight."** He sacrificed
himself to save the nation, and now he lives on, resurrected, in the American
political religion.

5.12

Thoughts on God's Will

ABRAHAM LINCOLN

(1861)

I am approached with the most opposite opinions and advice, and that by religious men who are equally certain that they represent the divine will. I am sure that either the one or the other class is mistaken in that belief and perhaps in some respects both. I hope it will not be irreverent for me to say that if it is probable that God would reveal his will to others on a point so connected with my duty, it might be supposed he would reveal it directly to me; for, unless I am more deceived in myself than I often am, it is my earnest desire to know the will of providence in this matter. And if I can learn what it is, I will do it.

(1862)

The will of God prevails. In great contests each party claims to act in accordance with the will of God. Both may be, and one must be, wrong. God cannot be for and against the same thing at the same time. In the present civil war, it is quite possible that God's purpose is something different from the purpose of either party; and yet the human instrumentalities, working just as they do, are of the best adaptation to effect his purpose. I am almost ready to say that this is probably true; that God wills this contest, and wills that it shall not end yet. By his mere great power on the minds of the now contestants, he could have either saved or destroyed the Union without a human contest. Yet the contest began. And, having begun, he could give the final victory to either side any day. Yet the contest proceeds.

Source: Philip Stern, *The Life & Writings of Abraham Lincoln* (New York: Random House, 1940) pp. 720, 728–729.

5.13

Proclamation of a National
Fast-Day (1863)

ABRAHAM LINCOLN

Whereas, the Senate of the United States, devoutly recognizing the supreme authority and just government of Almighty God in all the affairs of men and of nations, has by a resolution requested the President to designate and set apart a day for national prayer and humiliation:

And whereas, it is the duty of nations as well as of men to own their dependence upon the overruling power of God; to confess their sins and transgressions in humble sorrow, yet with assured hope that genuine repentance will lead to mercy and pardon; and to recognize the sublime truth, announced in the Holy Scriptures and proven by all history, that those nations only are blessed whose God is the Lord:

And insomuch as we know that by his divine law nations, like individuals, are subjected to punishments and chastisements in this world, may we not justly fear that the awful calamity of civil war which now desolates the land may be but a punishment inflicted upon us for our presumptuous sins, to the needful end of our national reformation as a whole people? We have been the recipients of the choicest bounties of Heaven. We have been preserved, these many years, in peace and prosperity. We have grown in numbers, wealth, and power as no other nation has ever grown; but we have forgotten God. We have forgotten the gracious hand which preserved us in peace, and multiplied and enriched and strengthened us; and we have vainly imagined, in the deceitfulness of our hearts, that all these blessings were produced by some superior wisdom and virtue of our own. Intoxicated with unbroken success, we have become too self-sufficient to feel the necessity of redeeming and preserving grace, too proud to pray to the God that made us:

It behooves us, then, to humble ourselves before the offended Power, to confess our national sins, and to pray for clemency and forgiveness:

Now, therefore, in compliance with the request, and fully concurring in the views, of the Senate, I do by this my proclamation designate and set apart Thursday the 30th day of April, 1863, as a day of national humiliation, fasting, and prayer. And I do hereby request all the people to abstain on that day from

Source: Nicolay & Hay (eds.), *Complete Works of Abraham Lincoln* (New York: Lamb, 1905), VIII, pp. 235–237.

their ordinary secular pursuits, and to unite at their several places of public worship and their respective homes in keeping the day holy to the Lord, and devoted to the humble discharge of the religious duties proper to that solemn occasion. All this being done in sincerity and truth, let us then rest humbly in the hope authorized by the divine teachings, that the united cry of the nation will be heard on high, and answered with blessings no less than the pardon of our national sins, and the restoration of our now divided and suffering country to its former happy condition of unity and peace.

In witness whereof, I have hereunto set my hand, and caused the seal of the United States to be affixed.

5.14

Second Inaugural Address (1865)

ABRAHAM LINCOLN

At this second appearing to take the oath of the Presidential office there is less occasion for an extended address than there was at the first. Then a statement in detail of a course to be pursued seemed fitting and proper. Now, at the expiration of four years, during which public declarations have been constantly called forth on every point and phase of the great contest which still absorbs the attention and engrosses the energies of the nation little that is new could be presented. The progress of our arms, upon which all else chiefly depends, is as well-known to the public as to myself, and it is, I trust, reasonably satisfactory and encouraging to all. With high hope for the future, no prediction in regard to it is ventured.

On the occasion corresponding to this four years ago all thoughts were anxiously directed to an impending civil war. All dreaded it, all sought to avert it. While the inaugural address was being delivered from this place, devoted altogether to *saving* the Union without war, insurgent agents were in the city seeking to *destroy* it without war—seeking to dissolve the Union and divide effects by negotiation. Both parties deprecated war, but one of them would *make* war rather than let the nation survive, and the other would *accept* war rather than let it perish, and the war came.

Source: Angle & Miers (ed.), *The Living Lincoln* (New Jersey: Rutgers University Press, 1955) pp. 628–630.

One-eighth of the whole population were colored slaves, not distributed generally over the Union, but localized in the southern part of it. These slaves constituted a peculiar and powerful interest. All knew that this interest was somehow the cause of war. To strengthen, perpetuate, and extend this interest was the object for which the insurgents would rend the Union even by war, while the Government claimed no right to do more than to restrict the territorial enlargement of it. Neither party expected for the war the magnitude or the duration which it has already attained. Neither anticipated that the *cause* of the conflict might cease with or even before the conflict itself should cease. Each looked for an easier triumph, and a result less fundamental and astounding. Both read the same Bible and pray to the same God, and each invokes His aid against the other. It may seem strange that any men should dare to ask a just God's assistance in wringing their bread from the sweat of other men's faces, but let us judge not, that we be not judged. The prayers of both could not be answered. That of neither has been answered fully. The Almighty has His own purposes. "Woe unto the world because of offenses; for it must needs be that offenses come, but woe to that man by whom the offense cometh." If we shall suppose that American slavery is one of those offenses which, in the providence of God, must needs come, but which, having continued through His appointed time, He now wills to remove, and that He gives to both North and South this terrible war as the woe due to those by whom the offense came, shall we discern therein any departure from those divine attributes which the believers in a living God always ascribe to Him? Fondly do we hope, fervently do we pray, that this mighty scourge of war may speedily pass away. Yet, if God wills that it continue until all the wealth piled by the bondsman's two hundred and fifty years of unrequited toil shall be sunk, and until every drop of blood drawn with the lash shall be paid by another drawn with the sword, as was said three thousand years ago, so still it must be said "the judgments of the Lord are true and righteous altogether."

With malice toward none, with charity for all, with firmness in the right as God gives us to see the right, let us strive on to finish the work we are in, to bind up the nation's wounds, to care for him who shall have borne the battle and for his widow and his orphan, to do all which may achieve and cherish a just and lasting peace among ourselves and with all nations.

5.15

The Uniter and Liberator
of America (1865)

GILBERT HAVEN

As Christ entered into Jerusalem, the city that above all others hated, rejected, and should soon slay Him, attended by those, but now lame and blind and deaf and leprous, whom He had cured, so did this, His servant, enter the city that above all others hated and rejected him, and would soon be the real if not intentional cause of his death, attended by thousands who had been saved from worse maladies than those bodily diseases, out of whom, in a moment, legions of devils that had long possessed them had been instantly and forever expelled by the same Divine Redeemer, through His appointed word. "Behold thy king cometh, meek," is most beautifully true here and now. The haughty tyrant is gone, the loving father is come. Well may their glad hearts dance for joy. Well may the air ring with their jubilant hallelujahs. Well may the paternal President feel the comfort and strength of the hour. The blessings of those that were ready to perish came upon him. His work draws near its close. The nation is united, the rebel subdued, the slave set free. His cup is full. He can well exclaim, " Now, Lord, lettest thou thy servant depart in peace, for mine eyes have seen Thy salvation, and the glory of Thy people Israel."

How near that departure was! This was his Palm Sunday. Ten days elapse, his Good Friday comes, and he follows his Divine Master, through like bloody hands, to his Savior's glorious eternity.

Thus did our king enter his strong city. Thus did he triumph over his Philistia. The story will be wrought in song and canvas, over the world and adown the ages, as a most beautiful and most rare expression of a Christian triumph. It will live with the last act of John Brown,—his kiss upon the slave-child's cheek,—each the perfect flowering of his earthly life. With such a word as the inaugural, and such a deed as this, we may truly feel that his life was rounded to a perfect close. He could properly hear the voice of the Master saying, "It is enough; come up higher! Thou hast been faithful over a few things, I will make thee ruler over many things. Enter thou into the joy of thy Lord."

His work is done. Ours is yet unfinished. His place in history, and, we trust, in heaven, is sure. Ours is yet to win. We shall show our admiration for him more by completing his work, than by standing too long gazing steadfastly into the heavens whither he has ascended.

Source: Gilbert Haven, *The Anti-Slavery Crusade in America* (New York: Arno, 1969 [from 1869]) pp. 578–579.

5.16

The Martyr (1865)

HERMAN MELVILLE

Good Friday was the day
   Of the prodigy and crime,
When they killed him in his pity,
   When they killed him in his prime
Of clemency and calm—
   When with yearning he was filled
   To redeem the evil-willed,
And, though conqueror, be kind;
   But they killed him in his kindness,
   In their madness and their blindness,
And they killed him from behind.

There is sobbing of the strong,
   And a pall upon the land
But the People in their weeping
   Bare the iron hand:
Beware the People weeping
   When they bare the iron hand.

He lieth in his blood—
   The father in his face;
They have killed him, the Forgiver—
   The Avenger takes his place,
The Avenger wisely stern,
   Who in righteousness shall do
   What the heavens call him to,
And the parricides remand;
   For they killed him in his kindness,
   In their madness and their blindness,
And his blood is on their hand.

Source: http://www.poetry-archive.com

There is sobbing of the strong,
 And a pall upon the land;
But the People in their weeping
 Bare the iron hand:
Beware the People weeping
 When they bare the iron hand.

5.17

Abraham Lincoln Walks at Midnight (1909)

VACHEL LINDSAY

It is portentous, and a thing of state
That here at midnight, in our little town
A mourning figure walks, and will not rest,
Near the old court-house pacing up and down,

Or by his homestead, or its shadowed yards
He lingers where his children used to play,
Or through the market, on the well-worn stones
He stalks until the dawn-stars burn away.

A bronzed, lank man! His suit of ancient black,
A famous high-top hat and plain worn shawl
Make him the quaint great figure that men love,
The prairie-lawyer, master of us all.

He cannot sleep upon his hillside now.
He is among us:—as in times before!
And we who toss and lie awake for long,
Breathe deep, and start, to see him pass the door.

His head is bowed. He thinks of men and kings.
Yea, when the sick world cries, how can he sleep?

Source: *Collected Poems of Vachel Lindsay* (Simon & Schuster, 1925; MacMillan Pub. Co, 1953), found at http://www.bartleby.com and used by permission in my book, *Abraham Lincoln*.

Too many peasants fight, they know not why;
Too many homesteads in black terror weep.

The sins of all the war-lords burn his heart.
He sees the dreadnaughts scouring every main.
He carries on his shawl-wrapped shoulders now
The bitterness, the folly and the pain.

He cannot rest until a spirit-dawn
Shall come;—the shining hope of Europe free:
A league of sober folk, the workers' earth,
Bringing long peace to Cornland, Alp and Sea.

It breaks his heart that kings must murder still,
That all his hours of travail here for men
Seem yet in vain. And who will bring white peace
That he may sleep upon his hill again?